Betrayal:

Obama's Corrupt Legacy of Lies, Deceit, Guns and Murder

By

Larry Gaydos and Andre Howard

Betrayal: Obama's Corrupt Legacy of Lies, Deceit, Guns and Murder

Table of Contents

Prologue i

Chapter 1 - Obama's Desperate Plan to Control Guns 1

Chapter 2 - Cooperating with Obama's DOJ, ATF, and FBI 23

Chapter 3 - Obama's "Anti-Drug Cartel Plan" - By Selling Guns? 55

Chapter 4 - They are "Just Mexicans" ... Until 87

Chapter 5 - "I'm Sorry, Gentlemen... You Are Just Not Credible"...... 117

Chapter 6 - Thank You for Your Help - Have a Serving of Retaliation 183

Chapter 7 - Stonewalling, Fake Privilege, Retaliation, Gun Control 211

Chapter 8 - Attorney General Holder - Perjury? Incompetence? Bad Memory? Or All of the Above? 236

Chapter 9 - What? Obama's in the Loop? 273

Chapter 10 - Hope for Justice Fades, But Prayers Continue 291

Epilogue 306

About The Authors 314

Sources and Acknowledgements 317

    Media Sources 321

    Judicial Sources 322

    General Background Sources 322

    Books 323

    Acknowledgements 324

Prologue

On September 11, 2011, Richard Serrano of the _Los Angeles Times_ wrote an article titled "Gun Store Owner Had Misgivings About ATF Sting". He interviewed Andre Howard, owner of the Lone Wolf gun store in Arizona, about this role in an outrageous Obama gun trafficking operation that supplied assault weapons to the Mexican cartels:

"In the fall of 2009, ATF agents installed a secret phone line and hidden cameras in a ceiling panel and wall at Andre Howard's Lone Wolf gun store. They gave him one basic instruction: Sell guns to every illegal purchaser who walks through the door. For fifteen months Howard did as he was told. […] He was assured by the ATF that they would follow the guns and that the surveillance would lead the agents to the violent Mexican drug cartels on the Southwest border.

"When Howard heard nothing about any arrests, he questioned the agents. 'Keep selling,' they told him.

"Some 2,000 firearms from the Lone Wolf Trading Company store and others in southern Arizona were illegally sold under an ATF program called Fast and Furious that allowed 'straw purchasers' to walk away with weapons and turn them over to criminal traffickers."

Serrano asked Howard if he had "second thoughts about helping law enforcement."

"Was I betrayed?" he said. "Absolutely yes."

This is a book about "Betrayal." First, it is about how the highest levels of the United States government betrayed one of its most loyal, patriotic, and law-abiding citizens. Through lies, deceit and retaliation attorneys and law enforcement agents of the Obama administration used him and then tried to destroy his livelihood and him personally.

Second, it is about how the Obama administration created a "deep state" of embedded top-level bureaucrats who betrayed thousands of brave, loyal, and dedicated frontline public servants and tarnished the reputation of the agencies they faithfully served.

Third, it is about how the Obama administration betrayed the Republic of Mexico, a loyal neighbor and ally whose cooperation is essential to the security of North America and vital to the mutual national interests of both nations. Both countries battle the escalating challenges of illegal immigration, drug trafficking, and extreme violence — cartel violence in Mexico and domestic violence in the United States.

The Obama administration first informed the Attorney General of Mexico about the existence of Operation Fast and Furious after it was terminated in January 2011. They provided no details about the Operation. Mexican government officials and media were understandably concerned and outraged. Their "supposed" loyal neighbor had been reporting through the press that both countries had been making great progress in addressing their mutual drug and firearms trafficking issues. Unbeknownst to the government of the Republic of Mexico, their United States partner had kept them completely in the dark about their fifteen-month program of letting lethal assault weapons "walk" into their country. The Obama administration conducted a clandestine program of providing assault weapons to the most violent drug cartels in Mexico knowing those weapons would "more than likely not" be used in the murder of innocent Mexican citizens, police officers, politicians, and even Mexican children.

Attorney General of Mexico Marisela Morales solemnly addressed the astonishing reports of the Obama administration program with extreme restraint:

"At no time did we know or were we made aware that there might have been arms trafficking permitted. In no way would we have allowed it, because it is an attack on the safety of Mexico."

She summarized her reaction to the shocking revelations of the reported United States government's Operation Fast and Furious succinctly:

"Allowing weapons to 'walk' would represent a 'Betrayal' of Mexico."

Obama's policy of lies, deceit, guns and murder, which started when he became president in 2009, is impacting the United States of America and President Trump's administration years after the end of his disgraceful presidency.

Most of the guns he "walked" during Fast and Furious are still unaccounted for. They continue to be used in violent crimes, including murders, not just by the drug cartels in Mexico, but also in ISIS terrorist attacks in the United States and Europe.

Obama and his administration do have a legacy for America that still remains — a "Legacy of Betrayal".

Chapter One

Obama's Desperate Plan to Control Guns

I was in my Dallas office at Haynes and Boone LLP on Monday morning, March 7, 2011, catching up on business that had come in the previous week. During that time I had been attending the American Bar Association's annual White Collar Crime Institute in San Diego. The three-day annual gathering of white-collar criminal attorneys started in 1987 with a small gathering of less than 100 white-collar practitioners. In 2011, it had grown to about 1,500 attorneys and forensic accountants from the United States and many other countries. It is now the premier white-collar crime networking and educational event, every year drawing participation by top judges, high-level Department of Justice (DOJ) officials, leading national prosecutors and defense counsel, and others related to the white-collar practice, including media that cover the practice.

Mid-morning, Stacy Brainin, my partner and one of my fellow co-founders of the white-collar practice group at Haynes and Boone in 1986, came into my office and handed me a torn piece of paper with some handwritten notes from a telephone call she'd answered on Friday. She said a gun shop owner from Arizona, Andre Howard, called and wanted to talk about retaining our firm to represent him in a matter involving the government's "walking" of thousands of firearms to the Mexican cartels. She said, "It sounds crazy, but call him if you think we should pursue it."

I called Andre that day and learned he was currently represented by Chris Rapp, an attorney in Phoenix. I called Chris to get a summary of the matter, and reviewed some documents that Andre sent me, including letters between Senator Grassley and the Obama administration. I agreed to represent Andre and called Assistant United States Attorney (AUSA) Emory Hurley in Phoenix to set up a meeting with the Phoenix Bureau of Alcohol, Tobacco, Firearms, and Explosives (ATF) agents and Phoenix DOJ attorneys on Friday, March 11.

I discussed the nature of the representation, "gunwalking of firearms to Mexican cartels", with various partners, friends, and family, and the universal reactions were the same:

"That is ridiculous!"

"There is no way the Obama administration would allow that."

"What possible rationale could ever lead to our government sending assault weapons to the most violent criminals in the world?"

"President Obama is against cartel violence and never has had any gun control agenda."

During my twenty-five years in the white-collar crime practice group, I had many cases involving state and federal government agencies, including the Securities and Exchange Commission (SEC), the Federal Bureau of Investigation (FBI), and the Department of Justice. I never had a negative experience. I had the utmost respect for the agents around the country and the various leadership teams of each agency. So, I entered the representation with a healthy skepticism about the idea that our government would ever have a program that would actually help the Mexican drug cartels kill innocent Mexican citizens. The unanimous skepticism of my colleagues and friends gave me some pause. Yet the documents I reviewed concerning the "alleged" Operation and its "alleged" connection to the December 2010 ambush-murder of Customs and Border Patrol (CBP) Agent Brian Terry made it clear that there was sufficient substance to Andre Howard's claims that merited additional investigation.

2

The January 2011 Phoenix indictment of twenty straw purchasers, many of whom purchased weapons from Andre's business, Lone Wolf Trading Company, also triggered concerns about my client's safety.

On my first day as co-counsel for Andre Howard, I raised those concerns with co-counsel Chris Rapp and with Assistant United States Attorney Emory Hurley. I asked AUSA Hurley to put my client's safety as the number-one priority on the March 11, 2011, meeting agenda.

AUSA Hurley, who was the lead prosecutor assigned to Fast and Furious, was reluctant to discuss anything substantive over the telephone, but he assured me the United States Attorney's Office (USAO) had been discussing the issue and at the March 11 meeting we would discuss WITSEC, the government's witness protection and security program. The unsealed criminal indictment of the Fast and Furious straw purchasers specifically alleged that more illegal purchasers made purchases at Lone Wolf than all other Federal Firearm Licensees (FFLs) combined.

On Tuesday, March 8, 2011, I had additional conversations with Andre and Chris Rapp about WITSEC. In the morning I received a call from Andre. He said, "You will never guess who is in my store right now — John Dodson." (John Dodson was the first ATF whistleblower to raise concerns about Operation Fast and Furious to Congress and the media.) He put me on the phone with Agent Dodson, who wanted to assure me that Andre had done nothing wrong, other than be a true patriot who trusted the word of corrupt ATF agents and DOJ attorneys. He also confirmed that two firearms recovered at the murder scene of CBP Agent Brian Terry were in fact weapons sold to a "straw purchaser" in Fast and Furious. The serial numbers on the firearms were positively traced and verified: They had been purchased at Lone Wolf Trading Company, and they had been allowed to "walk" to the Mexican cartels.

I spent the next two days reviewing internet blogs like Sipsey Street Irregulars, and newspaper articles in preparation for my Thursday afternoon meeting with Andre, my evening follow-up meeting with Andre and Chris Rapp, and our Friday meeting with the ATF and the DOJ. I also reviewed additional documents that Agent Dodson provided Andre.

On my Thursday flight to Phoenix, I had many unanswered questions. The number-one priority was my client's protection. He had been publicly identified as someone who sold numerous firearms to "straw purchasers" who were working for Mexican cartels. Those sales were illegal. The straw purchasers purchased the firearms on behalf of a third party who would not, or could not, make a purchase themselves. The indictments were largely for false statements the straw purchasers made on the purchase documents. The purchasers had stated that the firearms were for their personal use. They also lied about their criminal record, their residential address, and/or their status as an illegal alien.

The more pressing question was: "Why would our government do this?" To try to answer this question, and to try to address my law firm partners' reactions, the starting point seemed to be researching the underlying assumption that the Obama administration had no gun control agenda, and was only focused on combating drugs and gun violence in both the United States and Mexico. On its face, letting firearms "walk" to the Mexican cartels would be inconsistent with both of those objectives. My initial research quickly contradicted the first part of the assumption that President Obama and Attorney General (AG) Holder had no gun control agenda.

In January 1995, Eric Holder, who was then the U.S. Attorney for the District of Columbia, gave a speech to the

Women's Democratic Club. In that speech he addressed gun control. He said:

"What we need to do is change the way in which people think about guns, especially young people, and make it something that's not cool, that it's not acceptable, it's not hip to carry a gun anymore, in the way in which we've changed our attitudes about cigarettes."

He went on to say that the anti-gun message should be pushed in the schools "every day, every school at every level." He urged a nationwide campaign "to really brainwash people into thinking about guns in a vastly different way."

Eric Holder also wrote an opinion editorial in the *Washington Post* after 9/11, urging that the terrorist attack was a reason "to push for more gun control laws."

On January 15, 2008, United States Senator Obama spoke about "licensing and registering gun owners" at a Democratic Presidential campaign debate in Las Vegas. He explained his objective in a strange way. He said he favored "common-sense enforcement". He then defined that as making changes that would promote:

"the efforts by law enforcement to obtain the information required to trace back guns that have been used in crimes to unscrupulous gun dealers. As president, I intend to make it happen."

Ironically, the next significant pronouncements about gun control by Attorney General Holder and President Obama would not be made until Fast and Furious was exposed by the United States Congress in 2011.

On February 25, 2009, less than two months after President Obama's inauguration as president, Attorney General Holder held a press conference regarding the capture of more than fifty alleged members of the Sinaloa Cartel. The Sinaloa Cartel was viewed as the most powerful drug trafficking cartel in Mexico. Holder used the press conference to signal one of the most important, but understated, objectives of the young Obama administration:

"Well, as President Obama indicated during the campaign, there are just a few gun-related changes that we would like to make, and among them would be to reinstitute the ban on the sale of assault weapons. I think that will have a positive impact in Mexico, at a minimum."

The previous week "over fifty Democratic lawmakers sent a letter to President Obama urging him to enforce a ban on importing assault weapons, citing rising gun violence in Mexico. The Sinaloa Cartel […] is involved in drug and weapons trafficking in the U.S. and Mexico."

During his congressional confirmation hearings, Holder said: "he supported […] making the ban on assault weapons permanent." President Clinton's administration passed what was called "The Brady Bill" in 1994. The terrible attempted assassination of President Reagan in 1981 resulted in his press secretary, James Brady, being seriously injured and partially paralyzed for life. The Brady Bill required background checks for purchases of handguns and imposed a ten-year ban on the sale of assault rifles. The ban expired in 2004.

Holder also pointed out:

"During the campaign, Mr. Obama […] pledged to make the assault weapons ban permanent."

Although Holder was confirmed as Attorney General by a vote of 75-21, some Republican senators refused to support him because of his hostility to gun owners' rights and lack of support for the war on terror.

During his campaign, presidential candidate Obama signaled his secret desire for gun control, and perhaps his strategy for overcoming the significant opposition of Americans to any amendment or limitation of their Second Amendment rights.

Both Attorney General Holder and President Obama pledged gun control by reinstating former president Clinton's ban on the sale of assault weapons. They both acknowledged that there was strong American public opposition to any legislation that would materially infringe on Second Amendment constitutional rights. Their initial attempt to ban assault weapons on February 25, 2009, had to be abandoned before it was ever voted on in Congress. The proposed ban was opposed by most Republicans and a large number of congressmen from their own party.

Over the next eight months, from March to October 2009, high-level Obama administration officials held multiple meetings to address this dilemma. These meetings involved a wide range of executive branch law enforcement agencies, including the Drug Enforcement Agency (DEA), the Office of the Attorney General (OAG), the Federal Bureau of Investigation (FBI), the Immigration and Customs Enforcement Agency (ICE), the Customs and Border Patrol (CBP), the United States Marshals Service (USMS), and the Southwest Border state federal prosecutors, as well as some state law enforcement agencies like the Phoenix Police Department.

Clearly any hope of fulfilling President Obama's and Attorney General Holder's pledges to enact gun control would require something more than another futile attempt at "off-the-shelf" legislation. Any executive order that would try to circumvent legislation would probably be challenged in court as a violation of the United States Constitution.

In the Obama administration's first budget, President Obama included $21.9 million for the ATF to expand "Project Gunrunner". Project Gunrunner was a Bush administration initiative started in 2006 that focused on limiting the flow of firearms to Mexico by interdicting weapons purchased by straw purchasers and shutting down unlicensed dealers. Licensed dealers were trained to identify and report straw purchasers to their local ATF or DOJ officials. Andre was an active participant in the program.

The next substantive action by Attorney General Holder was to expand the mission statement in the existing Department of Justice Guidelines for the Organized Crime Drug Enforcement Task Force (OCDETF). The Task Force was originally formed and funded in 1982 to address the flow of illegal drugs into the United States. On April 27, 2009, less than four months into their administration, Attorney General Holder amended the DOJ Guidelines to include firearms trafficking as part of the OCDETF initiative. ATF could now use OCDETF to access additional funds, obtain support from other federal agencies, and utilize surveillance wiretaps under the DOJ Title III authorization process. Title III of the Omnibus Crime Control and Safe Streets Act of 1968 (Wiretap Act) is codified at 18 U.S.C.§2518. It is a law designed to protect the privacy of citizens. It requires a detailed application that must be approved by a Federal Court. The application must set out specific facts about why the wiretap is necessary. The application is submitted under seal. The proposed target of the requested wiretap obviously has no knowledge about the application and does not have any legal representation in the process. The legal statutes thus place a strict burden on the highest levels of DOJ to carefully review the application and vouch for its truthfulness when it is presented to the federal judge.

Adding firearms trafficking to the OCDETF process was a significant move by the Obama administration. First, it linked drug trafficking and firearms trafficking together for the first time. This directly targeted Mexican and other Latin American cartels and gangs. Second, it brought enforcement of firearms trafficking more tightly under centralized DOJ control.

ATF's history traces back to 1886 when it was called the "Revenue Laboratory" and was part of the Department of Treasury's Bureau of Internal Revenue. It became an independent agency within Treasury in 1927 during Prohibition. In 1930 it became part of the DOJ and briefly was part of the FBI. When Prohibition was repealed by the Volstead Act in 1933 it was returned to Treasury as the "Alcohol Tax Unit". The Prohibition era version of ATF was popularized by Elliot Ness and the "untouchables". In 1942 it became the primary agency responsible for firearms law enforcement. This responsibility was legislatively formalized in the Gun Control Act of 1968 and the ATF officially became the Bureau of Alcohol, Tobacco, and Firearms in 1972. In 2002 President Bush signed the Homeland Security Act of 2002 which transferred the newly named "Bureau of Alcohol, Tobacco, Firearms, and Explosives" from the Department of Treasury to the Department of Justice. From 2002 until 2009 ATF was involved in numerous controversial operations including Ruby Ridge and the assault on the Branch Dividian complex in Waco, Texas.

The Obama administration move was purposely designed to enhance DOJ control over ATF as a vehicle for their gun control agenda.

On June 29, 2009, there was an OCDETF conference in Albuquerque, New Mexico, on "Firearms Trafficking." The conference was attended by high-level Obama administration officials, including Deputy Attorney General (DAG) David William Ogden (who had been recently confirmed by Congress as the second highest official in the Attorney General's office on March 12, 2009); Acting Bureau of Alcohol, Tobacco, Firearms, and Explosives (ATF) Director Kenneth E. Melson (who was appointed April 8, 2009); Assistant Attorney General (AAG) Lanny Breuer (who headed the DOJ Criminal Division and was appointed on April 20, 2009); and Director of the Executive Office of U.S.

Attorneys (EOUSA) H. Marshall Jarrett (who was appointed April 8, 2009).

On August 19, 2009, Assistant Attorney General Lanny Breuer wrote a Memorandum for Attorney General Eric Holder titled "Recommendations of the Firearms Trafficking Group", which followed up on an April 2009 meeting between Attorney General Holder, Department of Homeland Security (DHS) Secretary Janet Napolitano, and Mexican Attorney General Medina Mora, held in Cuernavaca, Mexico, and the June 29, 2009, meeting of senior DOJ officials. At the April 2009 meeting, the Attorney General and DHS Secretary "committed to form a working group [...] to curb illegal firearms trafficking from the United States to Mexico." The two countries agreed that illegal firearms trafficking facilitated "much of the violent drug cartel activity in Mexico." One attendee at the meeting said that there was at least one secret closed-door meeting between Holder, Napolitano, and Mora. Some believe the secret topic discussed may have been gunwalking.

The working group formed was the Southwest Firearms Trafficking Strategy Group (SFTS Group) led by AAG Lanny Breuer and the DOJ Criminal Division with input from ATF, FBI, DEA, DHS, ICE, CBP, the Executive Office of U.S. Attorney (EOUSA), the DOJ Office of Legal Policy (OLP), and the DHS Office of General Counsel.

The mission of the high-level Firearms Trafficking Group was to "disrupt traffickers and dismantle their enterprises." The Group was required to "regularly report to the Attorney General and the DHS Secretary."

On August 13, 2009, Immigration and Customs Enforcement (ICE) and ATF entered a letter of intent with the Attorney General of Mexico "to improve intelligence sharing and cooperation in the investigation of smuggling and trafficking of weapons." Other United States agency participants included the National Security Division (NSD), the United States Marshals Service (USMS), the State Department, and the U.S. Embassy personnel in Mexico City. This was a significant development signaling a very different mission than the original mission of Project Gunrunner. There is no mention of interdiction of firearms or prosecution of straw purchasers in the new SFTS Group mission statement.

The avowed key to the interagency trafficking strategy was not to interdict illegal firearms sold to "straw and prohibited purchasers" but to "dismantle criminal organizations in their region of operation". The letter of intent focused on "intelligence gathering" and a strategy to "dismantling a cartel". These were real strategic shifts that would be the foundation of Operation Fast and Furious.

The next high-level executive agency conference on "Arms Trafficking Cooperation" was held in Phoenix on September 22, 2009, and was attended by officials from the FBI, ATF, DEA, ICE, CBP, the Arizona U.S. Attorney General's office, as well as prosecutors from the southwest border states and Utah.

This conference was quickly followed-up with a meeting in Phoenix between Deputy Attorney General Ogden, Arizona U.S. Attorney Dennis Burke, the Director of ICE, the Phoenix DEA Senior Agent-in-Charge (SAC), the Phoenix FBI, and the Phoenix U.S. Marshals Service. At this meeting, DAG Ogden unveiled the new OCDETF Arms Trafficking initiative, known as "An Intelligence-Driven Program." This was the first time the Obama administration confirmed a strategy change that differed from the traditional law enforcement practice of arresting and prosecuting illegal purchasers. Once the offenders were arrested, law enforcement would try to get them to "flip" and provide information about higher level traffickers in exchange for a favorable plea bargain.

The strategy change was finalized a month later on October 26, 2009, in a Washington D.C., teleconference between DAG Ogden, AAG Breuer, FBI Director Robert Mueller, Drug Enforcement Agency Administration Leonhardt, ATF Acting Director Melson, and top southwest border state prosecutors. They discussed the major decision the Obama administration made to target arms trafficking networks as opposed to low-level straw purchaser buyers. This was a different mission than the original focus of Project Gunrunner, which meant that enforcement agencies would require different methodologies.

Their conclusions were that gun trafficking enforcement needed to take "a new approach." It needed to gather information from straw purchasers as an "intelligence-gathering operation", and to focus on the ultimate prosecution or elimination of Mexican drug and firearm trafficking organizations, as opposed to lower level criminals within the organizations. This new approach for law enforcement was signed off on by Deputy Attorney General David Ogden; Assistant Attorney General Lanny Breuer (Criminal Division); Acting Director of the Bureau of Alcohol, Tobacco, and Firearms Kenneth Melson; Director of the Federal Bureau of Investigation Robert Mueller; DEA Administrator Leonhardt; and top DOJ federal prosecutors from the southwest border states at the teleconference on October 26, 2009. How could AG Eric Holder not know about this significant new strategy that was personally approved by at least five of the highest officials that reported directly to him?

On October 31, 2009, five days later, the first multiple purchases of firearms in Fast and Furious were made at Lone Wolf Trading Company by Jacob Chambers and Uriel Patino, two straw purchasers who were already known by the ATF. They both increased their number of assault weapon purchases within days.

Given the gun control views of Attorney General Holder and presidential candidate Obama, it only made sense to scrutinize the Obama administration's agendas and conduct during the nine-month period following President Obama's inauguration in January 2009, and leading up to the October 2009 initiation of Operation Fast and Furious.

First, the Obama administration increased the ATF budget by $21.9 million to expand Project Gunrunner. Project Gunrunner was originally a Bush administration initiative to target straw purchasers and unlicensed firearms dealers. Licensed federal firearms dealers, like Andre Howard, were trained to identify signs that a purchaser might be a straw purchaser and to report any suspicious purchasers to ATF.

Licensed firearms dealers received pamphlets listing key warning signs of a suspected straw purchase. Obvious red flags were things like multiple purchases of particular types of assault weapons preferred by the Mexican cartels, purchasers who lacked knowledge about the weapons being purchased, purchases with cash, purchasers who didn't care about price, purchasers who didn't appear to be able to afford large cash purchases, purchasers who did not buy ammunition for the gun they purchased, and purchasers who failed to engage in any conversation or discussion with the seller.

Andre cooperated fully in the program and made numerous referrals of suspicious purchasers to the ATF. He also assisted law enforcement in the prosecution of straw purchaser criminal cases, testifying as a fact witness or as an expert witness for the government.

Part of Project Gunrunner included partnering with law enforcement agencies from other countries, particularly Mexico and Columbia, where the governments employed Electronic Tracing Systems in coordination with the United States E-Trace System. This collaboration allowed both the

DOJ and ATF to get data about U.S. Firearms recovered at crime scenes in Mexico.

From 2005 to 2008, Project Gunrunner, under the Bush administration, resulted in 650 criminal prosecutions involving 1,400 offenders and the seizure of 12,000 illegally purchased firearms. There were no reported deaths in the United States or Mexico attributed to the project during that time period.

One of the Bush administration's operations under Project Gunrunner was a Tucson-based 2006 operation called "Wide Receiver". During this time, no purchasers working during Wide Receiver were prosecuted. Early in the Obama administration, top Obama government officials examined the prior administration's Wide Receiver Operation and decided to pursue criminal prosecutions. The decision to prosecute was made at a very high administration level that included, at a minimum, AG Eric Holder's Assistant Attorney General (Criminal Division), Lanny Breuer.

The Obama administration understood that Wide Receiver was a failed operation that actually resulted in 300 to 400 weapons crossing the border to Mexico. They characterized it as "gunwalking" and refused to acknowledge that Wide Receiver was not really intentional gunwalking. In Wide Receiver, the ATF attempted to coordinate with Mexican law enforcement. There was also a meaningful attempt to trace the illegal sales to the border and across the border. The operation was promptly cancelled when it was determined to be a failed "controlled delivery" program. A "controlled delivery" program was a strategy where the straw purchaser was not arrested but the guns purchased were followed all the way to the border, where Mexican law enforcement picked up the transfer and followed the guns until they were delivered to the cartel. They would then arrest and prosecute the cartel members who received the guns and seize the guns before they were used in crimes.

Wide Receiver was a Tucson ATF operation initiated in the spring of 2006, using cooperating FFL Mike Detty, owner of Mad Dawg Global. During the operation, 474 firearms were sold, but only 64 were seized. Radio frequency identification (RIFD) tracking devices were placed inside the gun stocks of the firearms, but the Raytheon battery life was too short to allow adequate tracking. Traffickers became suspicious about surveillance and let the guns sit in "stash houses" before being moved to the border. ATF used helicopter surveillance, but the gun traffickers knew the helicopters would have to refuel, and they moved the guns while they were refueling.

In addition to technology issues, there was poor coordination between ATF in Tucson and their counterparts in Mexico, who were supposed to take over the surveillance and tracking of the weapons as they crossed the border. The ATF could not cross the border so most of the guns got lost in Mexico.

In September 2007, the ATF made another attempt at "controlled delivery" of 200 guns to straw purchaser Fidel Hernandez. ATF Tucson informed Mexican law enforcement when the firearms crossed the border, but again, Mexican authorities "lost them". Assistant ATF Director of Field Operations William Hoover directed ATF Tucson SAC William Newell to shut the operation down in October 2007, six weeks after it started. A controlled delivery is a legitimate investigative technique, but it involves a number of variables that can't always be controlled by the ATF.

In 2008, ATF SAC Newell again allowed approximately 100 more firearms to be part of an attempted controlled delivery sold to straw purchasers Medrano and others over objections made by the Immigration and Customs Enforcement Agency. It also failed.

In August 2010, three straw purchasers from Wide Receiver were convicted, receiving sentences of thirty months, forty-six months, and fifty months in federal prison.

Meanwhile, the DOJ and the ATF, in Phoenix, were gearing up for what later would be called Operation Fast and Furious. The Phoenix OCDETF task force had been established in August or September 2008 during the Bush administration, with the limited mission of fighting illegal drug trafficking. After President Obama's inauguration, the Department of Justice issued a memorandum in April 2009 titled "Guidelines for Consideration of OCDETF Designation for Firearms Trafficking Cases Related to Mexican Drug Cartels." Part of the guidelines enabled the Phoenix ATF to access both additional funding and DOJ support to get Title III wire taps in an investigation "primarily targeting firearms trafficking [...] if there is a sufficient nexus to a Mexican drug cartel." ATF's access to OCDETF resources required that their operation was linked to a strategy targeting a drug cartel.

Around the time of the new guidelines, Phoenix ATF and Special Agent-in-Charge William Newell, a veteran of Operation Wide Receiver, got funding to start a new ATF Group, "Group VII." The sole mission of the new ATF Group VII was "to dismantle firearms trafficking organizations." Everyone at the DOJ and the ATF knew from years of frontline experience that arresting straw purchasers would not "dismantle" any firearm trafficking organization. Everyone also knew that SAC William Newell had already tried "controlled delivery" strategies with Mexican law enforcement that failed. Everyone knew that AG Eric Holder wanted to take down the infamous Sinaloa Cartel. For some reason, not everyone knew that Mueller's FBI and Leonhardt's DEA already had paid informants at various levels of the Phoenix firearms trafficking

16

organization and at a very high level within the Sinaloa Cartel leadership in Mexico.

Given what everyone knew and didn't know, what was the Phoenix OCDETF and the ATF Group VII plan to dismantle the Sinaloa Cartel's firearms trafficking organization?

First, they had to assemble a team in Phoenix. President Obama appointed his trusted colleague Dennis Burke as the U.S. Attorney for the District of Arizona. Burke was from Chicago, and was a senior policy analyst during the Clinton administration. Some, including Obama's confidant and White House Policy Analyst Rahm Emanuel, credit Burke for getting Clinton's ten-year assault weapons ban passed in 1994. Burke was nominated by President Obama on July 10, 2009, and Congress confirmed him on September 15, 2009 — one month before Fast and Furious started.

Dennis Wagner, reporter for the Arizona Republic, wrote:

"[G]un control was Burke's pet theme for his 23 years in Government." He fought to get the ban on assault weapons reinstated ever since it expired in 2004.

ATF SAC Newell made SA Hope MacAllister the acting supervisor of the newly formed Group VII until a more senior official, SA David Voth, replaced her on December 6, 2009. Newell then made SA MacAllister the lead agent on Fast and Furious.

U.S. Attorney Dennis Burke made AUSA Michael Morrissey section head of the newly formed USAO National Security Section in charge of "southbound gun smuggling". He also promoted AUSA Emory Hurley to a new position — "Senior Advisor and Trial Attorney for Firearms." Finally, he brought AUSA Patrick Cunningham to Phoenix to act as Criminal Chief." The Phoenix part of the Fast and Furious team was set.

On November 30, 2009, SA MacAllister told an ICE Agent involved with the Phoenix OCEDTF "she was working on a big straw purchaser case in which guns were being transported to Mexico." Everyone on the Phoenix team was on board with gunwalking.

On January 7, 2010, Deputy Attorney General Lanny Breuer issued the Justice Department's "Strategy for Combating Mexican Cartels". The strategy "was developed over several months by the Southwest Border Strategy Group, a newly created body that included representation from the office of the Deputy Attorney General, the Department's Criminal Division [...] and several federal agencies, including [the] ATF and the Arizona U.S. Attorney's Office."The new strategy was implemented to "use [...] intelligence-based [...] multi-agency task forces, that simultaneously attack all levels of, and all criminal activities of, the open operations of the [cartel] organizations."

The memorandum said: "merely seizing firearms through interdiction will not stop firearms trafficking to Mexico. We must identify, investigate, and eliminate the sources of illegally trafficked firearms and the networks that transport them."

In November 2010, the DOJ IG issued a report that was critical of the ATF's Project Gunrunner. Project Gunrunner was the overarching national program started in April 2006 to reduce cross-border weapons trafficking. One of the report's recommendations was that the "ATF focus on developing more complex conspiracy cases against higher level gun traffickers and gun trafficking conspirators." The ATF reviewed a draft of the report in September 2010 and "concurred with the OIG's recommendation". There is no documented evidence that the DOJ IG recommendation influenced the DOJ to initiate the new strategy, but was it made to provide cover and support for the new strategy which DOJ had already put in place a year earlier in September 2009?

Operation Wide Receiver was dormant from December 2007 until September 2009. In 2009, AG Holder's Assistant Deputy Attorney General Jason Weinstein assigned a DOJ prosecutor to review the case file. In April 2010, DAAG Weinstein and AAG Breuer decided that although guns had been walked, thus presenting a potential public relations challenge, the DOJ Criminal Division would proceed with prosecutions of the straw purchasers who were involved in Wide Receiver. Indictments were handed down in May 2010 and October of that same year. The May 2010 indictments were prosecuted in August 2010. The October 2010 indictments were filed under seal pending the end of Fast and Furious.

The DOJ IG, based on a November 7, 2011, letter request from the Chairman of the Senate Judiciary Committee, Democratic Senator Patrick Leahy, agreed to add Operation Wide Receiver to the scope of their review of Operation Fast and Furious. Adding it to the DOJ IG investigation would allow Holder to use his "ongoing criminal investigation" delay tactic to avoid answering questions or producing DOJ documents to Congress about their decision to prosecute the Wide Receiver cases.

Ironically, the Obama administration tried to use the gunwalking in the Bush administration as an excuse or justification for the gunwalking in Operation Fast and Furious. The Obama administration (including Weinstein, Breuer, and Holder) would get amnesia about the 2006/2007 gunwalking when they responded to Congress' January 27, 2011, investigation requests about the ATF gunwalking to Mexican cartels during Project Gunrunner.

Operation Wide Receiver, part of Project Gunrunner, was a far different type of gunwalking than Operation Fast and Furious, which was also part of Project Gunrunner.

Both operations used court-ordered electronic surveillance and consensual recordings made by a cooperating FFL, and both targeted higher level members of Mexican cartels, including the Arrellano Felix Organization and a crime family associated with the Sinaloa Cartel in Operation Wide Receiver, as well as the Sinaloa Cartel itself in Operation Fast and Furious.

Both operations were supervised by ATF Agent Williams Newell, but that is where the similarities end. Operation Wide Receiver was a flawed plan because it was executed incompetently. The cooperating FFL in Wide Receiver was selected by the ATF because he "had provided leads to ATF in the past, and [...] the FFL was a Good Samaritan informant with a clean record who wanted to do the right thing". While the same criteria was used to select Andre Howard and Lone Wolf Trading Company in Fast and Furious, the former FFL in Wide Receiver was made an official paid confidential informant, whose identity and security were protected. Andre Howard was not paid and was not given confidential informant status. Instead, Andre was lied to, deceived, and betrayed.

The Wide Receiver FFL knew for a fact the guns were going to Mexican cartels. The straw purchasers repeatedly told him on recorded conversations that the guns they purchased had gone, and were going, south. They even thanked the FFL on behalf of their "boss in Tijuana".

The DOJ and the ATF lied to Andre Howard and gave him assurances that all the straw purchases had been, and were being, interdicted in Phoenix. Operation Fast and Furious shut down surveillance while the firearms were still in Phoenix. It had no comprehensive tracking device plan. Fast and Furious officials betrayed our Mexican ally by keeping them completely in the dark. Fast and Furious was only shut down after a United States border agent was murdered.

The top Obama administration officials involved in discussing operation Wide Receiver indictments in 2010 described the Operation as "walking" guns. DAAG

Weinstein defined "walking" as "situations where agents had the legal authority and ability to interdict the firearms, but chose not to. Weinstein said 'walk' also included a reckless operation — that is if ATF was trying to follow and interdict firearms but their tactics were repeatedly unsuccessful [...] that also was 'walking'."

During Operation Fast and Furious, the ATF and the DOJ had numerous discussions about gunwalking in operation Wide Receiver because they wanted to publicize prosecutions in that matter. They had high-level discussions — both oral and written — about the issue, including:

> April 12, 2010 Weinstein memo to Carwile, Trusty (Carwile's Deputy)
> April 19, 2010 Carwile, Trusty briefing to Lanny Breuer
> April 28, 2010 Weinstein, Trusty meeting with Hoover, McMahon
> April 26, 2010 Newell and Voth memo to McMahon
> April 27, 2010 McMahon email to Newell
> April 28, 2010 Weinstein email to Lanny Breuer
> April 30, 2010 Breuer email to Weinstein

These discussions, early in Fast and Furious, show that gunwalking was being discussed between top ATF officials in Phoenix, (Newell and Voth), top ATF officials at ATF headquarters (Hoover and McMahon), and top DOJ officials in AG Holder's office (Weinstein, Carwile, Trusty, and Breuer).

These same groups also had detailed strategy discussions about gunwalking in December 2010, just before the end of Fast and Furious, when they were planning a joint press conference by AG Holder for January 2011 in Phoenix where AG Holder would announce the unsealing of the

October 2010 wide receiver indictments and the success of Operation Fast and Furious.

Their unanimous conclusion was that no one would care that guns were walked to Mexico because "they were just Mexicans."

In 2011, when the Obama administration had to answer to congressional demands for answers and documents about Fast and Furious, they used a far different definition of gunwalking to cover up their deceit and criminal false statements.

The DOJ attorneys who reviewed the Title III wiretap applications, or even the short OEO cover memorandum, could clearly tell from the facts stated in the applications that ATF agents did not take enforcement action to interdict the weapons or make arrests.

The wiretap applications were reviewed by numerous DOJ officials in AG Holder's office, and were signed by two of his top Deputy Assistant Attorney Generals in the Criminal Division between March and July 2010:

March 10, 2010 (DAAG Blanco)
July 1, 2010 (DAAG Blanco)
May 21, 2010 (DAAG Weinstein)
June 1, 2010 (DAAG Weinstein)
June 23, 2010 (DAAG Weinstein)

Between June 28, 2010, and August 9, 2010, the National Drug Intelligence Center provided seven weekly reports to the U.S. Attorney General and the Deputy Attorney General that referred to Fast and Furious. The reports stated "straw purchasers acquired 1,500 firearms that were supplied to Mexican gun trafficking cartels." But that was not evidence of any improper gunwalking?

Chapter Two

Cooperating with Obama's DOJ, ATF, and FBI

Andre Howard was born in San Antonio, Texas, the son of a World War II career Air Force pilot. He was a "military brat" who grew up in Arizona. Andre had a healthy respect for the military and the values of the military, like leadership, accountability, honesty, and country above any individual interests. His military background led him to also honorably serve in the United States Army.

After his military service, he pursued a career as a sales representative in the sporting goods industry. In 1991 he translated his sporting goods industry experience into an entrepreneurial position as owner of Lone Wolf Trading Company. He became a federal firearms licensee and grew the business into a very successful firearms sales business. Ironically, he has never been a member of the National Rifle Association (NRA), is not personally a gun enthusiast, and does not own a personal firearm.

Andre also has another passion as a private helicopter pilot and helicopter flight instructor, based in Phoenix. He built upon his military experience, and over the years sold firearms and provided flight training to many clients who were current or former military and law enforcement personnel in a wide variety of agencies, including the CIA, the Secret Service, the FBI, and the ATF. Many of those clients over the years became professional contacts and friends.

In December 2008, one of his FBI customers asked Andre if he would accept firearms from Glock Inc. for other FBI agent's personal purchases. He agreed. He wholeheartedly embraced the mission of Project Gunrunner in 2006, and regularly reported suspected straw purchasers to the ATF.

His sense of patriotism and love of country eventually led him to be used by the DOJ and the ATF as the primary cooperating FFL in Fast and Furious. In future congressional reports, DOJ IG reports, and internal DOJ and ATF documents about Fast and Furious, he is designated as "FFL 1". Why Andre? And how did he become cooperating FFL 1?

When the Clinton administration's ten-year ban on the sale of assault weapons expired in 2004, statistics showed the gun violence in Mexico had still continued to grow. The Bush administration developed Project Gunrunner, which launched in 2006. Project Gunrunner had two targets. First, unlicensed individuals who were illegally selling firearms. The second target was straw purchasers who were recruited by the cartels to purchase guns on their behalf. The straw purchasers were usually individuals who had no criminal history, so they could pass the FBI criminal background check necessary for the purchase of certain firearms. The actual purchases were all illegal because they were not made for personal use. Instead, the straw purchasers were paid $100 to $300 for each firearm they delivered to the cartel traffickers. Project Gunrunner focused on training the properly licensed FFLs to identify these potential straw purchasers. They asked for the licensed FFLs, like Andre, to train their employees and to cooperate with law enforcement by promptly reporting suspicious purchases by potential straw purchasers.

When Project Gunrunner launched in 2006, Andre was a seasoned FFL who had been in the firearms business for fifteen years. He already had a long history of compliance with the strict regulatory and reporting requirement the government imposed on FFLs to maintain their license. The ATF was the regulatory agency tasked with enforcing those regulatory, record-keeping, and reporting requirements. They used inventories, audits, and inspections to ensure compliance. They could impose administrative sanctions, including loss of license, for violations. They controlled the FFLs' right to do business and thus their livelihood.

Andre also had a long history of cooperating with ATF, the Phoenix Police Department, and other agencies in their enforcement actions against straw purchasers and other criminals. Prior to Gunrunner, he had already reported suspicious sales, he supported law enforcement in their investigations, and he assisted in their prosecutions, testifying in both state and federal court as a fact or expert witness. He routinely refused to sell to potential purchasers when he determined they were obviously illegal purchasers. During project Gunrunner, from 2006 to 2009, Andre was not involved in the Tucson area operation (Wide Receiver), but he continued his cooperation and reported suspicious purchases by suspected straw purchasers at Lone Wolf in Phoenix. Typically, those purchasers were trying to buy one or two firearms. He and his employees were adept at recognizing the red flags published in the ATF Project Gunrunner training materials and the pamphlet ATF provided to all FFLs.

Operation Wide Receiver was purely a Tucson-based Project Gunrunner operation in 2006 and 2007 that did not involve Andre or other Phoenix area FFLs. ATF used Mike Detty, a licensed FFL in Tucson, as the primary cooperating FFL in that operation. Detty also had a long history of compliance and cooperation with the ATF. In 2013, Detty wrote a book titled "Guns Across the Border — The Inside Story", where he details his own experience cooperating with the ATF. Detty, a former marine, sold firearms out of a showroom at his home and at gun shows. His book describes his three years of cooperation which "took several twists and turns," perhaps the cruelest of which was his "betrayal" by the very agency he risked everything to assist. In Wide Receiver, the ATF made Detty a paid confidential informant, having him act as an asset of the government. They also fully briefed him on the plan: "Let the gun be trafficked to Mexico". The ATF would coordinate with Mexican law enforcement and they would interdict the guns in Mexico. The ATF installed cameras in his business, recorded telephone conversations, put tracking devices in the stocks of the weapons, and arranged for straw purchasers to repeatedly purchase large quantities of firearms. They conducted surveillance of the sales and then attempted to track the trafficking to the border, where Mexican law enforcement was supposed to take over. The operation failed, and several hundred guns went into Mexico uncontrolled by either country's law enforcement. There were no prosecutions and there was no publicity about the operation. SAC William Newell was the ATF Special Agent in Charge of operation Wide Receiver. ATF headquarters was aware of the operation but the Bush administration's Attorney General, Mike Mukasey, was never briefed on the operation and none of his senior deputies were aware of it. Mike Detty is referred to in the Fast and Furious records and reports as "FFL 2". In the forward to Detty's book, Emmy award-winning investigative reporter Sharyl Attkisson wrote: "Like other gun dealers who assisted the ATF in this confidential effort, Detty felt 'betrayed' and set aside when he learned his efforts weren't helping arrest bad guys after all. Instead, he had inadvertently assisted them."

Andre did not participate in the operation and had no knowledge about it when he was approached by the ATF in 2009 and asked to be a cooperating FFL in a Phoenix "investigation" that would become known as Operation Fast and Furious.

In the summer of 2009, Andre started to notice an increase in the number of customers who wanted to buy multiple quantities of assault-type weapons. At first, it was a modest increase. Instead of two rifles, they bought three or four. In

September 2009, ATF SA Hope MacAllister started spending more time watching the customer traffic coming into Lone Wolf Trading Company. Andre described his initial involvement in Fast and Furious to Congress:

> "ATF, the regulatory agency that licenses me as an FFL, contacted me to enlist my cooperation in an ongoing investigation they claimed they were conducting in mid-September 2009.
>
> "Pursuant to their instructions, I was to sell weapons to suspected straw purchasers while ATF monitored these sales to these suspects.
>
> "Afterward, I was to fax all documentation to their office.
>
> "I kept asking them questions. They said the questions could not be answered because this was an ongoing criminal investigation.
>
> "I was informed that several Arizona FFL dealers were cooperating as well, in addition to my store.
>
> "I was constantly assured these weapons were being interdicted shortly after they left my store. They said the guns were typically seized a few blocks away so there would be no attention drawn to Lone Wolf.
>
> "I overheard ATF field agents saying this investigation involved dangerous individuals involved with terrorists in Mexico and that every Federal Government Agency was now involved in the case, including ICE, CBP, FBI, DHS, IRS, ATF, and DEA."

The straw purchasers that the FBI informants sent into Lone Wolf during Fast and Furious fit all of the ATF red flags contained in the ATF pamphlet distributed during Project Gunrunner:

- "Want to buy a large number of the same model firearm or similar firearms." Check.

27

- "Choose only tactical type semiautomatic rifles and large frame semi-automatic pistols." Check.
- "Order more of the same firearms within days." Check.
- "Attempt to conceal their conversations with each other." Check.
- "Do not haggle or question the price." Check.
- "Have little or no knowledge of the firearms they are purchasing." Check.
- "Lack the physical stature to handle the firearm." Check.

Andre definitely knew these purchasers were straw purchasers. The FBI authorized all the sales even though many were convicted felons or illegal aliens disqualified from purchasing firearms under federal law. Most also falsified other data on their purchase forms.

In addition to the obvious red flags that Andre was trained to monitor and report, the ATF had real-time data about the straw purchaser's financial situation and knew that none of the original straw purchasers like Jaime Avila, Jacob Chambers, Joshua Moore, and Uriel Patino had any identifiable source of income. When the straw purchasers were followed by the ATF, they always took their firearm purchases to known stash houses where the ATF already had installed outside pole cameras to monitor the firearm transfers to the next level of traffickers. The DOJ and the ATF received immediate verification of firearm traces to crime scenes, and were able to keep cooperating FFLs in the dark about crime scene traces coming from Mexican crime scenes. The ATF and the DOJ blocked delivery of traces to the cooperating FFL, thus preventing the FFLs from challenging their false assertions that all guns were interdicted. After a month or so, Andre became increasingly suspicious because there were no criminal cases being filed against these major straw purchasers. In addition, there would normally not be repeat purchases if the prior purchase was interdicted. The DOJ and the ATF both said "still sell".

The first three months of Fast and Furious, running from October to December 2009, were telling. All of a sudden six straw purchasers "known" to the ATF showed up at five different Arizona FFLs and started ordering twenty or more assault weapons each visit. They often paid several visits in a week. How is it that they were confident that FFLs like Andre would continue to sell them those weapons? Andre didn't carry a large number of AK-47s, FN Herstal Five-seven caliber pistols, or .50 caliber rifles in his store's inventory. The answer: FBI informants, at the direction of the DOJ, FBI, and ATF, steered them to these cooperating FFLs, particularly Andre. Some of the straw purchasers were FBI informants themselves.

They all bought the same weapons. Most of the purchases were AK-47 rifles and pistols. The AK-47 assault rifle, also known and the Kalashnikov, was first prominently used by the Viet Cong during the Vietnam War. It is now a popular choice of the Mexican drug cartels, and is the most popular semi-automatic rifle in the world. The Herstal FN Five-seven semiautomatic pistol is lesser known to most Americans but is often referred to as "the cop killer" because it is so powerful that it can pierce a Kevlar protective vest. Historically, the Herstal manufacturer would only sell their pistol to military and law enforcement customers. Although the Brady Foundation protested against allowing domestic sales in the United States, it was still available. Several Democratic congressmen unsuccessfully tried to pass legislation banning sales domestically. The last attempt at legislation, introduced after Army Major Hasan used the weapon in the Ft. Hood shooting, also failed. Over 300 U.S. law enforcement agencies, including the U.S. Secret Service, and many foreign militaries use the pistol. It is very popular with Mexican drug cartels and the Mexican armed forces. Finally, the Mexican cartels bought dozens of powerful Barrett .50 caliber rifles during Fast and Furious. One was used by the Sinaloa Cartel to shoot down a Mexican Army helicopter.

The majority of the original straw purchasers were already known to the DOJ, the FBI, and the ATF. The Justice Department also knew the straw purchasers were part of a trafficking ring run by Manuel Celis-Acosta. They also knew, through a search of their financial records, that none of them had any identifiable source of income, although they paid tens of thousands of dollars to purchase the weapons with cash (usually in stacks of $100 bills). The ATF surveilled the purchases and followed most of them to a parking lot where they were transferred to a vehicle owned by Celis-Acosta, or to his residence where they were then transferred to a stash house for transport to the cartels in Mexico.

By December 31, the top four purchasers bought at least 630 firearms that were all transported to Mexico. Sean Steward bought 242, Uriel Patino about 196, Jacob Chambers bought 117, and Joshua Moore bought eighty-one.

The ATF knew where they lived, and watched them illegally transfer possession to the next level trafficker. ICE, the DEA, and other border security law enforcement officials who happened to intercept shipments were told by the DOJ to "let them go". The DOJ then waited for the murders to take place. All this so the Obama administration could pad crime scene statistics, blame the "corrupt" FFLs of greed and illegal sales, and eventually pass gun control legislation.

In the government's November 19, 2012, sentencing memorandum in the criminal case *United States of America v. Sean Christopher Steward*, the second largest straw purchaser of firearms in Operation Fast and Furious, prosecutors argued for an enhanced criminal sentence, in part because he had a past criminal history. He was sentenced for prior crimes in 2001, 2002, and 2010. During Fast and Furious, the Department of Justice approved fifteen separate purchases to Steward, totaling 289 firearms from three different Federal Firearms Licensees, all of whom submitted appropriate documentation for government pre-approval of the sales. Ten of the government approved sales, totaling 246 firearms, were sold from Lone Wolf Trading Company. Despite his prior criminal convictions and prior illegal transfers of firearms to cartel traffickers, the FBI approved all the sales to Steward.

In November 2009, top officials at the ATF emailed each other about a "big success" in Operation Fast and Furious. On November 24, William Newell, Special Agent in Charge of the ATF Phoenix Field Office, sent an email to William McMahon, ATF Deputy Assistant Director (West), Office of Field Operations in Washington, D.C., who forwarded it to Mark Chait, the ATF Acting Assistant Director of Field Operations regarding a gun seizure in Agua Prieta, Sonora, Mexico.

On November 25, Mark Chait responded to Newell, McMahon, and Daniel Kumor, ATF's Chief of International Affairs:

"I just heard from OSII [the Office of Strategic Intelligence and Information] [...] that twenty more semiautomatic 7.62 Draco pistols were tied to this recovery on two multiple sales with a time-to-crime of one day. In light of how hot this info is, I just wanted to make sure we put all resources on this."

Newell responded:

"On it. It's part of an active Phoenix case belonging to SA Hope MacAllister, OCDETF Strike Force, I thought I sent this to you."

On December 9, 2009, Chait forwarded the email chain to William Hoover, Deputy Director of the ATF:

> "Phoenix was already on two of the straws and already had an OCDETF case open prior to the event."

In the first months of Operation Fast and Furious, ATF officials were bragging about the major "success" of a large firearm crime scene recovery of weapons purchased by two straw purchasers in Phoenix that has a "time-to-crime" of one day! They bragged that this was part of Agent MacAllister's OCDETF Strike Force case, i.e. Fast and Furious.

Why was top ATF leadership, from the ATF Agent in Charge in Phoenix up the chain to the number-two official at ATF headquarters,Deputy Director Hoover, happy about the fact that weapons purchased by straw purchasers in Phoenix were recovered by Mexican law enforcement at a crime scene in Mexico the next day? This was more of a success because this was a recovery of "more" weapons? Why didn't anyone in the ATF chain of command ask "how did they get to a crime scene in Mexico one day after they were purchased from an FFL where ATF had surveillance and the FFL sold the firearms at ATF/DOJ's direction?" No one thought there was a law enforcement problem? This was not a red flag?

Apparently there may have been a miscommunication between Chait and Hoover because Hoover's boss, ATF Acting Director Kenneth Melson, already got the message about the "big success" before December 3, when he shared the news with top DOJ officials Assistant Attorney General Lanny Breuer and Associate Deputy Attorney General Edward Siskel, who was appointed Associate Counsel at the White House a month later on January 11, 2011, where he was put in charge of handling oversight from Congress, including the executive branch responses to the congressional requests for information about Operation Fast and Furious that Senator Grassley sent to DOJ two weeks later, on January 27, 2011.

In a December 3, 2009 memorandum to Lanny Breuer titled "Weapons Seizures in Mexico", Melson reported to the leader of the Southwest Border Firearms Trafficking Strategy Group about the new "anti-cartel strategy" that was agreed to by the ATF, FBI, DEA, and DOJ in October 2009:

> "Lanny: We have decided to take a little different approach with regard to seizures of multiple weapons in Mexico. [...] Using the [crime scene] traces as intelligence and compiling the information from each trace investigation, we can connect the purchases, identify the traffickers, and use more serious charges against them. The intelligence analysis and linking of trace data and investigation results will be done at HQ out of our intelligence directorate."

The reason this new strategy is a "little different approach" is that the real mission of the ATF, and the real "articulated strategy" of United States law enforcement, was supposedly to stop guns purchased in the United States from being trafficked to Mexico and to prevent those guns from being used in violent crimes where Mexican citizens are wounded, maimed and murdered. Certainly that was the promise the United States made to the government of Mexico at AG Eric Holder's meeting in Mexico in April 2009, and in subsequent public statements by the Obama administration. The strategy is also "different" because it ignores stopping straw purchases, which was the official purpose of Project Gunrunner.

If AAG Lanny Breuer did not understand, or had issues with, these "differences" in this new strategy outlined by ATF Acting Director Melson, he should have discussed it with Melson. As the leader of the Southwest Firearms Trafficking Strategy group that reported regularly to AG

Holder and the Director of DEA, he had a duty to know what the ATF was doing. AAG Breuer certainly could not have failed to understand Melson's next statement:

> "The success of the strategy would depend on '[the] level of activity' and 'will depend on the number of Mexican seizures and whether they will trace the guns, or allow us to do it."

Mexico had been providing, and continued to provide, crime scene firearms information to the ATF and FBI so they could trace the U.S. guns sold in the United States that were seized at Mexican crime scenes. The strategy to gain enough intelligence to bring high-level prosecutions could only succeed if there were many crime scene traces in Mexico.

Melson ended the message to AAG Breuer saying:

> "We should meet again just to catch up on where we are on our gun-trafficking issues, and we could talk about the above ideas as well."

The next day, Assistant Attorney General Lanny Breuer responded to ATF Acting Director Melson, interestingly copying four other high level Department of Justice officials:

Associate Deputy Attorney General Edward Siskel; Deputy Assistant Attorney General Jason Weinstein; Principal Deputy Assistant Attorney General and Chief of Staff to AG Holder Mythili Raman; and Deputy Chief of Staff (to AG Holder) Steven Fagell:

> "Ken, we think this is a terrific idea and a great way to approach the investigation of these seizures. […] Our DOJ Gang Unit will be assigning an attorney to help you. […] I would love to see you to discuss this further. See you soon, Lanny."

In 2011, when Congress investigated the Fast and Furious debacle, every DOJ official, including AG Holder's Chief of Staff and Deputy Chief of Staff, steadfastly denied being in any loop involving gun trafficking strategy issues.

Very early in his cooperation in Fast and Furious Andre had concerns. SA MacAllister gave him assurances that everything was being done legally and above boards. After less than one month into the investigation concerns continued to mount and he requested a meeting with SA MacAllister's superiors.

Andre Howard's request for a meeting with AUSA Hurley and ATF Agent Voth in October 2009 was triggered by a significant increase in straw purchaser activity. He was concerned about the quantities of weapons being purchased and the obvious red flags that Mexican drug trafficking organizations (DTOs) were involved. Eventually, the DOJ and the ATF agreed to meet with Andre on December 17, 2009.

To fully appreciate the context of Andre's scheduled meeting with Phoenix DOJ and ATF officials on December 17, 2009, and the duplicity of their conduct, it is important to look at the escalating Fast and Furious activity the day of the meeting, the days immediately preceding the meeting, and the days following the meeting. It is also very important to note the escalating Fast and Furious sales, and crime scene reports, during the two month period between his request in October and the eventual meeting in December.

In his December 18, 2009, Phoenix Group VII biweekly update, SA Voth reported that between the start of Fast and Furious and the meeting with Andre Howard on December 17 "the large-scale conspiracy of over fifteen interconnected straw purchasers had purchased over 500 firearms, most of which are the AK 47 variant 7.62 assault rifles and/or the F.N. Herstal 5.7 mm pistols. [...] Approximately [fifty] have been recovered in Mexico [...] with a short time-to-crime, some as little as one day."

The day of the December 17 meeting, SA George Gillett, Assistant Special Agent in Charge, reported to Special Agent in Charge Newell and Group Supervisor Voth that SA Ray

Rowley, the ATF Southwest Border Coordinator, expressed "some concern regarding the total number of guns that have been purchased by this straw purchaser scheme [...] and mentioned the possibility of needing to shut the investigation down due to the large number of guns that already have been trafficked."

SA Gillett said he told Ray Rowley "we have slowed down the FFL on future purchases [...] and will slow the purchases down as much as possible, but we have not identified the network yet." Straw purchasers bought over "175 guns the week before."

Of course the representations that the ATF or the DOJ had slowed Andre Howard down were completely false. In fact, the ATF and the FBI had been actively setting up larger purchases and directing straw purchasers to Lone Wolf Trading Company on a regular, and accelerated, basis.

The title of the investigation was initially "Jacob Chambers" because he and his colleagues were the first purchasers during the gunwalking operation. That name was soon changed to Operation Fast and Furious. Sean Steward had already been identified as a major straw purchaser.

A December 8, 2009, Report of Investigation by SA Tonya English, Group Supervisor David Voth, and Special Agent in Charge William Newell demonstrates a typical Fast and Furious timeline:

On December 8, 2009, ATF Special Agents Tonya English, ATF Special Agent Hope MacAllister, ATF Agent John Dodson, ATF Agent Jesse Medina, ATF Agent A. Bogle, ATF Supervisor David Voth, ATF Task Force Officers, and Phoenix Police Department detectives and officials all conducted surveillance of Sean Steward.

The surveillance was triggered on December 7, when ATF SA MacAllister was informed by a "source of information" (SOI) that Sean Steward was in Lone Wolf Trading Company trying to arrange a purchase of twenty AK-47 rifles. The source of information was not identified, but was likely an FBI informant embedded within the straw purchaser and drug cartel organization.

That same day, ATF SA Medina "received information that a call was received by an FFL employee [from Andre Howard's Lone Wolf store]. The caller was identified as Joshua Moore. He was also trying to arrange a purchase of twenty AK-47 rifles.

On that day, more than ten ATF agents and Phoenix police set up a full day of surveillance at Lone Wolf, starting at 1230 hours. The next morning SA MacAllister drove by the residences of known affiliated straw purchasers, recorded their license plate numbers, and verified that Uriel Patino's alleged residence was a vacant property.

At 0905, SA MacAllister obtained more information from the SOI, other existing data sources, and recorded telephone data regarding others involved in the transaction, their residences, and telephone numbers. SA MacAllister coordinated with FFL Andre Howard and Lone Wolf employees regarding the expected timing of the weapons arrival at Lone Wolf from the distributor, and the arrangement for the illegal sales.

During the next twelve hours, the surveillance team watched Steward purchase at least forty AK-47s. He was accompanied by multiple Hispanic and Caucasian accomplices. The ATF followed the weapons to multiple transfer points and even coordinated a traffic stop of one of the trucks transporting twenty AK-47s. The police identified two of the three individuals in the truck as known firearms traffickers. They confirmed that Steward and known trafficker Manuel Celis-Acosta had the firearms in the truck, then let them go. Next stop: a Mexican cartel crime scene.

On January 20, 2010, when SA Tonya English completed the OCDETF investigation initiation form applying for Fast and Furious to be accepted as an OCDETF Task Force

Operation, she listed twelve prospective defendants. Three had assigned FBI numbers:

Manuel Fabian Celis-Acosta,

Sean Steward, and

Juan Martinez-Gonzalez

The fact that they had assigned FBI numbers indicates they were paid FBI informants.

During Fast and Furious, the DOJ, the ATF, and the FBI had a problem. When Andre raised his concerns about the quantity of firearms being purchased by straw purchasers sent into his store by the ATF, it was FBI informants embedded within the cartel's arms trafficking network that were making the arrangements. The ATF and the DOJ both agreed to set up a meeting with Andre in October 2009, but delayed scheduling it until December for reasons that are still known only to them. They knew the firearms they were putting in the hands of the cartel would be used in violent crimes, would be entered into the NCIS system, and would be "traced." The normal tracing process would first go to the manufacturer to obtain the name of the wholesaler that made the original purchase. The wholesaler would then identify the retailer that purchased the firearm for sale to the public. The FBI then sent the licensed retailer, Lone Wolf Trading Company, a crime scene trace request. Andre's concerns would be exacerbated because he would obviously know the guns were being walked. To cover up their "lie" that all the guns were being interdicted, they had to intervene and change the normal FBI NCIS tracing process for firearms walked in Fast and Furious. Their solution was reported in a Southwest Border briefing paper in March 2010. At that time, 500 firearms had been walked and "approximately fifty had been recovered in Mexico or near the Mexican Border."

To assure their superiors at the upper levels of the DOJ, the ATF, and the FBI that all bases were covered, and to keep Andre and other cooperating FFLs in the dark, they reported:

"[O]f those 500 firearms purchased by the group [...] approximately [fifty] have been recovered. [...] The serial numbers are continuallybeing updated and changed, thus affecting the trace results."

So when AUSA Hurley, ATF Agent Voth, and ATP Agent MacAllister lied to Andre on December 17, 2009, and said all the firearms sold in Fast and Furious were interdicted, Andre had no evidence to the contrary. When Andre and I met with the DOJ and the ATF on March 11, 2011, and AUSA Hurley as well as AUSA Morrissey lied to us, saying again that all firearms from Lone Wolf during Fast and Furious had been interdicted, Andre still had no evidence to the contrary other than the fact that two ATF Agents showed up at his store on December 15, 2010, to do a personal trace of two AK-47s recovered from the Brian Terry crime scene. AUSA Hurley and AUSA Morrissey still lied, saying no firearms from Lone Wolf were recovered at the Brian Terry crime scene. Unfortunately for them, Andre knew two of the guns at the Brian Terry crime scene were traced to Lone Wolf Trading Company. He sold those two weapons to Jaime Avila on January 16, 2010. Jaime Avila was clearly a straw purchaser. This raised a huge red flag that the Fast and Furious guns were not being interdicted.

In March 2011, when Andre decided to cooperate with Congress in their investigation of Fast and Furious, the DOJ, the ATF, and the FBI immediately flooded him with dozens of crime scene traces relating to Fast and Furious weapons that were previously recovered at crime scenes in Mexico and the United States, but were withheld from him during the Operation.

All FFLs are subject to strict federal regulation, including detailed record-keeping and reporting requirements. FFLs must maintain an Acquisition and Disposition Record, which is a book or a computerized log that records the acquisition (date and source) and disposition (date and transferee) of all firearms transactions. FFL's must file a report to ATF within five business days whenever they sell or transfer more than one handgun to the same purchaser. The ATF uses these multiple handgun sales reports to verify a gun dealer's acquisition and disposition records, to detect suspicious activity, and to generate investigative leads.

The FFL must require each customer to personally fill out ATF Form 4473, the Firearms Transaction Record, for every firearms transaction regardless of the type of firearm being purchased. That form requires the purchaser to list his basic identification information including actual name, residential address, and citizenship status. In addition, it requires the customer to answer other questions that would disqualify them from purchasing a firearm, such as whether they have ever had any felony convictions or any convictions regarding domestic violence. Finally, the form requires a certification that the purchase is for personal use (unless it is a gift). Purchases on behalf of a third party are illegal. False answers to any of these questions can be prosecuted as a felony false statement in federal court.

Andre relays the ATF Form 4473 directly to the FBI's National Instant Criminal Background Check System that same day. The FBI responds with one of three replies: proceed, delay (for three days), or deny. If the FFL receives a delay response, the FBI must provide further guidance within three business days or the FFL can release the purchase on the fourth day. The FBI can still call later to cancel the sale. If the FFL has already transferred the weapon after being told to proceed or delay (after the waiting period), the ATF can still confiscate the firearm directly from the purchaser but the FFL is no longer required to take any action.

However the FBI responds, the reason for their response is known only to the FBI and is not provided to the FFL dealer. So, if an FFL has a customer who buys a hunting gun for a relative each year for Christmas and the next year provides the identical information on Form 4473 but the sale is denied, it could be for any reason including new information about the purchaser's background or government retaliation against the FFL.

By the same token, if the FFL is suspicious of a purchaser, sends in Form 4473, receives a delay order, conducts his own research of local court records and finds felony convictions, then receives a proceed order the next day, the FFL has no legal basis to personally refuse to complete the sale to the purchaser. The FFL does not know why the FBI initially delayed then approved the sale. It could be for any reason. Maybe the FBI database did not pick up the felony conviction, or maybe the ATF wanted the sale to go through despite the felony conviction so the firearm could be walked to the Mexican cartels as part of Operation Fast and Furious.

After Fast and Furious, Andre obtained the help of friends and contacts and discovered evidence that during the operation, the delay/proceed directions were frequently used to authorize sales to both felons and illegal aliens.

The documents demonstrated that Obama's administration (FBI in coordination with the ATF) intentionally kept him in the dark about disqualifying background information so they could accelerate illegal sales and pad their statistics for use in their ultimate gun control agenda that they intended to provide to Congress.

After Fast and Furious, and Andre's cooperation with Congress, the FBI suddenly started issuing denials of sales to Andre's longtime customers without any legitimate reason. Andre provided extensive documentary evidence about this new practice to Congress as proof of some of the Obama administration's retaliation against him.

Before Fast and Furious, noncitizens were required to submit documents to the FFL showing that they legally lived in Arizona for ninety days before they attempted to purchase a firearm. The Obama administration did away with that requirement, so in Fast and Furious, they just checked a box that they were "legal aliens". Many of the straw purchasers in Fast and Furious were illegal aliens approved for purchase by the FBI.

The ATF has a National Tracing Center that traces the history of a firearm that is illegally possessed, or used in a crime, by using the serial number from the weapon and linking it to the ATF Form 4473 information, which in turn also links to the FFL's Acquisition and Disposition Record and the FFL's record files containing the original Form 4473 filled out by the purchaser at the time of purchase. That document would typically be introduced into evidence at trial in a prosecution for a felony charge of making a False Statement in violation of 18 U.S. Code §1001.

In Mexico, firearm sales are extremely regulated. Under Mexican law, all firearm sales must be conducted through the Mexican government.

ATF Industry Operation Investigators are authorized to review FFL records, inventory the firearms on hand for sale, conduct annual warrantless inspections to ensure compliance with federal record-keeping requirements, obtain an inspection warrant if needed, and obtain a reasonable cause warrant if there is evidence of violations. Violations can result in administrative revocation of an FFL's license, and even potential criminal charges.

Between October 2009 and the time of the December 17, 2009 meeting, Andre's concerns continued to grow. The quantity of weapon sales increased, repeat purchasers were coming in more frequently, and straw purchasers started coming into the gun store together with other prior straw purchasers. It became obvious that no arrests were being made.

When the straw purchaser activity intensified, ATF placed their cameras inside Lone Wolf Trading Company. The two

ATF technicians who installed the cameras told Andre the cameras would run twenty-four hours a day, seven days a week, and cover the entire store. Every sale to a straw purchaser was recorded and could be viewed in real time on any computer or mobile device by any federal agent with an access code.

Even Director of the ATF Melson, at ATF headquarters in Washington, D.C., could watch the sales on his office or home computer. The ATF also put a device on Andre's business phone line so conversations with straw purchasers could be recorded. The phone line was rigged so Andre could directly contact the ATF with a dedicated pin number. Finally, the ATF set up pole cameras to have video surveillance and recordings of the parking lot outside Lone Wolf Trading Company.

In Fast and Furious, the FBI and the ATF made some record and reporting changes specifically for that operation. Every firearm purchased by a Fast and Furious straw purchaser was recorded in a separate Suspect Person Database handled by the Violent Crime Analysis Branch.

The ATF guidance for use of this database said:

"Entries made to this program are firearms that have 'NOT' been recovered by law enforcement but [are] suspected to eventually be used in criminal activity."

The ATF and the DOJ knew that the weapons sold in Fast and Furious, which were all entered in the Suspect Person Database, were probably going to be used in criminal activity, and that criminal activity would probably involve violence and could very well result in murder.

The database also served a second purpose. It saved valuable time in processing crime scene trace requests. Another aspect of the Suspect Person Database was that once a Fast and Furious weapon was entered into the database, the ATF could control the dissemination of trace requests. ATF agents entering data were directed to:

"also indicate whether or not the National Tracing Center
can release trace history to other requesters."

The ATF officials in Fast and Furious stopped the National Tracing Center from sending trace requests to Andre so he would not know weapons from Lone Wolf were being recovered from Mexican crime scenes on a regular basis.

For example: On May 6, 2010, Heigi Nelson, Program Analyst, ATF National Tracing Center in West Virginia, sent an email to SA Hope MacAllister, SA Tonya English, and two other ATF officials, Mark Sonnendecker and Jose Medina, titled "Suspect Gun Firearm Recovered":

"The National Tracing Center has received a Trace request for the above listed firearm [a Fast and Furious firearm sold by Lone Wolf] […] to prevent the NTC from releasing information that may jeopardize your investigation. […] It is extremely important that if your case is still active, that you state whether or not we may conduct a trace on this firearm."

No trace was sent to Andre on this weapon because the ATF wanted to keep him in the dark about their gunwalking. Ever since he raised his concerns in October 2009, SA Hope MacAllister continually assured him the firearms were being interdicted. Andre still insisted on a meeting with her superiors.

Andre's requested meeting finally occurred on December 17, 2009. Andre described the meeting:

"Something wasn't right and I began insisting to the ATF case agent in charge that I requested a meeting with whoever was in charge of this case for reassurance. I wasn't getting anywhere and now was adamant they meet with me. […] Finally, on December 17, 2009, Case Agent MacAllister, ATF Group Supervisor David Voth, and Assistant United States Attorney Emory

Hurley, who was prosecuting the case, arrived at my store. We met in my office. "Mr. Hurley began with a long, drawn-out narrative that my help had been extremely important. He said a lot of other FFL dealers were also helping. I expressed my own concerns and asked if my store was being set up. I asked, 'Who are these people and why hasn't law enforcement moved to prosecute them? Are these sales legal?'

"AUSA Emory Hurley was vague and said that they could not go into any details of the case because it was an ongoing massive investigation involving several federal agencies, which I had already been made aware of by several agents. I challenged them that I needed clarification before I continued their requested cooperation. Hurley responded that my cooperation was essential, but he could not tell me what to do. I explained to him that was incorrect because I had already been doing everything at their specific request, and under their direction, since September, including sending copies of all forms, again at their request, to ATF headquarters.

"I had telephoned them at their request to report when known straw purchasers, which they identified to me at the start of their operation, came into my store to buy weapons. At their request, I stalled the straw purchasers until they could set up their surveillance in the parking lot. They assured me everything was legal as long as the FBI approved the sale.

"In many instances the case agent notified me that these people would be coming in beforehand. They told me the type of weapons and the quantity of weapons they wanted to purchase so I could order them from my wholesaler. I continually asked the ATF when they were going to arrest these people and when this case was going to end. The case agent simply said 'it was up to the federal prosecutors.' Hurley would not discuss any details, but assured me all weapons were confiscated in Phoenix near my store."

Other things troubled Andre in October 2009. Several FBI agents did FFL transfers of their personal Glock pistols to his store. ATF agents asked him to set aside the cash the straw purchasers used to make each purchase, but they never wrote down the serial numbers from the cash and never took pictures for evidence at trial. They just counted the money and released the money to him to put into his account.

Andre concluded:

"The ATF and the DOJ controlled my livelihood, and not cooperating with them could result in retaliation by them. I heard several agents say the Department of Homeland Security was involved, so the case might involve terrorists. Most importantly, two senior ATF agents and the lead federal prosecutor assured me the weapons had been interdicted and no one would be harmed. They told me to continue what I was doing."

More than forty different straw purchasers and/or FBI informants would soon be arriving to purchase weapons in 2010.

"How do lies lead to deceit? How does deceit lead to Betrayal?"
"Step one: you recruit patriotic, law-abiding American citizens
to help you. You lie to them, telling them:

'*You are helping us defeat the Mexican cartels, stopping the flow of illegal drugs from Mexico to the United States, and saving Mexican lives.*"

"*Step two: Keep them in the dark about the truth. Repeat step one when challenged.*"

Andre Howard Helicopter Pilot, Instructor, 2002, Bell 206
Ranger helicopter at Mesa Falcon Field

Outside of Lone Wolf Trading Company, Glendale, Arizona, 2018

Inside of Lone Wolf Trading Company, Glendale, Arizona, 2018

Andre Howard, Owner of Lone Wolf Trading Company
with Fox News Investigative reporter Katie Pavlich.

Larry Gaydos, Cadet Captain, United States
Military Academy, West Point, New York, 1973

Larry Gaydos, Cadet Captain, United States
Military Academy, West Point, New York, 1973.

Major Larry Gaydos, Second Meritorious Service Medal Presented by Colonel Rice, Commandant of The judge Advocate General's School, 1982.

Larry Gaydos, Gaydos Duffer, P.C., Arlington, Texas, 2016

Co-Authors Andre Howard, Owner of Lone Wolf Trading Company, and Larry Gaydos, Glendale Arizona, 2018.

Katie Pavlich, Fox News investigative reporter and author of "Fast and Furious – Barack Obama's Bloodiest Scandal and its Shameless Cover Up" interviewing Andre Howard about Fast and Furious, 2018.

Katie Pavlich, Andre Howard, and Larry Gaydos filming a segment on Fast and Furious for Fox Nation documentary, 2018.

Chapter Three

Obama's "Anti-Drug Cartel Plan" — By Selling Guns?

While the DOJ and the ATF were locking in Andre's cooperation, and the alleged cooperation of numerous other FFLs, what was really going on in Obama's DOJ, FBI, and ATF?

Although straw purchasers started making modest purchases in September 2009, October 31, 2009, marked the first sales to straw purchasers who were ultimately indicted and prosecuted under the new OCDETF. Four straw purchasers, including Chambers and Patino, each bought multiple AK-47s. These first official sales occurred five days after DAG Ogden, AAG Breuer, ATF AD Melson, FBI Director Mueller, DEA Administrator Leonhard, and top federal prosecutors in the southwest border states had their teleconference finalizing the new Obama administration's firearm trafficking strategy. The top DOJ officials changed the OCDETF gun-trafficking focus from individual purchasers/traffickers to trafficking networks. The program was initially called "Chambers et.al" because Chambers was the first official purchaser after the program was officially launched. It was soon changed to Operation Fast and Furious, and Patino would be the most prolific illegal straw purchaser.

The first response of most Americans when the details about Fast and Furious began to emerge in 2011 was "a few gun interdictions might have slipped through our enforcement network". The second response, after more details about the quantity of firearms involved emerged, was: "Who would possibly come up with a plan to arm the already dangerous and heavily armed drug cartels with some of the most deadly assault weapons in the United States? Under what kind of anti-cartel strategy could a plan like this possibly make sense? How could we prevent these weapons from being used to murder innocent people in Mexico?"

On November 24, 2009, Jaime Avila, a new straw purchaser recruited by Patino, made his first firearm purchase at Lone Wolf. He was accompanied by Patino, who would ultimately make the most firearms purchases. ATF was on-site, identified Avila's false address and automobile information, and conducted limited surveillance. The firearms he purchased that day had not been recovered as of January 2011. Avila was entered into the newly created ATF Suspect Gun Database on November 24, 2009.

Also on November 24, 2009, a large group of Fast and Furious firearms were seized at a crime scene in Agua Prieta, Sonora, Mexico. Crime scene traces were issued. Correspondence between ATF Special Agent-in-Charge Newell, ATF Deputy Assistant Director McMahon, Acting Assistant ATF Director Mark Chait, ATF Assistant Director William Hoover, and ATF Chief of International Affairs Daniel Kumor reported the event:

> "Twenty or more semi-automatic pistols were tied to this recovery on
> two multiple sales with a "time-to-crime" of one day. […] Hot info. […]
> Part of an active
> e Phoenix case belonging to SA Hope MacAllister, OCDETF Strike Force."

The ATF immediately forwarded the email to ATF headquarters, the Deputy Attorney General of the United States (Holder's number-two official), and other top Holder deputies and assistants.

So, in November 2009, a single gun recovery in Sonora, Mexico, of twenty firearms sold in Arizona that had been traced to Fast and Furious with a time-to-crime of one day was an event so important that every top ATF and DOJ official needed to know about it immediately. What made this so important? The new Obama administration strategy was one month old. The news about this crime scene recovery of U.S. guns in Mexico was not buried in some routine weekly or monthly report. It was clearly a big event for the DOJ and the Obama administration. All of these same top officials would all have amnesia about this event when they were called to testify about it before Congress and the DOJ IG a little over a year later. One of the Holder deputies copied on the email, Edward Siskel, would later be transferred to the White House as Senior Counsel to President Obama in charge of handling the congressional investigation. He and the other top officials had a copy of this email exchange, but none of them remembered it or deemed it to be in any way significant. They had never heard of Fast and Furious and never had any idea U.S. guns ever went to Mexico. Credible?

What really is important about this event is that it was the first large recovery of firearms sold during Fast and Furious. Even more important, the firearms were recovered in Mexico as part of a program these same officials swore under oath was a program where all the weapons purchased by straw purchasers were interdicted. The most important fact was that they were recovered at a crime scene in Mexico one day after they were sold in Phoenix at a gun store during ATF surveillance of the purchase.

Curiously, not one top official at the DOJ or the ATF who received the email asked a single question about any surveillance; how the guns crossed the border; whether Mexico was informed about the traces or the program; or whether anyone was injured, maimed, or murdered during the crime in Mexico.

Not one top DOJ official expressed any concern that the first reported crime scene recovery, which occurred within the first month of the new OCDETF program, occurred one day after the sale. The ATF had transferred dozens of agents from other jurisdictions to assist surveillance and stop trafficking, so why weren't these top officials disappointed?

The truth was they considered it a huge success! There was celebration! It was great news they wanted to share with every top ATF and DOJ official. The program worked!

In November 2009, the first official month of the new OCDETF, straw purchasers bought thirty-four firearms in twenty-four days. The guns were taken to a used auto repair shop ("stash house") for temporary storage. The repair shop specialized in repairing street race cars. The operation name was thereafter changed to Fast and Furious.

In the beginning of December 2009, ATF Special Agent-in-Charge of Fast and Furious, Hope McAllister, informed Andre Howard that the quantity and dangerous nature of the straw purchases was about to significantly increase. Andre reiterated his demands for a meeting with SA McAllister's superiors.

On December 3, 2009, Acting ATF Director Melson followed up on the November 24, 2009, news about the Sonora crime scene recovery with an email titled "Weapon Seizures in Mexico" to Deputy Associate Attorney General Edward Siskel, Assistant Attorney General Lanny Breuer, ATF Deputy Director William Hoover, Deputy Assistant Attorney General Weinstein, and Principal Deputy Assistant Attorney General and Chief of Staff Raman informing them about the "new approach, where firearms are seized at crime scenes and the criminal traces are used as 'intelligence' about the cartels."

Assistant Attorney General (Criminal) Lanny Breuer responded that he would assign a DOJ criminal attorney to work with the Strike Force. Breuer would later testify under oath before Congress that he first learned about the gunwalking tactic in the spring of 2010 and regretted that he didn't do anything to stop it.

On December 8, 2009, ATF Agent Tonya English wrote an ATF Report of Investigation about the surveillance of a new straw purchaser, Sean Steward. Steward made two separate purchases of twenty AK-47s. He was followed by at least twelve ATF agents and Phoenix police. They made a traffic stop, viewed the guns, and took no action. The DEA also mentioned the purchases and took no action.

On December 12, 2009, straw purchaser Jaime Avila again purchased five more AK-47s, which were not recovered.

The day after Andre's meeting with SA MacAllister, AUSA Hurley, and Phoenix ATF Group VII Supervisor David Voth, where they assured Andre that all firearms were interdicted, Voth filed a report regarding Fast and Furious progress to ATF Intelligence Officer Simpson:

> "From September to December 18, 2009, there were over 500 firearm sales; over [fifty] of which were recovered at crime scenes in Mexico with [a] 'short' time-to-crime, some as little as one day."

On January 9, 2010, Jaime Avila purchased three assault pistols, his third purchase since November 24, 2009. There was no action taken and no recovery made. One week later, on January 16, 2010, Jaime Avila purchased three AK-47s. Andre promptly faxed the paperwork to the ATF but they took no action, even though they had Avila in the Suspect Gun Database. This was his fourth purchase. He provided a false residential address on all his purchase forms, he did not have any reported financial income, and he was working with other straw purchasers like Patino in a network of traffickers. Two of the three firearms he purchased that day were recovered almost a year later, on December 14, 2010, at the murder scene of Border Patrol Agent Brian Terry.

One month after ATF SA Voth's December 18 report to ATF Division Operations Officer Simpson, Voth filed another report, on January 21, 2010, that there were now over 800 firearms sold, over 150 of which were recovered at crime scenes in Mexico — over 100 crime scene recoveries in one month.

He also reported on January 21, 2010, that all telephone calls to Andre Howard directing him to make large-scale firearm sales to straw purchasers were recorded by the LETS video/audio recording system made by Law Enforcement Technologies.

On January 26, 2010, the ATF received additional funding for Operation Fast and Furious through the reorganized OCDETF Strike Force run by the DOJ, which included the FBI, the ATF, the DEA, and ICE, along with Homeland Security.

The ATF filed detailed monthly reports and briefing papers on the progress of Fast and Furious:

	Firearms Sold	Mexican Crime Scene Recoveries
Dec. 18, 2009	500	50
Jan. 08, 2009	650	53
Jun. 14, 2010	1100	150
Jul. 16, 2010	1608	309
Oct. 21, 2010	1800+	360+

In a January 8, 2010, briefing paper by the ATF, the agency described the pace of sales from September 2009 to early December 2009 as a "blitz that was extremely out of the ordinary." At that time, over twenty straw purchasers had made purchases. On December 17, 2009, Assistant Special Agent in Charge George Gillett emailed his boss, Special Agent in Charge William Newell, that after being briefed at ATF headquarters, Ray Rowley, the ATF Southwest Border Coordinator, became alarmed at the number of firearms being trafficked. Gillett said he told Rowley that "we have slowed down the [gun dealer] on future purchases."

The January 8, 2009, briefing paper said "currently our strategy is to allow the transfer of firearms to continue to take place, albeit at a much slower pace. [...] Since early December, efforts to slow down the pace of these firearm purchases have succeeded and will continue, *but not to the detriment of the larger goal of the investigation* (emphases added)."

In January, the ATF briefed AUSA Burke, ICE, and the DEA on the progress of the operation. When the ATF got Operation Fast and Furious accepted into the OCDETF program and received extra funding on January 26, 2010, the operation actually expanded. It did not slow down.

On February 26 and 27, Newell emailed Burke and Hurley about two large recovery incidents in Mexico and stated that he believed each one would have firearms traced back to Operation Fast and Furious. "FYI: Big Mexican Army seizure last night in Sinaloa from 'Chapo' Guzman's guys. Seems like something big is brewing down there, which is why there's been such a flurry of gun purchasing activity [...] in SA Hope MacAllister's Fast and Furious OCDETF Strike Force Case."

US Attorney Dennis Burke replied, "This is good stuff."

Operation Fast and Furious subjects spent over $608,000 for more than 600 firearms from February 1, 2010, to May 31, 2010. The firearms were primarily cartel weapons of choice, paid for in cash, and bought primarily from FFL 1 (Andre Howard) by straw purchasers that the ATF already knew had very little or no income.

"In March 2010, ATF Deputy Director Hoover received a detailed briefing about Fast and Furious that left him sufficiently concerned about the size of the case to require that the Phoenix Field Division draft an exit strategy."

The ATF responded to Hoover's order and drafted an exit strategy on April 27, 2010, but the ATF and the DOJ never finalized it or executed it until March of 2011, when Holder issued a directive that changed the government strategy to require interdiction of illegal straw purchaser sales in the United States.

A key part of the new Obama administration strategy was to get intelligence from Title III wiretaps. On March 10, 2010, the ATF got approval from Assistant Attorney General (Criminal Division) Lanny Breuer to apply for wiretap applications in Fast and Furious. They were already listening to, and recording, conversations between informants and FFLs because at least one party to the conversation consented to being recorded. No judicially approved wiretap was required under those circumstances.

Now the ATF could get court-ordered wiretaps of any conversation the DOJ and the court deemed necessary to their criminal investigation. The DOJ and the ATF called Fast and Furious an "investigation", but the only thing being investigated was how many guns walked to the Mexican cartels would be recovered at crime scenes in Mexico and how many days it took from the time of the sale to the time of the crime. It wasn't any kind of investigation designed to prosecute eventual criminals and/or murderers in Mexico; it was really their gunwalking. As the statistics show, the bottom line was selling more firearms to the cartels.

On August 17, 2010, AUSA Emory Hurley wrote a self-serving memorandum of talking points: "[A]gents have pursued interdiction of firearms transferred to the conspirators where possible. Agents have not purposely let guns walk." The next day, AUSA prosecutor Laura Gwinn reviewed ATF agents' reports of investigation from Fast and Furious in preparation for trials she was assigned to potentially prosecute. "It was apparent to her when she reviewed the reports that ATF agents were not seizing weapons in Operation Fast and Furious."

Despite ATF's and DOJ's repeated representations that they never told FFLs to sell to the straw purchasers; they were told about purchases after they occurred; the guns were already gone when they arrived; and they had no legal basis to intervene with these "legal gun purchases," the truth is far different. The U.S. attorneys from San Diego who prosecuted the straw purchasers filed a memorandum in the case, *United States of America v. Sean Christopher Steward*, on November 26, 2012. It contained a detailed discussion about what really went on in a typical Fast and Furious sale.

Steward was charged and convicted of ten illegal purchases from Lone Wolf.

1.	Dec. 08, 2009 (12 p.m.)	20 AK-47 rifles	
	$12,130		
2.	Dec. 08, 2009 (8:45p.m.)	20 AK-47 rifles	$12,130
3.	Dec. 10, 2009	20 AK-47 rifles	
		10 AK-47 pistols	
		3 FN Herstal 5.7 cal. pistols	
			$20,145
4.	Dec. 12, 2009	20 AK-47 pistols	$12,000
5.	Dec. 14, 2009	36 AK-47 rifles	
		7 AK-47 pistols	$25,479
6.	Dec. 24, 2009	40 AK-47 rifles	$23,500
7.	Jan. 04, 2010	20 AK-47 rifles	
		1 .45 cal. pistol	$12,500
8.	May 6, 2010	8 AK-47 rifles	$ 4,850
9.	Jun. 2, 2010	10 AK-47 rifles	
		20 9mm pistols	
		1 .45 cal. pistol	$15, 235
10.	Jun. 23, 2010	10 AK-47 rifles	$ 5,500

246 weapons in 6+ months
$143,469

The government's pleading filed in court clearly demonstrates the real role of Andre's cooperation and how the DOJ and the ATF controlled him and directed his conduct.

Steward's indictment, which occurred Jan. 19, 2011, alleged a scheme ("conspiracy") between Steward and nineteen other defendants beginning on or about September 2009 through December 2010 to "illegally acquire firearms from Federal Firearms Licenses in Arizona to be shipped, transported, and/or exported to drug-trafficking organizations both in the United States and in the Republic of Mexico."

Steward was the second most prolific straw purchaser (after Uriel Patino), purchasing 289 firearms, 246 of which were purchased at Lone Wolf.

Were these sales truly free enterprise sales by an FFL, totally uninfluenced by ATF direction, unmonitored by the ATF, and lost before the ATF could arrive for surveillance and interdiction?

Was the ATF truly prohibited by the U.S. Constitution from stopping Steward, questioning him, arresting him, or seizing these weapons, as ATF, DOJ, and other Obama officials argued?

DOJ attorneys sure had a lot of details about these purchases in their sentencing memorandum filed on November 11, 2012.

On December 7, 2009, Andre Howard had never met, or even heard of, Sean Steward. At noon on December 8, 2009, Sean Steward purchased twenty AK-47-type rifles from Lone Wolf.

The Department of Justice memorandum stated:

"Prior to the first purchase, an individual using a telephone subscribed to Celis-Acosta called the FFL (Mr. Howard) and inquired about the availability of AK-47-style rifles."

Q: Did Mr. Howard carry [twenty] AK-47 rifles? No, he did not carry that much inventory.

Q: How did the government know who owned the caller's phone? Celis-Acosta was the Phoenix-area firearm trafficker who employed the straw purchasers. [The] ATF [and the] DOJ already knew who he was.

Q: How quickly could Mr. Howard run a background check and get approval of the sale by the FBI? Immediately at the time of the sale. The memorandum continues:

> "Following that call, Steward arrived at the FFL and purchased [twenty] rifles. Steward loaded the firearms into his Mitsubishi car and departed the area. He was subsequently seen meeting at a gas station with Celis-Acosta's trafficking organization, including a white Nissan pickup truck and a tan GMC Yukon SUV."

Q: What did the ATF already know about Celis-Acosta's trafficking organization and the vehicles registered to the straw purchasers and other members of his organization? A lot!

"After meeting with those individuals, Steward traveled to a parking lot where he transferred the boxes of rifles from his vehicle to a red Durango pickup truck."

At this point, the ATF knew that the purchaser, Steward, transferred the twenty guns to another trafficker who worked for Celis-Acosta. Steward lied on his purchase form when he said they were purchased for personal use. The ATF had plenty of probable cause to arrest him and question him. The memorandum continues:

> "Steward returned to the Arizona FFL later the evening of December 8, 2009, at 8:45 p.m., and purchased an additional [twenty] rifles. Surveillance agents observed Steward and two Hispanic males load the firearms into the bed of the white Nissan pickup truck observed earlier that day.
>
> "Phoenix Police Department Officers conducted a traffic stop of the pickup truck after it left the Arizona FFL. Celis-Acosta was identified as the front-seat

passenger and Steward as the rear-seat passenger. Steward advised officers that he purchased the firearms.

"After the traffic stop, surveillance agents observed the Nissan pickup truck arrive at Celis-Acosta's residence, where Steward and others unloaded the rifles from the bed of the pickup truck. Surveillance agents also observed Steward's Mitsubishi car and the GMC Yukon (observed earlier that day with Steward) parked at the Celis-Acosta residence."

Ironically, Celis-Acosta was the key target of the Fast and Furious investigation during this initial timeframe, yet no action was taken against him when the ATF and the DOJ had the clear opening to arrest him, seize/interdict a large cache of assault weapons before they left Phoenix, and prosecute him for significant felony offenses. If they wanted intelligence about cartel members above Celis-Acosta in the cartel hierarchy, they had a golden opportunity to flip Celis-Acosta and save the lives of dozens, if not hundreds, of innocent Mexican citizens. They also could have saved the life of Border Agent Brian Terry, but the illegal sales of assault weapons did not stop on December 8, 2009.

Over the next seventeen days, after the extensive surveillance of Sean Steward and the Celis-Acosta gang on December 8, 2009, Sean Steward made four more purchases for Celis-Acosta and the Sinaloa Cartel, including 133 AK-47 rifles and pistols from Lone Wolf.

The DOJ sentencing memorandum does go on to shed clear light on how, and who, directed additional walked gun sales to the cartels.

"In January 2010, Steward had several consensually recorded telephone calls with FFL 1 (Andre Howard), in which Steward acknowledged the illegality of his purchases and expressed concerns that law enforcement was investigating his illegal activities."

The ATF and the DOJ directed Andre to call Sean Steward from his business phone, which was recorded with Andre Howard's consent so no judicial wiretap was necessary.

"On January 5, 2010, *at the direction of ATF Agents* (emphasis added) FFL 1 (Mr. Howard) called Steward. In that recorded telephone call, Steward inquired as to the prices and types of AK-47-style firearms, which FFL 1 had available for sale."

The ATF program absolutely encouraged, promoted, and directed the illegal sales of weapons to the cartels. The ATF has complete regulatory authority over Federal Firearm Licensees. They can put them out of business at their discretion and they can refer them to administrative, civil, and criminal authorities for civil and criminal prosecution any time they deem expedient for regulatory or legal violations that are real or false. Their power over FFLs can't be overstated. Fast and Furious would prove that the ATF agents and DOJ attorneys were corrupt, and would lie to the courts, the United States Congress, and the American public. Retaliation, abuse, and criminal conduct were all part of their playbook of strong-arm tactics. As Andre Howard would learn, once they convinced an FFL to cooperate with their alleged "ongoing criminal investigation" to stop the cartels, there was no turning back.

The ATF used the consensually recorded dedicated phone line, along with government informants embedded in the straw purchaser network, to continue escalation of the illegal gunwalking and the inevitable murders that foreseeably would result. The DOJ sentencing memorandum discussed the recorded telephone call, from January 5, 2010, that FFL 1 (Andre Howard) made at the direction of ATF Agents:

"Steward also made statements to FFL 1 which show that he was straw purchasing the firearms by using funds provided by a third party. Specifically, Steward told FFL1, that he wanted to purchase an additional [twenty] AK-47 rifles but 'he had to wait for other people to do their part' before he had the money to buy firearms."

On January 11, 2010, Steward again spoke with FFL1 regarding the availability of firearms for sale. The DOJ again addressed their intercepted conversations between FFL1 and Steward:

"In that recorded telephone conversation, Steward told FFL1 that he would be buying 'a lot more' of the AK-47-style rifles, but again, that he had to wait 'for other people to do their part'.

"Steward also expressed concern about law enforcement learning about his purchases. He told FFL1 that he did not want any questions from anybody regarding his firearms purchases, and expressed concern that law enforcement was investigating him.

"When FFL1 asked Steward why a government agency would call him, Steward stated that it was because 'he bought [sixty] guns and [that he was] selling them.'

"Steward told FFL1 he was going to stop buying because he believed he was starting to attract attention from the 'wrong people', i.e. law enforcement."

As of January 11, 2010, Steward had purchased 239 firearms, including 197 firearms from FFL1 (Andre Howard). Steward stopped purchasing firearms from January 11, 2010 to May 5, 2010. The DOJ and the ATF had a ton of surveillance evidence regarding the transfers and trafficking of the 239 firearms, including may recordings of admissions Steward made on the government-monitored telephone line they placed in Lone Wolf's offices. A federal felony prosecution would have been easy. Instead, they did nothing.

On May 6, 2010, Steward resumed his illegal purchases from FFL1 that provided more recorded telephone evidence to the DOJ and the ATF. From May 2010 to June 23, 2010,

FFL1 sold Steward an additional forty-nine firearms at the direction of the DOJ and the ATF. As the agencies said in their sentencing memorandum:

"In June 2010, Steward also made statements to FFL1 which indicate that Steward was aware that the firearms he purchased were being transferred to other individuals to be used in the commission of other crimes."

On June 2, 2010, Steward purchased 10 AK-47 rifles and 20 9mm pistols from FFL1 (Andre Howard). In their Government Sentencing Memorandum DOJ described their surveillance as follows:

"Surveillance agents observed Steward load the rifle boxes into his Honda Pilot automobile, and drive to his apartment complex. At the apartment complex, Steward met with a male who was driving a black Camaro automobile. This automobile was previously identified as a car driven by Celis-Acosta. [...] They then met up with individual(s) in a red Nissan automobile. The vehicles then drove away in tandem, and engaged in evasive driving maneuvers. Agents temporarily lost surveillance of the vehicles but subsequently observed a possible transfer of the boxes of firearms to the red Nissan automobile."

On June 23, 2010, Steward purchased ten more AK-47-style rifles from Lone Wolf. The entire purchase was videotaped on cameras the DOJ and the ATF had placed in the Lone Wolf store to record, as potential future evidence, the actual purchases and discussions with the illegal purchasers. In the DOJ sentencing memorandum, they described part of this videotaped purchase:

"Steward spoke with FFL1 and asked if FFL1 was aware of the term 'RICO' (referring to a federal criminal statute, the Racketeer Influenced and Corrupt Organizations Act, 18 U.S.C§ 196, which permitted a firearms purchaser to be charged with a felony, if the firearm he purchased was recovered in the commission of another crime). In sum, based on the conversations with FFL1, (recorded in real time and monitored by the DOJ and the ATF) the evidence establishes that Steward was well aware that his straw purchases, and subsequent transfer of hundreds of firearms to third parties, was in violation of law. He was also aware that these firearms were being used to commit other felony offenses. For these reasons, Steward expressed his fear to FFL1 that Steward was risking law enforcement investigation and criminal charges."

Ironically, the only one on the recorded (audio and video) conversations that did not know the firearms were not interdicted, that they did go to Mexico, that they were used at multiple crime scenes in Mexico, and that many innocent citizens in Mexico were being murdered with these weapons, was FFL1, Andre Howard.

After his arrest in January 2011, Steward admitted that he knew Celis-Acosta through car racing and travelled with him to deliver firearms to the cartel in Juarez, Mexico, on June 6, 2010. While there, Steward allegedly heard a report that 47-49 innocent children in Juarez were killed in a shooting with an AK-47. He allegedly stopped selling firearms after June, 2010.

The DOJ and the ATF knew of Steward's connection to Celis-Acosta, knew about Celis-Acosta's drug and firearms trafficking to Mexican cartels, and knew about the extreme cartel violence in Mexico at the beginning of December 2009. They tracked and reported the death totals related to Fast and Furious on a monthly basis to their superiors in Washington, D.C. They knew, without any doubt, that innocent Mexican citizens were being killed every month by weapons they illegally let walk to the Mexican cartels.

When the DOJ prosecutors argued for an enhanced criminal sentence for Steward, their final argument was:

> "He engaged in delivering those weapons to the border so they could get across into Mexico, and he did so for one reason: It was to make money. He didn't care about the consequences. He didn't care that these weapons, as he knew, were the types of weapons of choice of Mexican drug cartels, knowing full well that they were going to go down and fuel further violence down there. He didn't care about that. [...] He may have been angered by violence that was going on down there, but if he had a chance to make money, he was going to make money. [...] This court should hold him accountable for the choices he made, the egregious criminal conduct he had."

DOJ prosecutors argued for a prison sentence of 108 months.

The ATF's June 15, 2010, Gun Runner Impact Teams report indicated that from the inception of Fast and Furious in October 2009 until June 15, 2010, sixty-two straw purchasers purchased 1,608 firearms and passed them through more than twelve stash houses. 309 firearms were recovered from crime scenes in Mexico.

If the United States Department of Justice could argue in a United States Federal District Court that Sean Steward should be held accountable for his egregious criminal conduct in walking guns to the Mexican cartels, why shouldn't Mexican and American citizens demand that the Obama administration and its law enforcement agencies that created a program specifically designed to provide Mexican cartels with weapons so that they could be traced to crime scenes in Mexico, also be held accountable for their egregious criminal conduct? Was it worse for Sean Steward to sell the weapons to second-level traffickers for cash commissions when he had no known source of any other income, or for DOJ officials to intentionally let the second level and subsequent levels of traffickers, transport the weapons to the Mexican cartel so they could commit murder — not for cash but to advance their political Second Amendment agenda? The DOJ controlled the last links in a chain of events that started with Steward making $100 to $300 per gun and ended in cartel murders in Mexico. It was top DOJ officials whom ultimately put the murder weapons in the hands of the cartel murderers. And let's not forget Steward could not have even made those purchases without embedded FBI informants arranging the sales, FBI agents manipulating NCIS reports to the FFL approving the sales, and ATF agents facilitating, encouraging, and setting up the purchases to Steward.

Andre was not the only FFL used and lied to by the DOJ and the ATF. Tucson-based FFL2, which was the primary FFL SAC Newell used in Operation Wide Receiver, was also used in Fast and Furious and also expressed his concerns.

FFL2 expressed concern about sales from his store in May 2010. ATF Group Supervisor Voth assured him that the firearms "would not be allowed to enter Mexico or be allowed to fall into the hands of individuals that could use them against law enforcement."

In August 2010, an obvious straw purchaser wanted to purchase a larger number of assault weapons than FFL2 had in stock. He asked ATF Group Supervisor Voth for guidance. Voth replied:

> "We [ATF] are very much interested in this transaction and would like to coordinate [...] the delivery of these firearms under our direction. [...] In summary, our guidance is that we would like you to go through with [the] request and order additional firearms."

ATF Group Supervisor Voth denied making "any assurance to [FFL2] about the conduct of the investigation."

FFL2 said "he continued to assist [the] ATF [...] because he feared retaliation from [the] ATF because the agency controlled his license to sell firearms."

The DOJ IG found that Agent Voth's guidance "reflected [the] ATF's influence over the FFLs, and its interest throughout the case that FFL2 and FFL1 continue making sales to the Operation Fast and Furious straw purchasers because doing so advanced ATF's investigative interests."

When the DOJ IG finally issued his September 2012 investigative report, it was clearly a cover-up designed to protect his superiors (AG Holder and his senior officials and President Obama). It was a disgracefully whitewashed set of findings and conclusions that ignored clear factual evidence, much of which was actually included in the report and its exhibits.

It was early in the morning on October 5, 2010, during Andre's continued cooperation with the DOJ and the ATF, when Andre received a telephone call from the Glendale Police Department telling him that during a routine patrol they noticed there appeared to have been a break-in at Lone Wolf Trading Company sometime during the night or early hours of the morning. Andre's reaction was that it wasn't possible.

Andre had a sophisticated security system and received no notice of any security breach. The burglars somehow bypassed his security system and none of his motion detectors were set off. Neither systems were disabled, just circumvented. When he arrived at his store, he discovered that burglars were somehow able to break through the wall of a church that shared an adjoining wall with Lone Wolf. They then broke into specific locked display cases and stole thirty-seven handguns. The Glendale Police conducted an investigation and issued a police report, but were unable to find any evidence or clues that were able to assist in identifying the perpetrators.

Since the ATF had cameras surveilling his entire store twenty-four hours a day, Andre notified SA MacAllister and asked for the ATF to provide the Glendale Police Department with relevant videotapes covering the period from 8:00 p.m., which was store closing time, on October 4, to 6:00 a.m., October 5, when the police discovered the break-in. She confirmed that their audio-visual surveillance system was not compromised during the break-in, but did not provide the police any information from that time period.

Later, the ATF said they could not provide the local police information from an ongoing federal investigation. The break-in remained unsolved. "What burglary?" was the response from both the DOJ and the ATF.

In 2011, during the congressional investigation of Fast and Furious, Congress requested the videotapes of the early October surveillance. The tapes were not provided to Congress for the same reason other documents were not provided to Congress: There was an ongoing federal criminal investigation.

When the ATF and the DOJ were still being pressured to produce the tapes to Congress, an ATF testifying witness tried to deflect the issue. Even though the witness was not asked any question about the tapes, he volunteered out of the blue that the surveillance camera only operated "during store hours". This directly contradicted what the ATF technicians who installed the cameras told Andre at the time of the installation. It also contradicted the testimony of prior ATF witnesses. It did not make sense that no one ever told Andre that was the case. Certainly, SA MacAllister never told Andre or the Glendale Police Department that in October 2010.

Still unsatisfied, the House Oversight Chairman issued the DOJ a subpoena for the tapes. The DOJ responded that they didn't maintain a "searchable" database of the tapes. That explanation was not plausible because they had tapes they used in various criminal cases years after the crimes were committed. Finally, they changed their story again and swore to Congress they couldn't locate the tapes. That was the Obama administration's fourth false excuse, and final lie, about why they would not comply with the congressional subpoena.

The circumstances of this break-in during Fast and Furious are highly suspicious given the sophisticated technology available only to the government, and detailed knowledge of Andre's systems that would have been required to pull off the crime undetected. The government had both the knowledge and technology at the FBI and their intelligence agencies. It is highly unlikely, if not impossible, that local hoodlums could have done this undetected.

On June 30, 2011, six months after the end of Fast and Furious, two Phoenix field agents from the Phoenix ATF office arrived at Lone Wolf to remove their surveillance camera monitoring equipment. Andre asked Agent Harvey, who had previously installed the equipment, about the operational timing of the cameras he installed and was now removing. Agent Harvey confirmed that the equipment recorded the store twenty-four hours a day continuously. Andre then asked Agent Harvey if he was aware that Lone Wolf had been broken into on October 5, 2010. Agent Harvey stated that ATF Assistant Special Agent in Charge Williams Needles instructed him to remove the equipment and not to talk to Andre.

At the time of the camera removal, none of the thirty-seven guns had been recovered.

News 4 Tucson investigators reported on the burglary on September 25, 2014, during congressional hearings:

> "Up until now, the Obama Administration has argued the operation [Fast and Furious] was only locally run out of Phoenix. But members of Congress are pressing the Obama Administration to reveal what was

contained in a […] document the Justice Department […] fought to conceal […]. A federal judge agreed [with Congress].

Documents showed "even more guns turned up missing and those were never revealed to congressional investigators. […] In October 2010 […] someone broke into the Glendale gun store, whose owner, [Andre Howard] had agreed to sell weapons to cartel gun-buyers for the ATF.

"Glendale Police Department reports the burglars broke into the adjacent church, then smashed down the wall separating the church from Lone Wolf Trading Company. Thirty-seven handguns were stolen."

An attorney representing Andre in a civil lawsuit later wrote:

"The […] United States either orchestrated the burglary to obtain even more weapons from Lone Wolf to place in the hands of wrongdoers, or advised others as to the secret location inside Lone Wolf where the guns were stored.

"Weapons from the theft turned up […] in Albuquerque, […] Arizona, […] and Hermosillo, Sonora, Mexico. [The] ATF had surveillance inside the store at the time. […] [The] ATF had mounted surveillance video cameras […] running on a loop at the time, and [the] ATF could have identified the burglars."

On February 12, 2018, The City of Glendale Police Department followed up on the October 5, 2010, burglary report to keep the missing weapons in the National Crime Information Center computer system. Although some were recovered at Arizona crime scenes, most were still not accounted for.

On Sunday, December 10, 2017, Legendary Guns, an Arizona gun store frequented by AUSA Hurley and ATF

Agent Gillett, was burglarized. As with the burglary of Lone Wolf in October 2010, the alarm system was bypassed and the motion detectors did not go off. Thirty weapons were stolen. Coincidence?

Andre received no reimbursement from his insurance company or from the United States government, who continued to deny that their video surveillance was operational.

ATF Agent John Dodson testified to Congress that most sales by Andre were directed in advance by the ATF. SA Voth would get on the phone with the FBI to make sure the sales would go through the background check, regardless whether the purchaser was a felon or an illegal alien. Dodson himself was in Lone Wolf behind the counter posing as an employee during at least one sale in June 2010. On another occasion, SA Voth sent Agent Dodson in with a letter directing Andre to sell Dodson AK-47 pistols without running any NCIS paperwork through the FBI because SA Dodson himself was undercover posing as a straw purchaser. On the backend, Andre was also kept in the dark because the ATF and the FBI stopped sending him crime scene traces. At one point, the DOJ and the FBI arranged for a mass straw purchaser, Sean Steward, to be issued an Arizona Concealed Weapon Permit, which allowed Steward to purchase firearms without any FBI background check required at all.

In his September 2012 report, the DOJ IG did not directly address the Obama administration gun control agenda in their conclusions and finding, choosing to cast their findings as negligence rather than intentional misconduct. Their "spin" was that top officials:

> "[R]an a 'flawed investigation'[…] in their failure to adequately consider the risk to public safety in the United States and Mexico" and didn't take "adequate measurements to minimize the risk to public safety in the United States and Mexico."

The DOJ IG ignored the facts that clearly demonstrated every top Obama administration knew the "risks to public safety" of sending thousands of assault weapons to the Mexican cartels.

They all knew innocent people would be killed.

They didn't "just fail to take adequate measures to minimize the risks" when traffickers (as opposed to low-level straw purchasers) actually were stopped at the border and the DOJ/ATF ordered those law enforcement agencies to let the guns go across to the cartels with no surveillance or other tracking. The entire strategy was to just wait until the weapons were used in a crime scene, be it murder, maiming, or other crimes, and then get the crime scene trace. When they got the trace, they did no follow-up to ask the original purchaser questions, and they made no arrests of the original straw purchasers or any of the other transferees they identified during surveillance, who actually transported the firearms to the border.

In his September 2012 DOJ IG report, the DOJ IG "found" no evidence of any underlying Obama administration gun control agenda. He overlooked many obvious facts in his report that suggested otherwise.

On March 12, 2010, ATF's senior leadership had their first monthly meeting with the new Acting Deputy Attorney General Gary Grindler. It was the "first time he had heard of the investigation and the title Fast and Furious."

"Grindler's handwritten notes from the briefing refer to 'long rifles' — multiple sales issues. Grindler said that ATF officials discussed with him their desire to require FFLs to report multiple sales of long guns (rifles)..."

Melson later testified to the DOJ IG that "Grindler's briefing included the long gun reporting issue because [the] ATF expected to send him a memorandum later that month on it."

On March 26, 2010, Melson did send a memorandum "requesting that [the] ATF be permitted to issue demand letters to FFLs in select states [including Arizona] requiring them to report certain rifle sales to enable [the] ATF to uncover more illegal activity and develop better intelligence about trafficking patterns."

The memorandum did not mention the Fast and Furious strategy of walking guns or FFL cooperative efforts, but instead highlighted "[twenty-five] individuals who purchased in excess of 1,130 firearms in the Phoenix area". The "firearms that were recovered in Mexico in the possession of drug traffickers affiliated with the Sinaloa Cartel", firearms "recovered in stash locations or during a crossing along the border"that were "destined for delivery to drug-trafficking organizations in Mexico", and the "extremely short time span, ranging from [one] day to less than one month between purchase and crime scene recovery."

The memorandum did mention an FFL, Andre Howard, but not as an FFL cooperating with the DOJ and the ATF, selling guns at the direction of the DOJ and the ATF. He also failed to mention that the DOJ and the ATF told Andre all guns were interdicted. The memorandum had a one-line conclusion:

> "The majority of the firearms were purchased at an FFL (Andre Howard) involving transactions of five to ten rifles at a time."

The set up began! They needed a Plan B backup if their gunwalking was exposed and a fall guy for later legislation.

The DOJ IG "found other instances later in the investigation where [the] ATF used Operation Fast and Furious to exemplify the need […] for a long gun reporting requirement."

"Grindler said [and his notes confirmed] that ATF officials told him that ATF had used trackers to follow firearms."

ATF Acting Director Melson renewed his gun control request "again on December 6, 2010."

Based on Melson's apparently uncorroborated testimony, the DOJ IG concluded that "no one [at ATF staff] ever suggested that [Operation Fast and Furious] was being done for the purposes of supporting our position on the long guns [...] and that the sales to Mexican cartels [...] were not done for purposes of supporting our position on the long guns."

The DOJ IG, without saying anything about who they interviewed about this issue, what steps they took to investigate the accuracy of Melson's testimony, or the explanation for Grindler's notes concluded: "we found no evidence that contradicted Melson's statements to us."

There were many facts and material omissions from his emails that did, or at least should have, raised serious red flags about Melson's truthfulness and credibility. There is nothing in the IG's 472-page report or its extensive appendices to indicate the DOJ IG ever followed up on the clear evidence of an Obama administration gun control agenda.

On November 24, 2010, during Fast and Furious, Jenny Durkan, the U.S. Attorney for the Western District of Washington, emailed Dennis Burke, the U.S. Attorney for the District of Arizona:

> "I want to discuss our approach to enforcing gun sale laws at FFLs and gun shows. We have just finished an undercover operation that looks promising,— but I think [the] ATF is getting cold feet."

U.S. Attorney Dennis Burke responded:

> "We are about to indict around [redacted] clowns for a gun-trafficking to Mexico operation [Fast and Furious}. It's a T-III [DOJ wiretap] investigation that we have been working with [the] ATF for a long time. [...] It's going to bring a lot of attention to straw purchasing of assault weapons. Some weapons bought

by these clowns in Arizona have been directly traced to murders of elected officials in Mexico by the cartels, so Katie-bar-the-door when we unveil this baby."

U.S. Attorney Jenny Durkan replied:

"What a great investigation. What is the ETI (estimated time of indictment)?"

In 2010, James Grimaldi and other reporters from the *Washington Post* did a series of investigative reports about guns and violence in Mexico. Since 2006, more than 60,000 weapons were used in Mexican crimes. Their articles were initially critical of the Obama administration's reluctance to take any actions that would "upset the gun lobby in Congress", particularly the Democratic members who opposed the assault weapons ban Eric Holder proposed in 2009, Obama's first year in office.

Grimaldi criticized "the Obama administration's lax response in 2010" which "really put the gun stores in the front lines of defending or preventing this flow of guns to Mexico."

In 2003, Congress passed the Tiahrt Amendment, which prohibited [the] ATF from releasing gun trace data to anyone, including media requests for information under the Freedom of Information Act and releases of any data to the gun shop owners. Somehow, Grimaldi was able to get gun tracing data in December 2010, and they published a list of the U.S. gun dealers with the most firearms traced to crime scenes over the past four years.

Grimaldi claimed that "the *Post* obtained hundreds of thousands of state and local police records and did its own tracing and analysis." Grimaldi only cited two actual examples — Maryland and Virginia — yet their article purports to cover the entire nation over a four-year period. The original Tiahrt Amendment was amended by the Obama administration in 2009 to allow state and local police access to the data for legitimate law enforcement purposes, but it tightened restrictions on any public disclosure of the information. It seems unlikely the *Post* could possibly recreate a national database from tens of thousands of local police and state police records that had "tightened restrictions" on public disclosure. It seems much more likely that the *Post* somehow got access to the FBI NCIS database information through a massive Obama administration intentional leak designed to further their gun control agenda.

Grimaldi' s article, published in December 13, 2010, said the top seven dealers were in Columbus, Ohio; Charlotte, North Carolina; Indianapolis, Indiana; Memphis, Tennessee; Jonesboro, Georgia; Milwaukee, Wisconsin; and San Leandro, California.

Lone Wolf Trading Company was listed as eighth in the nation for number of crime scene traces in the past four years, but was number one, over the last two years, in number of crime scene traces from Mexico with 185 traces.

Numbers nine and ten nationally were in Decatur, Georgia, and Jacksonville, Florida. Of course the real number one in traces from Mexico in 2009 and 2010 was the U.S. Department of Justice and Fast and Furious.

From February 1, 2010 to May 31, 2010, ATF agents conducted surveillance of approximately twenty-five Fast and Furious straw purchasers. By April 15, Uriel Patino had purchased over 490 firearms for over $380,000 and at least sixty-three of the firearms had already been recovered at Mexican crime scenes, many of which had extremely short times-to-crime. On April 16, 2010, the ATF watched Patino purchase three powerful .50 caliber rifles from Lone Wolf Trading Company. They followed the transfers to Celis-Acosta's residence and the residence of another known trafficker affiliated with Celis-Acosta.

AUSA Morrissey shockingly testified at the DOJ IG hearing that in the summer of 2010 "he began to question why ATF was apparently failing to identify how firearms were getting to Mexico."

In a July 26, 2011, follow-up *Washington Post* article titled "Operation Fast and Furious: A gunrunning sting gone wrong", reporter Sari Horwitz quoted an anonymous Obama administration official: "We have never been up so high in the Sinaloa Cartel, the largest and most powerful drug cartel in the world. […] This is an open, ongoing investigation." The official bemoaned the interruption of the operation by the congressional investigation: "It is so unfair."

The *Washington* reporter pointed to the initiation of the program — a series of discussions at the end of October 2009 between "the directors of the FBI, Drug Enforcement Administration, [the] ATF and the Deputy Attorney General at the Justice Department." The plan had the legal backing of U.S. Attorney Dennis K. Burke in Phoenix, and had been approved and funded by a task force at the Justice Department. The article continued:

"ATF and Justice didn't tell Mexican officials about the [fifteen]-month operation until it became public. […] Darren Gill, ATF attaché to Mexico and his deputy, Carlos Canino, were alarmed by the large number of weapons being recovered at bloody crime scenes in Mexico and being traced to Phoenix. […] Gill recalled yelling at his boss: 'Shut this damn investigation down'."

ATF special agents "Dodson [and] Casa, and two other agents were furious about letting guns walk. They watched guns being transferred for transport to Mexico. They were told to stand down. Dodson tried to contact ATF headquarters, the ATF Chief Counsel, the ATF ethics section, and the Justice Department's Office of the Inspector General."

ATF Special Agent in Charge Newell's response: "Fast and Furious was a phenomenal case, the largest ever

Mexican gun-trafficking investigation." When asked by a local reporter whether the ATF purposely allowed firearms to enter Mexico, he answered, "Hell no!"

ATF Phoenix supervisor Pete Forcelli's reaction:

"I was appalled [...] [b]ecause it was a blatant lie."

Representative Issa's reaction:

"Who authorized this program that was so felony stupid that got people killed? I do have serious concerns that the attorney general should have known a lot more than he says he knew."

John Stewart on *The Daily Show* quipped:

"The ATF plan to prevent American guns from being used in Mexican gun violence is to provide Mexican gangs with American guns. If this is the plan they went with, what plan did we reject?"

During Fast and Furious some of the crime scenes where firearms were recovered included:

January 2010 — Juarez, Mexico — cartel members burst into a home, killing sixteen people — mostly teenagers — at a birthday party. "Family members of those killed appeared before the Mexican government demanding to know what happened. [...] Who's going to pay for this?"

December 2009 — Juarez, Mexico — Mexican hit men carried out a massacre of eighteen young men in a rehabilitation center.

On April 2, 2010, SA Voth sent a congratulatory email to the entire Phoenix Group VII:

"Sinaloa — March statistics — 187 murders in March, including eleven policemen. [...] Our subjects purchased 359 firearms during the month of March alone, [including] numerous Barrett .50 caliber rifles. I believe we are righteous in our plan.

"[A]gents within Group VII described Voth's reaction to all this gun violence in Mexico as 'giddy'.. [...] Group Supervisor Voth presented to us [that] this is proof that we are working a cartel, the guns that our guys are buying […] are being found [at crime scenes] with very short time-to-crime rates in Mexico in known cartel-related violence, and the violence is going through the roof down there. We are onto a good thing here.

"Wherever he would get a [crime scene] trace back […] he was jovial, if not giddy, but just delighted about that, hey, [twenty] of our guns were recovered […] in Mexico last night."

When SA Dodson complained about the horrendous consequences Mexican citizens were suffering at the hands of cartel members using the Fast and Furious firearms to murder teenagers, policemen, and other innocent Mexicans, Voth replied: "If you're going to make an omelet, you have got to scramble some eggs."

In October 2010 the Department of Justice in Washington, D.C., began planning a big press conference strategy to promote their success in their "anti-cartel" plan. They would unseal their indictments in Operation Wide Receiver and announce prosecutions in both Operation Wide Receiver (AUSA Laura Gwinn's Tucson prosecutions) and Operation Fast and Furious (AUSA Emory Hurley's yet-to-be-indicted straw purchaser cases).

On October 17, 2010, Deputy Assistant Attorney General Jason Weinstein and the DOJ's Gang Unit Acting Chief James Trusty communicated about having AAG Breuer as the highlight speaker at the event. DAAG Weinstein wrote:

"Do you think we should try to have Lanny participate in press when Fast and Furious and Laura's Tucson case are unsealed? It's a tricky case given the number of guns that have been walked, but it is a significant set of prosecutions."

Trusty responded about a November or December event:

"It's not going to be any big surprise that a bunch of U.S. guns are being used in [Mexico], so I'm not sure how much grief we get for 'gunwalking!'"

The clearly callous and immoral position of the Obama administration throughout Fast and Furious was reflected in this exchange between two top DOJ officials under AG Eric Holder. "They are just Mexicans."

Chapter Four

They are "Just Mexicans" ... Until

By December 2010, approximately 2,000 firearms were sold to the Mexican cartels, resulting in the murder of an estimated 300 Mexican citizens. Most of the 2,000 firearms were still unrecovered. Operation Fast and Furious was still in progress despite growing concerns from some top DOJ and ATF officials who had started to formulate an exit strategy, plan a shutdown, and issue a joint press release about their Wide Receiver and Fast and Furious prosecutions. AG Holder planned to personally present the press release at a big press conference in Arizona. Ironically, on December 14, 2010, AG Holder's Deputy Chief of Staff Monty Wilkinson notified U.S. Attorney Dennis Burke that "the AG's office is now expressing interest in the AG coming out for [the press conference announcing the takedown of Operation Fast and Furious]." The press conference was being planned for sometime in January.

Late in the evening of December 14, 2010, Customs and Border Patrol Agent Brian Terry was on patrol with three other border agents in Peck Canyon, Arizona. They discovered a group of five suspected illegal aliens carrying assault weapons. They were probably a rip squad planning to rob drug smugglers or illegal alien traffickers. The border agents identified themselves as police and ordered them to drop their weapons. One of the suspects fired at the Agents. Agent Terry returned fire with a weapon that fired non-legal bean bags. During the firefight that ensued, Agent Terry was struck by a bullet that killed him on the scene. One suspect, Manuel Osorio-Arellanes, was wounded. The other four suspects fled and escaped. Three of the suspects' weapons, including two AK-47s, were seized at the crime scene.

Early in the morning of December 15, 2010, two ATF agents showed up at Lone Wolf Trading Company to personally conduct an emergency crime scene trace. The agents told Andre that a border patrol agent had been killed during the night. The trace confirmed that the two AK-47s from the crime scene were positively traced to firearms sold during Fast and Furious to straw purchaser Jaime Avila on January 16, 2009.

Andre was horrified at the thought that his firearms were recovered at the crime scene where a United States law enforcement officer was murdered, and he prayed that they were not the actual murder weapon.

> "I immediately called SA MacAllister for an explanation as to how those weapons slipped through. Her demeanor was very different. She seemed unnerved and did not want to talk. She said that she and her supervisor would meet with me soon to talk about how we are going to deal with this. She told me not to talk to any other people, including other agents or the media, about this."

At 5:19 p.m., the AUSA in charge of the Tucson office, Shelley Clemens, issued a press release on behalf of the Arizona District U.S. Attorney's Office about the Brian Terry murder. She released no details other than time, place, and a limited description of the crime.

Andre retained Phoenix criminal attorney Chris Rapp to "advise me personally regarding the incident and to assist me in finding out what happened." Chris Rapp's brother was an Assistant United States Attorney in the Phoenix United States Attorney Office.

At 9:41 a.m. on December 15, U.S. Attorney Burke sent an email with details about the murder of Agent Terry to AG Holder's Deputy Chief of Staff, Monty Wilkerson.

Wilkerson responded twenty-three minutes later:

"Tragic. I've alerted the AG [Eric Holder], the Acting Deputy Attorney General [Gary Grindler], Principal Associate Deputy Attorney General [Lisa Monaco], etc."

Wilkerson followed up at 11:15:

"Please provide any additional details as they become available to you."

Burke forwarded additional information about the killing at 1:21 p.m.

Wilkerson replied twenty-four minutes later:

"Thanks, Dennis. Terrible situation."

Two hours later, Burke responded:

"Thanks […] The guns tie back to Emory's [Hurley] Fast and Furious case."

Burke also notified Wilkerson that the "guns found in the desert [...] connect back to the investigation [they were going to have a press conference about in January] — they were AK-47s purchased at a Phoenix gun store."

The AUSA in charge of the Tucson office, Shelley Clemens, was informed about the two seized firearms tied to the ongoing Phoenix ATF investigation before she made the U.S. Attorney's Office press release at 5:19 p.m. That information was not released.

The next day ATF Deputy Director William Hoover also sent a separate email notification to Brad Smith, Senior Counsel to the Deputy Attorney General and Mark Michael, Special Assistant to the Deputy Attorney General:

"Here are two briefing papers re: Az. The first will give you an update on our Fast and Furious investigation. The second [...] gives you the information re: the firearms recovered at the scene of the homicide of CBP Officer."

Smith informed Grindler that "the weapons recovered at the scene of Agent Terry's murder had been purchased by someone the ATF and the U.S. Attorney's Office had been investigating since November 2009." Avila had been entered in the Suspect Purchaser Database in November, but was allowed to illegally purchase assault weapons at least three more times, including the fateful purchase on January 16, 2010. ATF officials watched from the parking lot and/or on live video streamed to their mobile electronic devices and computers. They could have, and should have, arrested Avila and seized the murder weapons. The blood of Agent Terry's murder is on their hands. None of them cared, expressed guilt, or even condolences, to the Terry family. Andre was devastated, and conveyed his feelings and support to the family, through their attorney, on multiple occasions.

On January 3, AG Holder announced that Grindler would be his new Chief of Staff starting January 17, 2011.

The context of these email exchanges with top DOJ officials clearly demonstrates two important points:

First, top DOJ officials definitely knew about Fast and Furious well before Agent Terry's murder. They were planning an AG Holder press conference about Fast and Furious. They also received "updates" about the operation after the murder. They never asked: "What is Fast and Furious?" Deputy Chief of Staff Monty Wilkerson obviously knew what U.S. Attorney Burke meant when Burke referenced "Emory's Fast and Furious case." No one asked for any briefing about the details of the operation, or how the murder suspects managed to get assault weapons from an OCDETF multi-agency operation that was staffed with dozens of additional DOJ agency agents from around the country.

Second, top DOJ officials, and the FBI, who was investigating the murder itself, definitely knew with certainty that the two AK-47s recovered at the Terry crime scene were sold to Jaime Avila by Lone Wolf Trading Company in January 2010 at ATF's direction, as part of Operation Fast and Furious. It was Avila's fourth purchase of illegal firearms — all of which were made after he was a registered suspect in the DOJ/FBI/ATF database in November 2009. No one at the ATF or the DOJ notified the Terry family that the guns found at the scene of their son's death were part of an ATF/FBI/DOJ Strike Force operation.

Not surprisingly, on December 21, 2010, U.S. Attorney Burke and Deputy Chief of Staff Wilkinson agreed that AG Eric Holder should not announce their "big victory" in Arizona at a big press conference in January.

Andre heard nothing from the ATF. His attorney, Chris Rapp, met with the ATF and the DOJ without Andre to find out what was going on. Chris Rapp reported back:

> "Mr. Rapp informed me that the two AK-47s purchased from my store were recovered at the Brian Terry crime scene and were part of the 'ATF investigation' [Operation Fast and Furious] that I cooperated in [...] That ATF and DOJ admitted that false statements had been made by the DOJ regarding these facts and [the] [DOJ] [was] awaiting further instructions [from the Attorney General's office]. He also advised me that they said: 'We were all in the same boat and it would be OK as long as we stayed together.'"

After DOJ officials received notification of the Terry murder on December 15, 2010, and the notification that same day that two weapons seized at the crime scene were purchased by Jaime Avila during Fast and Furious, DOJ officials wasted no time starting their cover-up.

Step one was to arrest Jaime Avila on December 15, not for illegal firearm trafficking, but for providing a false address on the purchase forms (ATF Form 4473). This DOJ decision was made so that the media and others would not connect the Avila arrest to the Brian Terry murder, and so the illegal gun sales to Avila, at the direction, and under the supervision of the ATF and the DOJ, would not trigger scrutiny of Operation Fast and Furious. Avila provided a false address on the ATF Form 4473 for his November 2009 purchase, and the other three purchases, before his January 16, 2010, purchase of the Terry crime scene weapons. He could have been arrested at any time during, or after, the other purchases.

Step two was the January 25, 2011, indictments of Avila and nineteen other Fast and Furious straw purchasers, which were also designed to mask the fact that most of these arrests and indictments could have been done in 2009. Again, the DOJ executed this charade in a way that purposefully disguised the fact that the firearms that were purchased illegally were intentionally walked to the Mexican drug cartels, and many were traced to violent crime scenes and murders in Mexico. The indictments were initially filed under seal, but were unsealed the next day.

Step three was the creation of a false CYA document to retroactively paper over the events leading up to the Avila purchased firearms being seized at the Brian Terry murder scene. On January 28, 2011, AUSA Emory Hurley was tasked with creating a memorandum titled "Jaime Avila, Jr." Knowing that Fast and Furious agents created a detailed paper trail of suspects, purchases, and the use of cooperating FFLs, Hurley had to blend the undisputed facts already available to congressional investigators, with a fictitious revisionist history, to create an exculpatory story.

The factual portion of the memorandum was that Avila first illegally purchased five FN Herstal Five-seven pistols on November 24, 2009, from Lone Wolf Trading Company. Avila was accompanied by Uriel Patino, who was already a known suspect (i.e. a straw purchaser targeted by the ATF, and a past purchaser of illegal Fast and Furious weapons).

On or near October 31, 2009, the ATF "initiated an investigation into suspected gun trafficking by Patino, and the ATF had already filed grand jury subpoenas for evidence about his phone records and his financial records. They conducted an extensive background check and had all this information about his residences and vehicles (past and present). They reviewed surveillance tapes of related stash houses, reviewed videos from FFLs regarding his purchases, entered the serial numbers from his firearm purchases into the ATF Suspect Gun Database and entered Patino in the ATF case management system as a suspect. All of these procedures were official Fast and Furious standard operating procedures.

AUSA Hurley's CYA memorandum acknowledged that on November 25, 2009, when Avila purchased five Herstal assault pistols and his companion Patino purchased five AK-47 assault rifles, Avila was immediately entered into the ATF case management system as a suspect in arms trafficking.

Avila's next purchase from Lone Wolf Trading Company was on December 12, 2009. He purchased five AK-47 assault rifles. The ATF was notified by Andre Howard at the time of the purchase, and an ATF Form 4473 regarding the purchase was immediately provided to the ATF.

Avila's next purchase of illegal Fast and Furious firearms was on January 9, 2010. He purchased three Herstal Five-seven pistols. This purchase was entered into the ATF suspect gun database on January 14, 2010. That same day, the U.S. Border Patrol pulled over a vehicle that was transporting the three firearms purchased by Avila and five AK-47 assault rifles purchased by Patino, in Columbus, New Mexico (a border town). The guns were not seized and the vehicle was allowed to proceed.

On the evening of Friday, January 16, 2010, Avila purchased three firearms from Lone Wolf Trading Company. This purchase included the two AK-47 assault rifles found at the Agent Terry murder scene in December 2010. AUSA Hurley said that the ATF did not receive notice of this purchase until they received the ATF Form 4473 three days later, on January 19, 2010, and then it was "too late" to act.

However, Avila also purchased firearms on June 15, 2010. The ATF was notified promptly. They knew the address on the form was false, but they still took no action.

The Hurley memorandum fails to point out what surveillance the DOJ and the ATF actually did regarding each of Avila's purchases, leaving the impression that they were previously unable to arrest him, or interdict the weapons. They claimed they had no knowledge that his address on the ATF Form 4473 was false until August 2010, when he changed his driver's license to reflect a different address. Avila admitted after his arrest that he had not lived at the address he listed on his ATF Forms for over two or three years. AUSA Hurley also failed to note that the ATF Form 4473 relating to the fateful sale of the murder scene weapons the evening of Friday, January 16, was actually faxed to the ATF on Saturday morning, January 17, when Andre Howard came to work. Apparently, no one was at the ATF office Saturday, Sunday, or Monday, which was Martin Luther King Jr. Day.

Hurley also fails to mention that every Avila purchase was captured on live video cameras that the ATF installed at Lone Wolf Trading Company. The videos were streamed in real time to the laptops and computers of all ATF agents involved in Fast and Furious, including ATF Acting Director Melson. He also did not mention the live pole cameras installed in the parking lot outside of Lone Wolf and at every single stash house where the weapons were transported. These pole cameras also provided twenty-four-hour live video. Before the January 16, 2010, Avila purchase, the DOJ and the ATF had overwhelming proof that Avila's firearms were being transported to Mexico.

Step four of the cover-up was for the DOJ to "leak" Hurley's exculpatory memorandum to the *New York Times*, which they did on June 14, 2011.

The leaked Hurley memorandum also falsely addressed the December 17, 2009, meeting Andre Howard requested because of his concerns about the increasing quantity of illegal sales he was being directed to make to straw purchasers. Hurley said that at the meeting, held in Andre's office at Lone Wolf Trading Company, AUSA Hurley, ATF Group Supervisor David Voth, and ATF Special Agent Hope MacAllister told Andre Howard:

> "[T]hat they could not tell him who he could or could not sell to and that they could not instruct him to make a sale in violation of the law or to refuse to make a lawful sale. He was advised by the agents that, as an FFL, he has to comply with all the statutes and regulations that govern the sale and transfer of firearms, and cannot sell firearms unless the required paperwork and background check were completed. As long as the required forms were properly filled out and the FFL did not *know or have reason to know that the firearms were part of a straw purchase* or intended to be used in a crime, that he could complete the transfer." (Emphasis added.)

Hurley also said in the memorandum that they told Andre Howard that "the information he provided to the ATF regarding large firearms transactions, particularly sales involving only long guns, was very important and useful to ongoing ATF investigations".

AUSA Hurley's version of the meeting, which was leaked to the media, and was also provided to the DOJ IG, and congressional investigators, was an absolute lie!

At the beginning of Fast and Furious, both the DOJ and the ATF provided Andre Howard the names of straw purchasers who would be coming to Lone Wolf Trading Company within days to make straw purchases. Every sale at Lone Wolf was surveilled by agents in the parking lot and/or videotaped on live streaming cameras. At the December 17 meeting, AUSA Hurley, Supervising Agent Voth, and Special Agent MacAllister assured Andre Howard that all the firearms sold to straw purchasers from Lone Wolf were, and would continue to be, interdicted.

Those same representations were repeated by the DOJ and the ATF on March 10, 2011, at the meeting in Phoenix I attended with Andre Howard and Attorney Chris Rapp. At the March 10, 2011, meeting, AUSA Hurley specifically admitted he told Andre Howard all Fast and Furious firearms had been interdicted when they met in December 2009. At the March 2011 meeting he said he told Andre the truth: They were all interdicted. He then doubled down, saying as of March 10, 2011, it was still absolutely true and accurate that all weapons sold from Lone Wolf had been interdicted: "Not a single firearm crossed the border into Mexico." AUSA Morrissey and everyone at the meeting from the ATF confirmed the interdictions.

Step five of the cover-up: deflect attention toward the FFLs, primarily Andre, as a part of the Obama gun control strategy.

On January 25, 2011, U.S. Attorney Burke issued a press release announcing: "five cases against thirty-four defendants accused of assisting Mexican drug-trafficking organizations." The press release included the fifty-three-count Avila indictment from Fast and Furious, which was unsealed that day.

The forty-three-page indictment mentioned Lone Wolf Trading Company ninety-six times. U.S. Attorney Dennis Burke's two-page press release did not mention Lone Wolf Trading Company or Andre Howard, at all. Instead of acknowledging Andre's extraordinary cooperation, and without giving a heads-up" that his business would be thrown out to the media in a bombshell release to the media, the DOJ and the ATF chose to blindside him and open him up to cartel retaliation, as well as public criticism and business boycotts. The DOJ should have protected Andre's identity by redacting his name and business from the unsealed indictment or using a convention like "FFL#1". U.S. Attorney Burke's press release said: "Our office is committed to stopping the illegal flow of guns into Mexico. […] The massive size of this operation sadly exemplifies the magnitude of the problem: Mexican drug lords go shopping for war weapons in Arizona."

Assistant Attorney General Lanny Breuer, who distanced himself from anything associated with Fast and Furious during the investigation by Congress, did take the opportunity to be quoted in the January 25 press release. He might have declined if he knew that two days later Senator Grassley would expose the scandal in his January 27 letter to Acting ATF Director Melson, which revealed shocking internal DOJ and ATF evidence provided by the ATF whistleblowers. Instead, Breuer touted the Justice Department's role in combating gun trafficking:

> "These indictments are important steps in the Justice Department's effort to curb gun trafficking along the southwest border. […] The criminal division is working hard with its partners in the U.S. Attorney's offices and colleagues in Mexico to find and prosecute those who seek to transport weapons illegally across our borders."

So, "working hard" with your partners in Mexico included keeping them totally in the dark about the operation, keeping DOJ employees like ATF Agent Gill, who was ATF's liaison to Mexico, in the dark, and lying to them for fifteen months?

Bill Newell, Special Agent in Charge of the ATF Phoenix Field Division, also jumped on the glory train in the press release:

> "This investigation is further proof of the relentless efforts by Mexican drug cartels, especially the Sinaloa Cartel, to illegally acquire large quantities of firearms in Arizona […] for use in the ongoing Mexican drug war. […] This investigation is also further proof that those individuals that knowingly falsify ATF firearms forms in order to supply Mexican drug cartels with firearms *have as much blood on their hands as the criminals that use them.*" (Emphasis added.)

This is an interesting and hypocritical unknowing admission by SA Newell. First, he knew the Fast and Furious guns were going to the Sinaloa Cartel. Second, he knew, and believed, some of the people who were involved in getting the guns in the hands of the Mexican cartels would be in the same position as the criminals who used them and "have as much blood on their hands."

The straw purchasers were actually low-income people who acted as intermediaries in buying firearms to get a modest commission — approximately $100-$300 per weapon. They did lie about details on their purchase form. They did understand the firearms were intended to go to the Mexican cartels. They didn't know that they were actually guaranteed to go to the Mexican cartels because they didn't know that the ATF, DOJ, FBI, DEA, ICE, IRS, and other United States government agencies would not interdict them. Or maybe they did! So the straw purchasers, who were the first step in the illegal process, did go to jail but the people who were the key link to the guns actually getting to the cartels so they could kill people never went to jail. They got promoted, retired, or went on with their lives with *blood on their hands*!

After the January 25, 2011, DOJ press conference announcing the Fast and Furious takedown, ATF Assistant Director (Field Operations) Mark Chait emailed ATF Special Agent in Charge William Newell and copied Deputy Assistant Director (Field Operations) William McMahon:

> "[I]n light of our request for Demand Letter 3, this case could be a strong supporting factor if we can determine how many multiple sales of long guns occurred during the course of this case."

According to Newell, "ninety-five percent" of the "2,000+ guns involved in Fast and Furious were AK-47s. Demand Letter 3 was the Obama administration gun control proposal involving the sale of assault rifles.

Less than one month later, the House of Representatives overwhelmingly voted to block the Obama administration's Demand Letter 3 proposal which would have required border state FFLs to report sales of two or more semiautomatic rifles (of a certain type) to the same person within five consecutive business days of the sale.

The ATF previously tried to get the regulation approved in January 2010 "on an emergency basis." It, too, failed.

No one in the DOJ, ATF, DEA, ICE or the U.S. State Department ever warned Mexican law enforcement or the Mexican government that over 2,000 dangerous firearms were allowed to walk to the Sinaloa, El Teo, and La Familia cartels. Most went to the Sinaloa Cartel, who AG Holder targeted in numerous speeches as the most violent cartel in Mexico. Even the ATF agents assigned as attaches to Mexico City were kept in the dark about Fast and Furious until the summer of 2010, when they figured out for themselves that the number of crime scene traces in Mexico must mean gunwalking. The DOJ and ATF headquarters never informed them about the operation, nor did they provide them any details when specifically confronted about the obvious fact that guns had been walked.

The scope of the crimes the cartels committed using Fast and Furious weapons ranged from shooting down a Mexican Army helicopter (with a .50 caliber weapon), to the execution of Mexican attorneys and officials,the murder of children, and the killing of opposition cartel members.

Every reported cartel murder in Mexico severely disturbed Andre, who processed crime scene trace request after crime scene trace request following Agent Terry's murder. The evidence mounted that the government attorneys and law enforcement agents he trusted were not telling him the truth about interdicting the firearms in Arizona.

On February 1, 2011, *Arizona Republic* reporter Dennis Wagner again focused on Lone Wolf Trading Company and Andre in an article titled "Senator links gun buy to border agent's death."

"Grassley said he had information that the AK-47s recovered at the shooting scene were traced to Project Gunrunner. [...] Individuals purchased three assault rifles with cash in Glendale, Arizona, on January 16, 2010. Two of the weapons were then used in a firefight, killing CBP Agent Brian Terry."

That same day, February 1, Sari Horwitz and James Grimaldi also wrote an article in the *Washington Post*:

> "Whistleblowers [...] allege that federal agents allowed guns, including AK-47s, to be sold to suspected straw purchasers who transported the weapons throughout the region and into Mexico. The AK-47s [...] at the scene of a fatal shooting of a Border Patrol agent in December [...] have become part of a southwest border crackdown on firearms known as Project Gunrunner.

"ATF and other federal officials said the Fast and Furious case was a 'major success.' U.S. Attorney Dennis Burke said the announced indictments were part of 'breaking up a network linked to the Sinaloa drug-trafficking cartel.' The massive size of this operation sadly exemplifies the magnitude of the problem."

The Grimaldi article also linked the firearms seized at the Brian Terry crime scene to Avila's purchase of "700 weapons" from Lone Wolf Trading Company. He defended the Fast and Furious tactics as a "response to criticism from the Justice Department's inspector general that the firearms bureau was bringing too many minor cases against straw purchasers."

How could the DOJ IG later do a supposedly independent investigation of DOJ officials and ATF officials when the media pointed to the DOJ IG himself as at least one of the reasons that the OCDETF task force initiated the gunwalking strategy? President Obama should have granted Congress' request for appointment of a truly independent special counsel to investigate Fast and Furious and prosecute wrongdoers.

The truth is, the Obama administration didn't want the truth to come out and did not want wrongdoers to be punished. They knew the DOJ IG would protect AG Holder and AG Holder would protect President Obama. Their only exposure was from the investigations by Congress, and they planned to obstruct those investigations.

Curiously, seasoned investigative reporters Horwitz and Grimaldi said: "Owner Andre Howard could not be reached for comment." No one tried to get Andre's story. Andre went to his business every day, and Congress, the ATF, and others in the media never had any problem contacting him. ATF officials who were contacted said "they have no indication that Lone Wolf Trading Company is doing anything wrong or illegal." Of course, they did not disclose their role in the 185 guns being traced to crime scenes in Mexico in 2009 and 2010. They also never admitted their role in letting guns walk.

On December 17, 2010, the *Arizona Republic* did a follow-up story to the *Washington Post* article, highlighting Lone Wolf Trading Company and Andre Howard. Their article, titled "Glendale Store Tops List of Guns in Mexico Crimes", also quoted "Michael Vice, a senior attorney at the Brady Center to Prevent Gun Violence [who] called for reform on 'weak laws' that allow 'a few bad gun dealers' to operate, some despite numerous violations and warnings."

This defamatory comment ignored the fact that Andre and Lone Wolf Trading Company did not have any violations and did not receive warnings. Andre fully cooperated with the ATF and sold the firearms at issue at the direction of ATF, and under the supervision and surveillance of the ATF. The *Arizona Republic* said: "Local and federal officials from [the] ATF did not return the *Republic's* calls for comment on Lone Wolf Trading Company."

On December 20, the *Arizona Republic* doubled down on its defamatory attack on Andre and Lone Wolf Trading Company, still without contacting Andre to give him an opportunity to defend himself, and still without ATF and DOJ comment. Again they quoted Michael Vice:

> "He hailed the [*Washington Post*] news report for shining a light on what he described as a few 'bad apples' flooding the illegal-gun market with guns used for crime. [...] He said he "isn't surprised by Lone Wolf's presence on the list. [...] It was among the top so-called crime-gun dealers in lists going back to 1996 and 2000. The ATF defines crime guns as any firearm that is illegally possessed, used in a crime, or suspected to have been used in a crime."

Unfortunately Arizona was the focal point for gun control again on January 8, 2011, when Representative Gabrielle Giffords and others were targeted in a shooting in Tucson that killed six people and wounded thirteen others. The incident was not related to Fast and Furious, but it did keep the spotlight on Andre and gun control in the border states.

During the week of January 17, 2011, the world's largest annual gun tradeshow opened in Las Vegas. It sparked heated debate about gun control. Sari Horwitz of the *Washington Post* wrote about the gun show on January 20:

> "[T]here is a serious side: During the four-day convention, the ATF holds seminars to teach dealers how to adhere to federal laws governing the sale of firearms and how to watch for straw buyers who are illegally buying guns for others prohibited from purchasing one. They teach dealers how to properly fill out federal forms that allow the ATF to trace a gun recovered during a criminal investigation."

Sari Horwitz had nothing to say about ATF's role in Fast and Furious.

Senator Grassley's first public release of information about the Fast and Furious investigation was the letter to ATF Acting Director Ken Melson on January 27, 2010. The first media report was from Dennis Wagner, a reporter for the *Arizona Republic,* on February 1, 2011, titled "Phoenix area gun store, ATF sting may be linked to shootout... Senator links gun buy to border agent's death." In the article, Wagner quotes: "a source within the justice system familiar with the case." That source "confirmed to the *Arizona Republic* last week that one or two weapons recovered from the border shootout had been traced to Lone Wolf Trading Company, a

Glendale gun store." This would not be the first leak from the DOJ trying to put the focus and blame on Andre.

A week before, on January 25, "[the] ATF and the U.S. Attorney's office announced indictments of [thirty-four] people in connection with firearms smuggling to Mexico. [...] According to the justice system source [...] no one has been charged [in the murder] of the Agent Brian Terry. An indictment was expected against the wounded suspect [who was arrested at the crime scene].

"In a statement Monday, Lone Wolf Trading Company owner Andre Hunter (sic) said he has been cooperating with authorities: 'We have worked closely in conjunction with several federal agencies.'"

Reporter Wagner also quoted ATF officials but did not ask them how they had been cooperating with Andre. Instead, the author chose to portray the situation in a way that left the reader with the impression that Andre was personally selling guns to the cartels without ATF knowledge or participation:

> "Newell was asked if agents purposely allowed firearms to enter Mexico as part of an investigation. He answered, 'Hell no.'
>
> "Tom Mangan, an ATF spokesman in Phoenix, said he was 'unaware of any guns allowed to go south of the border' either intentionally or inadvertently."

This article followed up on the December 13, 2010, article by Sari Horwitz and James Grimaldi of the *Washington Post* that "uncovered the names of the dealers, all from border states, with the most [crime scene] traces from guns recovered in Mexico over the past two years [...] of the leading stores with Mexican traces, Lone Wolf Trading Co [...] is No. 1 on the Mexico list over the past two years. It had 185 of its guns recovered and traced south of the border."

Senator Grassley's January 27, 2010, letter to the DOJ the ATF was based on interviews with ATF whistleblowers, the first of whom was ATF SA John Dodson, and internal ATF documents provided to Congress. The January 27, 2010, letter was addressed to Acting Director of ATF Ken Melson. Melson sent it to the Office of Legislative Affairs at the Department of Justice.

The letter from Senator Grassley requested information about firearms sales to straw purchasers and the connections between those firearms and the Terry murder:

> "Members of the Judiciary have received numerous allegations that the ATF sanctioned the sale of hundreds of assault weapons to suspected straw purchasers, who then allegedly transported those weapons throughout the southwestern border area and into Mexico."

This is absolutely what happened. Under any reasonable interpretation of the allegation, it was true. If anything, it is understated. Not only did the ATF sanction the sales, they arranged the sales with the straw purchasers, directed and supervised the sales by the FFLs, and conducted video-taped and on-site physical surveillance of the sale. It is likely ATF even funded many of the purchases!

The second part of the allegation "straw purchasers who then [...] transported these weapons [...] into Mexico" is also absolutely true, both factually and legally. According to the DOJ's own indictments, the straw purchasers were members of a firearm trafficking conspiracy. They agreed to purchase firearms for the agreed purpose that they would be transported to the Sinaloa Cartel in Mexico. They were the first overt acts in furtherance of a conspiracy to illegally transport firearms to Mexico. On some occasions the straw purchasers actually accompanied the driver, or next transferee in the conspiracy, to the border. In other cases, they went back to the FFL to purchase the next batch of illegal firearms to be transported.

Surely the senior DOJ officials,which included numerous lawyers who practiced white-collar criminal law for decades at prestigious law firms in Washington, D.C.; New York City; and other major cities would advise their clients to either admit those two allegations or assert their Fifth Amendment rights. Or would they? There are legal ethics rules that provide long accepted guidance in this area suggesting strongly that they should not lie to Congress or encourage others to lie to Congress.

There was one other specific allegation raised by Senator Grassley: that one of the Fast and Furious straw purchasers purchased three assault rifles with cash in Glendale, Arizona, on January 16, 2010.

As the DOJ's internal email exchanges showed, every key official at the ATF and the DOJ knew this to be true no later than December 17, 2009.

They also knew that two of the weapons were then recovered at the scene of the firefight on December 14, 2010, where Customs and Border Protection Agent Brian Terry was killed.

Grassley also advised the DOJ that "these extremely serious allegations were accompanied by detailed documentation which appears to lend credibility to the claims and partially corroborate them."

Only the FBI, the ATF, and the Obama administration know the real truth about what weapon actually killed Agent Terry because the real and complete forensic ballistics reports have still never been released to the public. If they don't know the truth it is because, as some insiders claim, AG Holder did not want the FBI to conduct a complete forensic test. We know that multiple shell casings were recovered at the crime scene, but we don't know if any were fired from the two AK-47s that were recovered. We do not know what weapon, type of weapon, or any other information about the actual murder weapon. The DOJ and the ATF originally said: "forensic tests excluded those two AK-47s from being the actual murder weapon." When challenged, the DOJ and the FBI said tests were "inconclusive" because the bullet was "too damaged" to do conclusive testing. Nothing else was ever released. Were either of the two guns fired during the firefight? That would be an easy test to conduct. Was the bullet from an AK-47? Again, that could be an easy test to conduct. What were the test results on the shell casings? Were fingerprint tests done? Cover-up?

Andre received further guidance from the DOJ. After the DOJ received the Grassley letter, the department told his attorney, Chris Rapp, "Senator Grassley would jeopardize their cases against the straw purchasers if Andre spoke to anyone in his office or any other congressional officials. If Senator Grassley's office tried to subpoena Andre, through Senator Leahy, Democratic Chairman of the Senate Judiciary Committee, they would quash the subpoena."

Andre did not know that brave ATF agents had come forward as whistleblowers to expose the truth about Fast and Furious, so Andre did not know the truth... yet.

Senator Grassley had a meeting with Attorney General Holder on January 31, 2011. At the meeting, Senator Grassley personally handed Attorney General Holder his January 27 letter asking ATF Director Melson to address the gunwalking allegations generally and the weapons seized at the Agent Terry crime scene specifically. He also handed Attorney General Holder a letter dated January 31, 2011, about alleged retaliation against ATF whistleblowers who were cooperating with the congressional investigation.

Attorney General Holder testified under oath before the DOJ IG that he did not recall any conversations with Senator Grassley about the letters or the failure to interdict weapons.

He also supposedly did not know about the Attorney General Office's response to the letter from Congress.

The DOJ/ATF February 4, 2011, letter replying to Senator Grassley (copying Senator Patrick Leahy and signed by an assistant attorney general) stated:

> "[The] allegation [...] that [the] ATF 'sanctioned' or otherwise knowingly allowed the sale of assault weapons to a straw purchaser who then transported them into Mexico, is false.

> "[The] ATF makes every effort to interdict weapons that have been purchased illegally and prevent their transportation to Mexico."

It then goes on to cite the success of Project Gunrunner since its inception in 2006. Senator Grassley's letter specifically asked about "guns transported to Mexico" during Project Gunrunner, which was still ongoing, and which included Operation Wide Receiver and Operation Fast and Furious. According to the DOJ, both operations walked guns to the Mexican drug cartels. In Fast and Furious, the ATF made no effort at all to interdict them. In fact, the ATF actively stopped other government agencies like Customs and Border Patrol, the DEA, and ICE from interdicting them or seizing them at the border.

According to the DOJ IG report, the February 4, 2011, letter from the DOJ and the ATF to Congress "contained inaccurate information". It was not corrected or withdrawn by AG Holder until December 2011, despite repeated efforts by Congress to provide factual evidence that categorically proved the key statements in the letter were false. The "inaccurate information" was not due to a mistake, an oversight, a flawed drafting process, or a failure to proofread. It was a blatant lie intended to mislead Congress, thwart their investigation, cover up criminal misconduct, and obstruct justice. The written official lie to Congress was followed up by DOJ and ATF witnesses who supported it under oath in testimony at the DOJ IG investigation and before Congress.

The explanations witnesses tried to give defending the accuracy of the letter ranged from laughable to absurd, if they weren't actually criminal.

"The DOJ Office of Legislative Affairs at Main Justice, the Arizona U.S. Attorney's office, and ATF headquarters assumed responsibility for drafting the response."

Between January 27 and February 4, there were multiple "iterations of the proposed response, which were circulated for review and comment by dozens of officials in the DOJ Criminal Division, the Office of the Deputy Attorney General, the Office of the U.S. Attorney General, the U.S. Attorney's office in Phoenix, and at the ATF headquarters."

According to the Office of Legislative Affairs, "everyone who knows, or is responsible for, information in that letter signs off on it." That list included:

> "Attorney General Eric Holder, Deputy Attorney General James Cole, Chief of Staff to the Attorney General Gary Grindler, Assistant Attorney General for the Criminal Division Lanny Breuer, ATF Director Melson, Deputy ATF Director Hoover, U.S. Attorney for the District of Arizona Dennis Burke, Senior Counsel to the Deputy Attorney General Brad Smith, Deputy Assistant Attorney General Jason Weinstein, OLA Attorneys Burton and Weich, as well as countless lower level attorneys and officials."

The Obama administration's testimony ran the gamut of every ridiculous explanation except "my dog ate the draft of the letter they sent me to review."

Faced with the media onslaught generated by the indictment, the misleading press release by the DOJ, the inaccurate reporting by the local press, and the admonitions and veiled threats about obstruction of justice if he talked to the media or Congress, Andre drafted his own response the next day:

"Lone Wolf Trading Company
"January 26, 2011
   "So there remains no confusion to the accuracy regarding these events culminating with the Federal Indictment and arrests Monday, and to set the record straight and assure the public, we have issued the following statement:
   "We have worked closely in conjunction with several Federal agencies including the Phoenix office of the ATF within the guidelines of both the Southwest Border Initiative and Operation Gunrunner, as well as within the guidelines of being an existing Federal Firearms Licensed dealer, as well as many other licensed Arizona dealers as well.
   "Due to the sensitivity and nature of any ongoing Federal Investigation, we obviously are precluded from making any further statement other than we defer respectfully to the United States Attorney's Office and the Phoenix ATF field office on our behalf for any further comment they determine appropriate at this time.
   Thank you."

Some of the Obama administration responses to this media and investigation crisis were questionable at best:

1. "Gunwalking" was defined as an ATF agent physically putting a firearm in the straw purchaser's hand and personally watching them take it across the border into Mexico.
    This interpretation was offered by many DOJ and ATF officials who had many meetings about gunwalking

during Operation Wide Receiver and Operation Fast and Furious. In those meetings no official ever adopted, used, or discussed this contrived, and extremely narrow, definition of gunwalking.

"Technically, the straw purchasers did not transport the weapons into Mexico; someone else did." Co-conspirators are legally liable for all of the acts of their other co-conspirators.

2. "The sales were not illegal — they were all to individuals who could have been legal purchasers." They knew every purchase was going to a third-party cartel member, thus they were all illegal.

3. "It would have been unconstitutional to refuse to sell the guns or to seize the guns without probable cause. Probable cause required an admission from the purchaser that they lied when filling out their Form 4377." Every white collar attorney in the United States knows this is legally incorrect. There are thousands of law enforcement actions based on probable cause taken every day without any prior admission of guilt by the suspect.

ATF never stopped or questioned any straw purchasers because the suspect would get suspicious, so of course there were no admissions. Oh, they actually did make admissions in their recorded telephone conversations about taking the guns to Mexico.

4. "They never told or directly encouraged FFLs to sell firearms." There is overwhelming evidence to the contrary.

5. "They 'forgot about' Wide Receiver — it was a prior administration program." They actually planned a joint press release about Wide Receiver and Fast and Furious for January 2011, to be presented by AG Holder.

6. "They thought Grassley made a mistake when he asked about gunwalking in Project Gunrunner, they thought he was just asking about Fast and Furious." Wide Receiver and Fast and Furious were a part of the same DOJ press release planned for January, and they were both part of Project Gunrunner.

7. "Avila purchased the weapons seized at the Agent Terry crime scene before Fast and Furious started." False! Fast and Furious started in September 2009 and the weapons were purchased in January 2010.

8. "Avila was not known to be a straw purchaser at the time he purchased the Terry Weapons." False! He was entered in the Suspect Database in November 2009, and the sale was in January 2010.

9. 9."Tests showed that the Avila guns were not the murder weapon." False! The official FBI ballistic report regarding the crime scene weapons was supposedly "inconclusive". The FBI never released or published any other conclusions about the actual murder weapon.

10. "The three-day delay in getting the faxed information from the FFL is what hindered them from arresting Avila when he purchased the crime scene weapons." False! They didn't go to work, or check their recorded video, for three days and still had multiple opportunities to arrest him.

11. "We didn't know that these weapons left the United States." False! Read the crime scene traces from Mexico!

12. " AAG Breuer had nothing to so with the false February 4 letter to Congress." AAG Breuer received several drafts of the February 4 to Congress, the signed February 3 letter, and the final letter for review and comment, but he said that he never reviewed them because it was difficult to read documents on his

blackberry. It was a one-and-half-page letter, he got 4 versions, and he never corrected the letter afterward.

13. "Weapons wouldn't have been sold if Congress had passed assault weapon legislation." The sales allowed by the FBI and the DOJ were illegal under existing laws.

14. AG Holder and Deputy AG Cole testified they didn't review the final February 4 letter before it went out.

The two key false statements in the February 4 letter to Congress were in every prior draft of the letter and in the signed February 3 letter sent to both of their offices.

On February 9, 2011, Senator Grassley sent a letter to AG Holder saying "the allegations I received are supported by documentation." He attached nine documents regarding the Avila purchases, directing Holder's attention to the indictment and the missing weapons. He also added that FFLs were forced to make sales, and the Terry family had not had any contact with the government since Agent Terry's murder. He concluded the letter by saying: "The Terry family deserves answers."

On February 16, 2011, Senator Grassley sent another letter to AG Holder reiterating his questions about "persuading reluctant FFLs" and he again requested that document be produced.

On March 3, 2011, Senator Grassley sent Holder a letter with more documents that "demonstrated that the Department's claims in the February 4 letter were not accurate." Even if you believed the unlikely testimony that AG Holder and Deputy AG Cole really did not review the February 4 letter before it was sent, what action did they take when they got three letters from Congress within the next month pointing out that it was clearly false? They did nothing to correct it, temporarily pull it back, question their senior officials, or even read the letters from Congress calling them liars?

Instead, the Attorney General responded by deferring to the new DOJ IG investigation that he just requested.

The obvious fact is that there was chaos in the Obama administration. That chaos started on December 15, 2010. They lost their plausible denial strategy when the victim was a United States border agent, and the firearms were traced to a known Fast and Furious suspect. Too many people knew too much, too quickly. The Obama administration had to scramble to deal with ATF whistleblowers, mounting interest from the media — both bloggers and mainstream sources — and now Congress. They were in control when the victims "were just Mexicans". Now they had to undertake major damage control. The February 4 letter was their story and they were sticking to it.

Sticking to their story would prove to be more difficult than AG Holder and President Obama originally anticipated. Everyone learns growing up that the number-one problem with being a liar is you inevitably must admit you lied, or make up more lies to cover up your earlier lies. Even though dozens of top-level subordinates had initially lied in numerous high-level internal communications, those could be kept from seeing the light of day through a long string of technical ways that would prevent, or at least delay, the public from ever gaining access. Congress was a co-equal branch in the United States system of separation of powers, so their investigation could be handled by claiming interference with their executive branch investigation, assertions of various alleged privileges, or getting Democratic Party members to object. Obfuscate and obstruct!

The media was becoming interested in the matter, but the most powerful media sources could be an asset. They were controlled by liberal Democrats who could manipulate and spin any adverse information that came out of the smaller, less powerful media sources. The deep-state executive branch officials could, for the most part, be handled by the executive branch political appointees through persuasion backed by threatened retaliation and actual retribution. That only left the others on the fringe, like Andre, who they thought could be handled through his attorney, Chris Rapp. Mexico could be handled by Secretary Clinton and the State Department. Other potential adversaries could be attacked on a case-by-case basis by retaliatory intelligence assaults on their privacy, IRS harassment, lawsuits, smear campaigns, or retaliation from other resources within the United States government, as needed.

Some potential issues had already been handled by the Obama administration during the first two months of chaos:

Acting ATF Director Melson was silenced. DOJ forbid him from communicating with anyone, including members of his staff, or responding to the January 27 letter he received from Congress;

FBI Director Mueller was on board with lying, and hiding forensic information from the American public; and

DHS Secretary Janet Napolitano silenced the other border agents who were on patrol with SA Terry the night of the ambush murder.

It became obvious to Andre that the Department of Justice was working through his attorney, Chris Rapp, to get him to obstruct justice and involve them in orchestrating a cover-up by refusing to cooperate with the congressional investigation. Andre's response: "I retained Mr. Gaydos from Texas at the beginning of March 2011 to oversee [...]this matter."

On March 9, 2011, AG Holder had DAG Cole send out a policy to DOJ law enforcement. In the U.S. Attorney's office in Arizona, Shelley Clemens forwarded the policy to the local ATF and FBI:

> "We received a directive from the DAG, instructing on DOJ's policy regarding guns going south into

Mexico. 'We should not design or conduct undercover operations which include guns crossing the border. If we have knowledge that guns are about to cross the border, we must take immediate action to stop the firearms from crossing the border, even if that prematurely terminates or otherwise jeopardizes an investigation.'[…] Please distribute this to your agents to ensure they are clear on this policy."

It is interesting that this new policy was sent out by AG Holder a month after he and his top officials sent the February 4 letter to Congress denying that any guns went across the border during Fast and Furious. It was not sent out as a reminder of the DOJ's existing policy. It also implicitly acknowledges that stopping guns before they cross the border may "prematurely" impact an active investigation. The only active investigation in Arizona that included guns crossing the border as part of the investigation was Fast and Furious. The Obama administration officially denied that the investigation called Fast and Furious involved any investigative strategy involving guns crossing the southern border.

This raises some other questions others need to explore. How many other Obama administration programs around the United States included firearms being trafficked to other countries? What about Operation Castaway? We all know of that and many other code names but we don't know any details, about any of those operations. They were never investigated by the DOJ IG or the Congress.

Is there any way Congress would back off and let the Obama administration stick to their denial strategy?

Would anyone challenge the credibility of the Obama administration's strategy?

Chapter Five

"I'm Sorry, Gentlemen... You Are Just Not Credible"

On Thursday morning, March 10, 2011, my American Airline flight landed in Phoenix, Arizona, and I checked into my downtown hotel. In a couple hours I would meet my client, Andre Howard, for the first time at the hotel to prepare for our Friday meeting with the DOJ and the ATF. After meeting for several hours, we would have a scheduled meeting with Chris Rapp, who had been Andre's attorney for the three months since the murder of Border Agent Brian Terry.

I asked Andre why he wanted a Dallas attorney to represent him in this matter. He didn't hesitate to say that he did not trust any attorney in Phoenix. Chris Rapp's brother was an Assistant United States Attorney in the Phoenix U.S. Attorney's Office and was a colleague of AUSA Emory Hurley, who directed Operation Fast and Furious. Chris Rapp had several meetings with Hurley and other attorneys in his brother's office. He never had Andre attend any of those meetings, and the messages that he brought back to Andre were: (1) The DOJ confirmed there were two guns from Lone Wolf sold during Fast and Furious retrieved and traced to Lone Wolf from the crime scene where Agent Terry was murdered; and (2) the DOJ and the ATF would take care of Andre as long as he trusted them and did what they told him to do. I was very concerned that Chris Rapp might be conflicted in his loyalties because of his brother's position at the DOJ.

Andre brought me some documents to review in preparation for the next day's meeting. He also provided two copies of the *Arizona Republic* newspaper.

The first paper ran a front-page article about Lone Wolf on February 20, 2011. The article had a front-page photo of Andre's gun store, Lone Wolf. The article was titled "Arizona has few rifle-sale limits — Law allows big purchases that feds say supply cartels." The article discussed firearm sales that were disclosed in the January 25, 2011, indictment of twenty straw purchasers.

"Over [...] several months, federal agents say, the same man, Uriel Patino of Phoenix, will return to Lone Wolf Trading Co. [eighteen] times, buying a total of forty-two handguns and 190 semiautomatic rifles. Patino tells store clerks that all 232 guns are for his personal use.

"But federal authorities say Patino was acting as a straw buyer of guns for the Sinaloa drug cartel in Mexico when he purchased guns from Lone Wolf [...] between November 2009 and August 2010.

"It is unclear to what extent Lone Wolf cooperated with authorities in the gun cases. But Lone Wolf has been repeatedly named by authorities in smuggling cases and has been linked to guns found at crime scenes in Mexico.

"Lone Wolf owner Andre Howard refused to discuss gun sales or seizures.

"To set the record straight and assure the public [...] we have worked closely in conjunction with several federal agencies, including the Phoenix office of the ATF,' Howard said in a written statement.

"Lone Wolf and J&D sales are at the top of the list of U.S. stores that sold guns traced to crimes in Mexico in 2009 and 2010, according to a recent investigation by the *Washington Post*."

An unnamed ATF spokesperson did tell the reporter that none of the FFL sales to straw purchasers listed in the indictment were illegal under Arizona laws. That ATF statement was of course, a lie.

The second front-page article was published in the *Arizona Republic* on Saturday, March 5, 2011, and was titled "ATF sting scrutinized — Agency accused of losing track of guns that wound up with drug cartels." The tenor of the press investigation changed:

"Newly released U.S. records and assertions by a government whistleblower support allegations that government agents allowed hundreds of firearms to be smuggled across the Arizona border and into the hands of Mexican drug cartels. […] Investigators have confirmed that two weapons connected to the ATF operation were found at the scene of a gun battle near Rio Rico, Arizona, where Border Patrol Agent Brian Terry was killed by suspected border bandits.

"[The] ATF came in for criticism from the Justice Department's Office of the Inspector General last year because […] [the] [ATF] was only catching straw buyers — small fish in the smuggling business.

"The newly released ATF documents make it clear the bureau sought to overcome such criticism by allowing firearm smugglers to make purchases […] so they could be traced to bigger fish south of the border. […] Gun dealers were encouraged to make sales to known traffickers, sometimes under surveillance.

"At a news conference, William Newell […] was asked if agents knowingly allowed guns to be smuggled into Mexico. 'Hell no,' he said."

On March 9, 2011, James Grimaldi at the *Washington Post* wrote an article titled, "ATF's tactics to end gun-trafficking faces a federal review." Grimaldi was the lead reporter of a series of gun-control articles titled "The Hidden Life of Guns", which included the article citing Lone Wolf as the number-one firearm dealer in sales traced to Mexican crime scenes in 2009 and 2010. Congress had already publicly raised the issue of gunwalking in their January 27, 2010, letter, and other media sources like CBS News (Sharyl Attkisson) and the Center for Public Integrity were well on their way to publicly exposing the scandal. Sharyl Attkisson was the first mainstream media investigative reporter to report on Fast and Furious on February 22, 2011, on the CBS evening news. She followed that up with an exclusive interview of ATF whistleblower John Dodson on March 4, 2011. Despite the direction the real story was taking, Grimaldi decided to double down on his, and the Obama White House, gun-control agenda:

> "The controversy highlights the difficulty ATF agents face in complex cases against increasingly sophisticated gunrunning rings, said former and current government officials. [...] Because of weak gun laws and investigative limitations imposed at the urging of the gun lobby [...] many gun-running cases end with little more than paperwork violations."

Grimaldi tried to defend the tactics used by the ATF by quoting Andre:

> "It appears that any state or federal agency [...] are damned if they do, and damned if they don't."

Blogger John Richardson on "onlygunsandmoney.blogspot.com" attacked Andre without knowing the context of the quote, and without ever contacting Andre:

> "Howard was probably paid twice on the guns he sold. Once, by the straw purchasers, and second, by the ATF, as I understand he was a paid confidential informant."

That was totally false. Andre was not paid by the ATF. He was not a confidential informant. He did not knowingly participate in gunwalking. He was a victim caught in the middle of a very heated political issue. It was a no-win situation.

On March 11, 2011, Andre, Chris Rapp, and I met for the last round of preparation before the meeting with DOJ and ATF representatives. After reading articles from the local newspapers, which squarely linked Andre and Lone Wolf to the indictments of twenty straw purchasers with cartel connections, and highlighted his extensive cooperation with ATF over a fifteen-month period, my priority was to address the safety and security of Andre and his family.

I did not know specifically who was going to attend the meeting other than AUSA Emory Hurley, with whom I had discussions about the Witness Security program. When we arrived at the US Attorney's office, we were escorted to a large conference room filled with DOJ and ATF officials. In addition to AUSA Emory Hurley, other attendees included AUSA Michael Morrissey (Chief of the National Security Section), ATF Assistant Special Agent in Charge James Needles, ATF Agent Tonya English (Co-Leader of Fast and Furious), and a new ATF agent.

I began by expressing my concerns about Andre's safety. AUSA Morrissey took the lead for the government, but AUSA Hurley said they would address Andre's safety. They designated ATF Agent Needles as their point of contact to call me the next week. They asked me why I had concerns about Andre's safety, so I recounted the newspaper articles and specifically pointed out that two of the weapons from the Agent Terry crime scene were traced to Andre's store and were sold to a straw purchaser during Operation Fast and Furious. To my great surprise AUSA Morrissey said those newspaper accounts were all false: "No firearms at the Agent Terry crime scene were sold as part of Fast and Furious and none came from Lone Wolf!" Morrissey said I should not believe everything I read in the newspapers; the truth would come out, but they could not discuss it with me because there was an ongoing criminal investigation. He assured me "the truth would come out in court during the trials of the indicted straw purchasers. [...] The government could not fight the battle for truth in the press."

On the table in front of me I had a file folder of internal ATF and DOJ documents dated December 15, 2010, with their names on the documents, which said the crime scene firearms were traced to Lone Wolf. The argument that details about the Terry crime scene would be litigated at trials of straw purchasers made no sense. The only issue at their trials would be whether they lied on the ATF Form 4473.

I then brought up the newspaper reports and the congressional correspondence about gunwalking firearms to Mexican cartels during Fast and Furious. AUSA Morrissey said that was not true: "It never happened." I confronted AUSA Hurley about his December 2009 meeting with Andre Howard and asked him directly whether he told Andre that all firearms sold from Lone Wolf, at their direction, had been interdicted near his store soon after the sales. AUSA Hurley said, "That is what I said."

"It was the truth then, it continued to be the truth, and it is the truth now as we sit here today."

I also raised the question about a possible congressional subpoena for Andre's testimony. Morrissey and Hurley said: "that would not happen. They would handle it and get it quashed." I assumed they planned to use the standard DOJ mantra—"ongoing criminal investigation"—to avoid compliance with any subpoena related to their investigation or investigation witnesses.

At this point Chris Rapp, who had been told by Hurley and others that the guns from the Terry crime scene did come from Lone Wolf, became ill and had to leave the meeting. He was escorted out of the U.S. Attorney's offices by AUSA Hurley. AUSA Morrissey continued to deny that any weapons went to the Mexican drug cartels. My documents proved otherwise. When AUSA Hurley returned to the meeting, I addressed the entire group of DOJ and ATF attendees: "I am sorry, gentlemen. You are just not credible." Andre and I left the meeting.

I returned to Dallas. I talked to Andre the next day. He said that when AUSA Hurley walked Chris Rapp out, he told Rapp, "Your client is in the same boat as us. If we row together and stay on the same sheet of music, he will be OK." This was a clear message that the government wanted Andre to refuse to cooperate with the congressional investigation and that he should obstruct justice. Andre and I left the March 11 meeting extremely disappointed and disillusioned. I'd had many dealings with the government law enforcement officials and government prosecutors over my twenty-five-year career in white-collar criminal defense. I had opposed them in criminal trials and investigations. I represented many audit committees of public companies in internal investigations and shared my internal investigation findings and documents with them, so they could investigate and prosecute wrongdoers. I had taken cooperating witnesses to them to help them expose and prosecute public corruption cases. I had allowed clients to wear wires to assist them in gathering evidence. Although I have not always agreed with them, and we may disagree about what alleged evidence means, this was the first time a federal law enforcement officer, or federal attorney, flat-out lied to my face. It took me several days to process the fact that four federal officials, sworn to uphold the U.S. Constitution, would blatantly lie to both of us. Chris Rapp obviously had an immediate visceral response to their contradiction of what they previously told him about the Terry crime scene weapons.

Andre and I decided that if Congress contacted us, we would fully cooperate with them.

In Operation Wide Receiver, Charles Highman, the ATF Resident Agent in Charge at the ATF Tucson office, told the cooperating FFL that the ATF would conduct a threat assessment and potentially relocate him when the case went to trial.

The DOJ IG found that "the failure to consider and take adequate precautions to ensure his safety during the investigation violated ATF order 3250.IA3(a)(21), which required agents to take into account the risk of harm to the FFL and his immediate family."

Having dealt with witness protection issues in the past, and given the precarious nature of Andre's position, we decided to proceed with the DOJ's offer of WITSEC protection. On March 14, 2011, I contacted ATF SA Needles to pursue protection for Andre and his family. Over the next two weeks I had numerous conversations with SA Needles and SA Hope MacAllister about both protection and compensation issues. The bottom line was they needed a proforma threat assessment, and documentation about the financial impact the government conduct had on Andre and his business. We supplied the requested documentation and expressed immediate willingness to participate in a threat assessment interview. It quickly became clear that they were slow rolling the process because they wanted to make sure Andre was on board for obstructing Congress.

The week before Andre and I had our March 11, 2011, meeting with DOJ and ATF in Phoenix, the DOJ was busy trying to get their stories coordinated. On March 2, Tracy Schmaler, the Deputy Director of the Office of Public Affairs for the Department of Justice, received a list of five questions about Fast and Furious from John Solomon. Solomon was a very prominent investigative reporter. He was the former national investigative correspondent with the *Washington Post* and former editor-in-chief of the *Washington Times*. In March 2011, he was President of the Packard Media Group and Executive Editor of the Center for Public Integrity. The Center for Public Integrity was a nonprofit investigative journalism organization. Their mission was "to reveal abuses of power, corruption, and dereliction of duty by powerful public and private institutions in order to cause them to operate with honesty, integrity, accountability, and to put the public interest first."

The Obama administration could not afford to ignore this request, but unwanted attention from the Center for Public Integrity was a potential powerful threat to their denial strategy.

Solomon wrote to Tracy Schmaler:

"Here are the questions for which we need on the record answers from the DOJ."

1. "What did the main justice know about the operation code-named Fast and Furious in Phoenix? Did the Attorney General or Lanny Breuer know about ATF's efforts to let guns flow to straw buyers as part of a larger strategy to make bigger cases against Mexican drug organizations?

2. Why did lawyers from the U.S. Attorney's office in Phoenix meet with FFLs and encourage them to keep selling guns to known straw buyers, including [redacted] after [redacted] was already listed in ATF's database as a suspect buyer? How did DOJ lawyers address the concerns of gun sellers about civil liability or future prosecution if they continued to let the gun sales proceed?

3. Does the DOJ believe its answers last month to Sen. Grassley were accurate and complete? If so, why?

4. Is the DOJ contemplating any action against ATF agents who talked to Sen. Grassley about their concerns?

125

5. What, if any, concerns does [the] DOJ have if ATF agents are monitoring the sales of guns to suspected straw buyers or begin seeing the guns they have been monitoring show up in crimes on both sides of the border?"

Before answering any of the questions, Tracy Schmaler asked Solomon for the facts surrounding the premise of the first question.

Solomon responded:

"I have confirmed this with DOJ employees and internal DOJ memos. If you read the F&F case summary sent to main justice, there are specific numbers given for the number of weapons ATF permitted to be sold to known straw and suspect buyers and then monitored between October 2009 and January 2011. If you want to dispute that premise, I'll be glad to quote you."

Unfortunately, the document that contained the DOJ's draft responses to these five questions listed the questions, but redacted all the draft responses as "protected deliberative privilege."

We do know that after March 2, the DOJ circled their wagons to refine their denial strategy.

In March 2011, SA Newell and SA Needles were transferred to ATF headquarters in Washington, D.C., to help the ATF get ready for the DOJ IG inquiry and the congressional investigations.

With the assistance of U.S. Attorney Dennis Burke, AUSA Patrick Cunningham, AUSA Morrissey, AUSA Emory Hurley, and DOJ spokesman Robbie Sherwood, Newell and Needles drafted responses to anticipated questions DOJ officials might be asked to answer under oath at either investigation.

Examples of their responses: In a March 25, 2011, email to Matthew Axelrod, Senior Counsel to AAG Lanny Breuer, titled "Six Smith Questions and Proposed Answers". they advised how to reply to Senator Lamar Smith:

> Question: "How many weapons have been allowed to pass to Mexico under the program known as Fast and Furious?"

> Answer: "None. Neither the USAO nor the ATF ever allowed weapons to pass to Mexico."

This is clearly not a credible response, and had already been refuted by dozens of government documents and congressional testimony by ATF Agents.

If a question involved sanctioning or encouraging FFLs to sell firearms to straw purchasers, the standard Obama Administration response was:

> "ATF agents and lawyers from the U.S. Attorney's Office did not encourage any FFL to keep selling guns to known straw buyers. [...] Those decisions were up to FFLs, as are all decisions to sell left up to the FFL to evaluate the sale and determine whether it is lawful. [...] There was no mistake as to the clarity of the agent's and attorney's message. [...] FFLs need no encouragement to sell guns as this is their actual business, selling guns. By the time that the government met with owners, they had made many multiple sales and the guns were gone."

This was also clearly not credible. There were fifteen-months of ATF Reports of Investigation and DOJ wiretap applications that totally contradict this response. It is patently false.

The ATF not only got advance notification of straw purchases from the FFLs, they also received advance notice from their FBI informants embedded within the firearms trafficking organization. They listened into telephone calls between the straw purchaser and the FFL (with the FFL's permission and cooperation) arranging the details of each large purchase, including the order, the delivery date and time, and the purchase time and date. They also had live video when known straw purchasers showed up at an FFL to make a scheduled or unannounced "show-up" purchase. Finally, starting by at least February 2010, they set up a coordinated system with the FBI at the FBI National Instant Criminal Background Check System. The ATF gave the FBI a list of straw purchasers for them to flag. FFLs had to enter potential purchases into the NCIS system to get FBI approval of the sale. If it was a potential purchase by a flagged straw purchaser, the NCIS system automatically sent an email notification to the ATF. The FBI could delay the purchase for up to three days to allow the ATF to set up any necessary surveillance. A typical notification was:

"At 5:36 a.m. March 11, 2011, Eric Moore, ATF NCIS liaison specialist, sent an email to ATF SA Voth titled 'another hit'. The email went to Phoenix Group VII and attached AZ SWB (Arizona Southwest Border) tracking information that provided details of the proposed purchase."

There was never any excuse for any ATF failure to monitor a Fast and Furious straw purchase other than incompetence. They had augmented agent resources for the operation and had complete control over where and when a purchase was made.

The government's standard response regarding general questions about whether there was gunwalking was:

"The number-one concern for the DOJ is interdicting guns that are unlawfully transferred to persons in the United States and in Mexico who will then commit crimes with those guns. The purpose of this investigation [Operation Fast and Furious] was to [...] interdict those guns and bring those responsible for their unlawful purchase [...] to justice."

Again, there are many internal ATF and DOJ documents that specifically say this was not the purpose of Operation Fast and Furious. The purpose, however fanciful and misguided, was to not arrest straw purchasers, but let the guns be transported to Mexico, and take down arms trafficking networks and Mexican cartels using information from crime scene traces.

Ultimately their standard response had to loop back and include a comment that contained a gun-control spin:

> "If they are buying only long guns, they may not become a suspect until guns they have purchased can be traced after being recovered at a crime scene."

This was their backup response if confronted with evidence that a gun was illegally purchased. "Current regulation and laws don't allow law enforcement to do anything until they receive a crime scene trace." Actually, every firearm purchased, and every purchaser, was entered into their Suspect Database when it was purchased, and every purchaser could have been arrested in Phoenix, criminally charged, and prosecuted on one or more felony offenses immediately after the purchase.

These are the talking points developed in March 2011 as part of the Obama administration's denial strategy. These talking points were developed by at least ten Phoenix Fast and Furious agents and attorneys working together after the leadership of the DOJ sent their February 4 letter to Congress.

Those ten agents and attorneys (and others who consulted with or assisted them) included:

SA Newell
SA Needles
U.S. Attorney Burke
AUSA Cunningham
AUSA Hurley
AUSA Morrissey

129

AUSA Kelly
DOJ spokesman Sherwood
AUSA Scheel and
AUSA Hernandez

These are just the seven DOJ attorneys, two ATF agents, and one DOJ spokesman who were actually listed on the emails drafting these false and misleading responses intended to be given to Congress and the DOJ IG.

SA Newell and SA Needles were brought to Washington, D.C., to support the lies in AG Holder's false statement to Congress on February 4. The February 4 letter, which responded to Senator Grassley's January 27 note, was not the product of some low-level, uniformed ATF agent.

It is not possible to reconstruct the entire Obama administration process in creating the denial strategy, but it was clearly finalized on February 4, 2011, was re-iterated and confirmed officially on May 2, 2011, and remained the Obama administration's official response until December 2, 2011.

Based on the DOJ IG report issued September 12, 2012, and the Congressional report dated June 7, 2017, the denial strategy was developed in seven days (January 28 — February 3).

DOJ Office of Legislative Affairs Special Counsel Faith Burton was the point person for drafting the actual February 4 false statement, but reports and supporting documents reflect that dozens of top Obama administration officials had input into the strategy. Special Counsel Burton testified that "everybody who knows or is responsible for information that's in the letter signs off in it."

Based on that sworn testimony, the documents and reports reflect that the following Obama administration officials signed off on the February 4 false statement to Congress:

Attorney General Eric Holder
Acting Deputy Attorney General James Cole

Chief of Staff to the Attorney General Gary Grindler

Deputy Chief of Staff Monty Wilkinson

Principal Associate Deputy Chief of Staff Lisa Monaco

Chief of Staff to the Deputy Attorney General Stuart Goldberg

Senior Counsel to the AAG (Criminal) Matthew Axelrod

Senior Counsel to the AAG (Criminal) Deborah Johnston

Senior Counsel to the Deputy AG Bradly Smith

Assistant Attorney General (OLA) Ronald Weich

Attorney Advisor Molly Gaston (SMO)

Assistant Attorney General, Criminal Division, Lanny Breuer

Principal Deputy AAG and Chief of Staff Mythili Raman

Deputy Chief of Staff and Counselor to the AAG Amy Pope

Deputy Assistant Attorney General Jason Weinstein

Attorney Advisor Paul Colburn (SMO)

Attorney Advisor Mark Agrast (SMO)

(OLA) Mary Gonzalez

(USAEO) Anne Pings

(JMD) Jamie Kralovec

U.S. Attorney Dennis Burke

AUSA Cunningham

AUSA Tarango

AUSA Hurley

ATF Acting Director Kenneth Melson

ATF Chief of Legislative Affairs Gregory Rasnake

ATF Deputy Director William Hoover

ATF Special Agent in Charge William Newell

ATF Assistant Director Mark Chait

ATF Deputy Assistant Agent in Charge James Needles

ATF Group VII Superior David Voth

ATF Assistant Director for Public and Government Affairs James McDermond

ATF Chief Counsel Stephen Rubinstein

ATF Associate Chief Counsel Barry Orlow

ATF Chief of Public Affairs Seth Thomasson

As well as "other officials at the Office of Legislative Affairs, other officials at the Office of the Deputy Attorney General, dozens of officials in the DOJ Criminal Division, and others at ATF headquarters."

Altogether, over twenty-five DOJ officials and over twelve ATF officials were involved in drafting a one-and-a-half-page false letter sent to Congress. The few officials that dared to even suggest that anything in the draft letter might not be completely accurate were immediately and forcefully rebuked.

During the first week of April 2011, Andre and I were contacted by Chairman Issa's staff regarding cooperation with the House of Representatives Committee on Oversight and Government Reform and the Senate Committee on the Judiciary. We agreed on a process. Andre would be interviewed in Phoenix. The interview would be under oath and would be kept confidential. We asked for a subpoena so the DOJ could not intervene and threaten us with obstructing an ongoing criminal investigation, which they hinted at during a fake threat assessment discussion. We never signed any nondisclosure agreement that they wanted us to sign pursuant to some unspecified national security law. Their attempts to cloak Andre's testimony as protected or privileged national security information seemed highly suspect to me, especially because they wanted it to be retroactively effective. I never researched the law regarding whether such a procedure would shield someone from complying with a subpoena from Congress. We certainly were not going to sign false documents, and back date them, to avoid testifying. Their proposal was clearly fraudulent and would have been illegal.

Representative Issa's staff (Steve Castor) and Senator Grassley's staff (Jason Foster and Brian Downey) were very professional and extremely honest and respectful of Andre's precarious position.

The Obama administration generally, and AG Eric Holder's Department of Justice particularly, had no credibility with us. The next few weeks, and next couple of months, validated our distrust of the DOJ and embracement of the congressional search for the truth.

On April 15, 2011, the House Committee on Oversight and Government Reform issued Andre a subpoena for documents and to appear for testimony on May 18, 2011, in Phoenix.

The document subpoena was limited to five categories of documents that related to communications between Andre and the DOJ or the ATF, relating to Fast and Furious, between September 1, 2009, and May 2011.

One document request stood out. It was no surprise to either Andre or me, but probably was to the Democratic committee members on the minority side of the House. It called for:

> "All records or communications relating to any meeting between (1) representatives of the Department of Justice and (2) Andre Howard during 2011, in which DOJ officials told Mr. Howard that he would not or should not communicate with any staff members of the U.S. Congress or that he would not or should not testify before any congressional committee."

We agreed to provide our documents prior to Andre's May 18 testimony, and they agreed to meet with us, non-publicly, in Phoenix on May 18 to give us advance notice of the documents they would show Andre at his testimony, and go over the lines of questioning he would be asked.

On April 15, 2011, I received a telephone call from Susanne Grooms and Donald Herman, who were both on the staff of Representative Elijah Cummings. Cummings was the Ranking Member of the House Oversight Committee on the minority side (the Democratic side). They wanted to know if we had received a subpoena yet and said "the committee" asked them to see if Andre would appear and testify without a subpoena from the committee. Then they gave me a detailed explanation about how the only thing Congress can do is hold someone in contempt if the subpoenaed witness refuses to testify. The minority staff then commented that most cases of refusing to testify do not rise to the level where the committee would actually initiate a contempt proceeding. I thought it was odd that they would be calling to explain their contempt policy and procedures when we already voluntarily accepted service of the subpoena and fully intended to testify. But it soon became clear what their motives were. They then asked whether Andre was "willing to pursue that path", i.e. refuse to show up and force "contempt proceedings." They argued that Andre's compliance with the subpoena (sent by the majority party on the committee) "would compromise an ongoing criminal investigation." They indicated that they would oppose a contempt charge if Andre refused to testify.

I told the minority staff that Andre and I did not want to intentionally compromise any investigation being conducted by either Congress or the Justice Department, and I wasn't aware of any legal basis for not complying with the congressional subpoena we received on April 15. I knew there was no risk of compromising any criminal investigation, and that argument was an unfounded pretext to actually obstruct the congressional investigation of AG Holder and the Department of Justice.

They then suggested I contact the Office of the General Counsel in the House of Representatives for assistance in understanding Andre's rights if he ignored the subpoena and refused to testify. I responded that I didn't think that was necessary because Andre intended to comply with the subpoena and fully cooperate with the committee's investigation.

On April 22, 2011, I reported this telephone call, which was clearly an attempt by the minority party to obstruct the majority party's investigation, to Steve Castor, who was Representative Issa's lead staff attorney.

Andre did testify before Steve Castor and Senator Grassley's staff attorney, Jason Foster, on May 18, 2011, in Phoenix.

On June 6, I received another telephone call from minority staff attorney Don Sherman, who asked if I had received a subpoena yet for Andre to testify before Congress in Washington, D.C., on June 15, 2011. I told him I did not. The next day he called back and said: "The committee asked him to call to see if Andre would appear in Washington, D.C., and testify without a subpoena." I told him Andre would testify if that was what Committee Chairman Issa wanted. I then sent a message to Steve Castor for verification. He replied that there was no request for Andre to testify in Washington, D.C., and for some unknown reason, the minority staff intentionally misled me. Andre and I were already scrambling to make our last-minute travel plans. I never learned what the minority's plan was, but on June 13, Steve Castor sent me an email saying Ranking Member Elijah Cummings asked Chairman Issa to give the DOJ a copy of Andre's interview transcript. Castor wrote: "This is an improper request in our view, and we do not intend to provide the transcript to anyone." He also said they intended to raise objections about the improper contacts we received from the minority party staff.

The Obama administration's attempts to obstruct the congressional investigation had several prongs. Trying to get Andre to refuse to testify was one prong. When he did testify confidentially, the DOJ teamed with the minority staff to try to find out what Andre said in his interview.

The minority staff said Andre was subpoenaed to testify in Washington, D.C., on June 15, 2011. This was a lie. They intentionally mislead us hoping to spring a trap and get him to talk to the minority staff and the DOJ without a subpoena once he got to Washington, D.C. That didn't work. They then asked Representative Issa for a copy of Andre's interview transcript. Representative Issa refused.

The second prong was the denial strategy that began with their February 4, 2011, response letter to Senator Grassley and the Senate Judiciary Committee.

The Department of Justice February 4 letter to Congress, which the DOJ IG later characterized as an "error" caused by a flawed drafting process, was anything but a "mistake, error or over-reliance on subordinates for facts." It was a criminal false statement. It was a calculated spear in the ground attempt by Attorney General Holder, President Obama's top administration officials, and President Obama's White House staff to cover up Fast and Furious and the murder of hundreds of Mexican citizens.

Attorney General Holder and his top deputies knew about the Brian Terry murder, and they knew about the ATF whistleblowers. Senator Grassley provided them documents. Associate Deputy Attorney General Edward Siskel, who was responsible for the ATF portfolio during Fast and Furious, was also the key DOJ point of contact for ATF Acting Director Melson. Siskel was transferred to an Associate Counsel position on President Obama's staff in January 2011, where his primary responsibility was to coordinate with congressional oversight. He was the linchpin to the cover-up, and the orchestration of the plan to protect Obama and his top political appointees.

On February 4, 2011, congressional investigators knew the DOJ letter was an official false statement prosecutable as a federal felony offense.

Title 18 of the United States Criminal Code lists the elements of many key federal felony offenses. One of the most commonly charged offenses is a violation of 18 U.S.C.§1001, which covers False Statements.

It provides:

(a) "[w]hoever, in any matter within the jurisdiction of the […] legislative branch of the Government of the United States, knowingly and willfully:

    (1) Falsifies, conceals, or covers up by any trick, scheme, or device a material fact; or

    (2) Makes any materially false, fictitious, or fraudulent statement or representation; or

    (3) Makes […] any false writing or document knowing the same to contain any material false, fictitious, or fraudulent statement or entry;

    Shall be fined under this title and imprisoned not more than five years.

(c) with respect to any matter within the jurisdiction of the legislative branch, subsection (a) shall apply to

    (2) any investigation or review, conducted pursuant to the authority of any committee, subcommittee […] or office of the Congress."

Congress intentionally made this law extremely broad. 18 U.S.C.§1001 (a) also applies to "matters within the executive or judicial branch of the government." It covers statements and writings made to, or submitted to, the Department of Justice Inspector General's investigation, to wiretap warrant applications submitted to the Judiciary under Title III, and to letters sent to a congressional committee. The problem in this situation is that Congress doesn't have the power to prosecute the criminal case. It would have to be prosecuted by the Department of Justice, or a special prosecutor.

Former Associate Deputy Attorney General Siskel and Acting Deputy Attorney General Grindler attended a detailed briefing about Fast and Furious on March 12, 2010, that included what Congress characterized as "overwhelming evidence of illegal straw purchasing" by thirty-one straw purchasers involving 1,026 firearms. The briefing included a discussion about the "stash houses where weapons bought during Fast and Furious were stored before being transported to Mexico", and the "unique investigative techniques [the] ATF was using during Fast and Furious." Finally, the briefing included a map of Mexico with detailed location information about where Fast and Furious weapons were recovered at crime scenes.

As early as March 12, 2010, two of AG Holder's top senior deputies knew that Fast and Furious assault weapons were illegally transported to Mexico, were not interdicted, and were recovered at multiple crime scenes in Mexico. Associate Deputy Attorney General Siskel was the top official in AG Holder's office responsible for the oversight of the ATF. ADAG Grindler was the second highest official in the Office of the Attorney General and reported directly to AG Eric Holder.

At the time the false February 4 letter was sent to Senator Grassley and the United States Senate Judiciary Committee, ADAG Grindler had been moved to the Chief of Staff position within AG Holder's Office of the Attorney General. Former Associate Deputy Attorney General Siskel was transferred to President Obama's personal White House staff as the Senior Legal Counsel in charge of handling oversight of the congressional investigation of Operation Fast and Furious.

When questioned under oath by Congress, Senior White House Counsel to the President Siskel testified: "I don't remember the briefing and I don't remember this PowerPoint presentation." The PowerPoint included the map of where hundreds of firearms allowed to walk to the Mexican cartels were recovered at crime scenes, invovling the murder of hundreds of innocent Mexican citizens.

Really? What was more important and memorable that day? An appointment for a haircut? What to have for lunch? A review of the *New York Times*? And when Siskel signed off on the false February 4 letter, subject to a federal felony charge, he apparently also forgot that two Fast and Furious firearms were recovered at the crime scene of Border Agent Brian Terry's murder. He didn't remember when Deputy Chief of Staff Monty Wilkerson spread the word on December 15, 2010, about that "tragic, terrible" event to the Attorney General and other key officials in the Attorney General's office?

It was less than a month later that Siskel took that knowledge to the White House, where he took charge over the handling of the congressional investigation into Fast and Furious, which started that same month.

When Chief of Staff Grindler, former number-two official at the Department of Justice, was questioned by Congress he admitted he attended the March 12, 2010, briefing along with ADAG Siskel. He had to admit it because Congress had a copy of his handwritten notes that he took at the briefing, which included notes about Fast and Furious. He said that he then "forgot about it" because he "believed that Ed Siskel [...] who maintained responsibility over the ATF had handled it." Did he still think it had been handled in March 2010 when he read Senator Grassley's January 27, 2011, letter? Did he still think Siskel had handled it when he signed off on the false February 4, 2011, letter to Congress? Despite its implausibility, he stuck to his out-of-sight, out-of-mind defense.

My response to both Siskel and Grindler: "I'm sorry, gentlemen, but you are just not credible."

And, by the way: You both probably violated 18 U.S.C.§1001, a felony offense, at least once. The good news is you were not alone. There were plenty of felony offenses committed by other officials in the Obama administration.

On April 14, 2011, Senator Grassley again sent Attorney General Holder a letter urging the Department of Justice to "revisit" their position taken on February 4, before the Attorney General's scheduled testimony before the House Judiciary Committee on May 3, and the Senate Judiciary Committee on May 4.

On May 2, 2011, Senator Grassley followed up with a conference call to Attorney General Holder in which he "personally expressed [...] his concern [...] about the accuracy of the Department's letters to Congress" and his "concerns about whistleblower retaliation". Several ATF agents had provided Congress detailed testimony about DOJ retaliation against them. He also raised his serious concerns that DOJ officials "were intentionally obstructing the congressional investigation."

That afternoon, the DOJ "decided it wanted to memorialize its position (in writing) before the Holder hearings", saying:

> "It remains our understanding that ATF's Operation Fast and Furious did not knowingly permit straw buyers to take guns to Mexico."

The DOJ IG found that "by the date of its May 2 letter to Senator Grassley, Senior Department Officials [...] knew or should have known that the ATF had not made 'every effort to interdict weapons purchased illegally and prevent their transportation to Mexico.' However, the DOJ IG would only say that the May 2 letter was 'carefully crafted' (i.e. deliberately misleading and intended to deceive), was 'troubling', and 'the department should not have made that statement.'" There was no accountability and no consequences other than that many of the officials involved received promotions from Attorney General Holder, with President Obama's blessings.

The DOJ IG's rationalizations that the ATF was technically not aware that the straw purchasers themselves personally took the guns physically across the border is disingenuous, false, and directly intended to be part of the Obama administration cover-up.

First, the DOJ had no surveillance at the border and thus had no idea, or report, on who physically transported most of the guns across the border to Mexico. Second, documents in the DOJ files clearly did reflect that known Fast and Furious straw purchasers actually did transport some weapons to Mexico. Third, the context of the May response was that it affirmed the DOJ support of the February 4 letter, which was undeniably false and contained material misrepresentations. This is especially true because there was no retraction or correction of anything in the February 4 letter, and the May 2 letter refers back by saying "it remains our understanding". This second attempt to deceive Congress once again should not have gone unpunished. If any ordinary citizen or corporate officer, not protected by President Obama, made such a statement, obviously intended to deceive Congress, the Obama government would have indicted and criminally prosecuted them without hesitation.

On May 3 and May 4, 2011, Eric Holder testified under oath that he first heard about Fast and Furious a "few weeks earlier", i.e. in April 2011.

The intentionally ambiguous and parsed May 2 letter did not fool Congress, which called Holder out on May 3: "It is particularly disturbing that the department would renew its denial [...] despite the growing evidence in support of the allegations." When AG Holder was required to testify before Congress again in June/July of 2011, his top staff discussed a game plan for dealing with his obvious perjury during his testimony on May 3. The response of Holder's former Deputy Attorney General Gary Grindler and four other senior DOJ officials - Director of the Office of Legislative Affairs Matthew Miller; Chief of Staff to the Deputy Attorney General Stuart Goldberg; future Assistant Attorney

General Stuart Delery; and Deputy Chief of Staff Margaret Richardson was:

> "We need to focus on how to 'clarify' the testimony of the AG at the hearing on May 3."

The first "brilliant" strategy was proposed by Stuart Delery:

> "Say that time flies."

That probably was the first thing that came to mind because "flies" rhymes with "lies". AG Holder's staff, top officials, and staff of attorneys thoroughly prepared him for his May 3 testimony. AG Holder refused to tell the truth because he was still maintaining that Fast and Furious gunwalking was a fiction and right-wing propaganda. His insistence that "all the guns were interdicted" could only be explained as arrogance or delusion.

In May 2011, Obama made Eric Schulz the White House press official for Fast and Furious. He was the former spokesperson for New York Senator Charles Schumer.

On May 16, 2011, two weeks after Holder falsely testified before Congress, Congress submitted Questions For the Record (QFRs) to Attorney General Holder.

The QFRs repeated requests made in a prior letter to Holder on February 16, 2011, which was ignored by the Department of Justice. Congress tried to work with the DOJ by prioritizing their requests, to eliminate excuses like "too burdensome", "part of ongoing criminal prosecutions against indicted straw purchasers", etc. For over three months AG Holder and DOJ stonewalled the prioritized request for (1) communications between the ATF and Andre Howard, including records relating to his December 17, 2009, meeting with DOJ and ATF; (2) a thirty-page memo from SAC Newell to ATF headquarters following the death of CBP Agent Brian Terry and the arrest of Jaime Avila on December 15, 2010; and (3) a copy of a 200-page presentation that ATF Group VII Superior Voth made to officials at ATF headquarters in the spring of 2010.

There were never any prosecution trials against any indicted straw purchasers because they all pled guilty. Andre had been cooperating with Congress since March 2011, and the December 17, 2009, meeting was fully discussed at the meeting Andre and I had with the DOJ and the ATF on March 11, 2011. At the meeting, AUSA Hurley admitted he told Andre all firearms purchased at Lone Wolf Trading Co. had been, and would continue to be, interdicted. Still the Obama administration would not respond to these three simple requests.

In May 2013, the DOJ IG issued a "Report of Investigation Concerning the Improper Disclosure of U.S. Department of Justice Information to a Member of the Media". This report focused on two leaks of internal DOJ documents to the media.

It did not mention the false retaliatory media attacks DOJ personnel made against Andre and Lone Wolf, but it did address a complaint of retaliation by ATF Agent Dodson's attorney (and Dodson's threatened lawsuit). The Obama administration's retaliation against ATF whistleblower John Dodson are discussed in detail in his book "The Unarmed Truth: My Fight to Blow the Whistle and Expose Fast and Furious", which was published in 2013.

In May 2010, Agent Dodson proposed going undercover as a straw purchaser in Fast and Furious.

In June 2010, Agent Dodson was tasked to act in an undercover capacity as a straw purchaser and deliver the firearms to a suspected firearms trafficker. Dodson purchased six firearms from Andre and another FFL and sold them to the suspected trafficker. There was surveillance of the transaction until the purchaser entered a gated storage facility. The experiment went nowhere — the guns presumably went to Mexico. SA Dodson wrote an internal

ATF memorandum regarding the experiment, which he provided to his ATF and DOJ superiors.

U.S. Attorney Burke was one the Obama administration's key co-conspirators in executing their denial strategy. On January 31, 2011, three days after AUSA Hurley circulated his memorandum about Jaime Avila's straw purchasing history, including his January 16, 2010, purchase of the guns found at the Brian Terry crime scene, U.S. Attorney Burke wrote that the Avila purchase of the crime scene weapons was before Fast and Furious:

> "New (warped) standard — you should have stopped this gun from going to Mexico even before your investigation began, even though the sale is legal, even though the dealer has no reporting requirement, even though the dealer never volunteered this info."

Actually, the Avila purchase of the Terry crime scene weapons was over two months after Fast and Furious started. It was also Avila's second purchase of multiple assault weapons within a one-week period, and Avila was in the ATF Suspect Database. It was an illegal purchase because Avila lied about his residential address and Andre did report the illegal purchase.

Agent Dodson testified before Congress on June 15, 2011, as a whistleblower. The day before, the *New York Times* published an article discussing AUSA Hurley's memo about Jaime Avila and his illegal purchases, including the weapons found at the Brian Terry crime scene. A copy of the internal DOJ memo AUSA Hurley wrote was leaked to the *Times*. The leaked memo included a fax banner at the top showing it came from U.S. Attorney Dennis Burke. After being confronted with this irrefutable evidence, Burke accepted responsibility for the leak on June 27, 2011. He admitted that he had DOJ spokesperson Robbie Sherwood send it to the *New York Times*. Deputy Attorney General Cole "admonished" Burke for his illegal conduct on June 28. Even though the intentional leak could have been criminally prosecuted, Burke received the lowest level of DOJ disciplinary action. The leaked memo contained false statements about Andre's December 2009 meeting with AUSA Hurley. On June 29, the very next day, Burke arranged to have the memo about Dodson's straw purchase leaked to Fox News to discredit Dodson's June 15 testimony before Congress. Burke was reprimanded, and he resigned. Again, the leak could have and should have been criminally prosecuted because it was leaked to discredit, and retaliate against, a whistleblower for cooperating with Congress. All Fast and Furious cases were transferred from Phoenix to the U.S. Attorney's Office in San Diego the next month.

Although the Obama administration knew about these illegal leaks in 2011, it never revealed these crimes publicly, or to Congress, because it didn't fit their denial narrative. They were not disclosed until May 2013 (almost two years later).

Congress knew that Attorney General Holder's letter of May 2, effectively denying that any firearms were intentionally allowed to be transported to Mexico was not true and that his sworn personal testimony to Congress on May 3, that he first heard about Fast and Furious in April, was also false.

On June 15, 2011, the House Committee on Oversight and Government Reform and the Senate Committee on the Judiciary created a PowerPoint which included the following "facts":

> -ATF documents in their possession, written during Fast and Furious, stated: "Currently our strategy is to allow the transfer of firearms to continue to take place in order to further the [Fast and Furious] investigation, and allow for the identification of additional co-conspirators who would continue to operate and

illegally traffic firearms to Mexican DTO's [Drug Trafficking Organizations]."

-They purported to justify this strategy as "in compliance" with an ATF policy. That alleged justification was in no way accurate, and the ATF whistleblowers all testified that the ATF policy did not allow the transfer of firearms that could have been interdicted. The DOJ and the ATF were actually also co-conspirators in illegal trafficking.

-The ATF leaders believed letting Mexican cartels kill people in Mexico with illegal weapons was a legitimate means to a larger end of dismantling cartels because "merely seizing firearms through interdiction will not stop firearms trafficking to Mexico."

The Obama administration really had no plan how their strategy could reasonably have any chance of dismantling any cartel, especially without any coordination with Mexican law enforcement. Early in the operation, the ATF learned that the two main targets within the Sinaloa Cartel, which were the ATF's ultimate target, were actually serving as paid FBI informants. They ignored this information. So, the FBI paid cartel informants to buy firearms through straw purchasers and the firearms purchased with the FBI (US taxpayer money) were freely transferred to the Sinaloa Cartel to use in violent crimes. There was no plan beyond this point.

The Congress PowerPoint also had charts showing Uriel Patino was identified as a suspect October 31, 2009, and was on an ATF video surveillance purchasing thirty-four firearms in twenty-four days, starting November 5, 2009. The weapons were recovered at a Mexican crime scene on November 20, 2009. On November 24, 2009, Patino purchased weapons with Jaime Avila (the purchaser of the Brian Terry crime scene weapons in January 2010).

Other powerful PowerPoint documents proved that the DOJ and the ATF were directing FFLs to make illegal sales to known straw purchasers.

On August 25, 2010, an FFL sent an email to ATF SA Voth and to an official at the DOJ (name redacted) that he "received a telephone call from Uriel Patino [...] one of the individuals your office has interest in [...] looking to purchase twenty FN-FNX 9mm firearms." The FFL only had four in stock and would need to order sixteen more specifically for this purpose. [...] I am requesting your guidance as to whether [sic] or not we should perform the transaction."

The DOJ/ATF guidance was: "We would like you to go through with Mr. Patino's request. [...] Obtain a partial down payment. [...] We (the ATF) are very much interested in this transaction."

As of June 25, 2011, 1,964 firearms had been purchased. The top five purchasers were identified as suspects between November 19, 2009, and January 28, 2010. They purchased 203 firearms before they were identified and purchased 988 more after January 28, 2010.

This statistic belies the repeated assertions that "sales slowed down" and "FFLs were told to reduce sales" after concerns were raised by the FFLs and ATF officials in December 2009.

This PowerPoint supports congressional concerns about the truthfulness of the Attorney General's office in both written statements and, sworn testimony, to both the House of Representatives and the Senate.

On May 21, 2010, President Obama nominated James Cole for the position of Deputy Attorney General. Cole had a questionable professional background. In 2004, Cole was hired by the AIG in an agreement with the SEC to serve as Independent Counsel to monitor AIG's regulatory compliance, financial reporting, whistleblower protection, and employee retention policies. He reported regularly in confidential reports to the DOJ and the SEC. In 2005, the AIG became embroiled in a financial scandal that resulted in a $100 billion bailout by the United States government/taxpayers in 2008.

Senator Grassley and Republican senators blocked Cole's confirmation largely based on the AIG debacle. On December 29, 2010, President Obama installed Cole (as a recess appointment) as Acting Deputy Attorney General. Congress continued to block his confirmation.

On June 27, 2011, after over a year of refusing to confirm Cole, Attorney General Holder agreed to end his eighteen-month refusal to produce documents that had been requested and subpoenaed by Congress in their Fast and Furious investigation, but only if Congress would first confirm Cole as the Deputy Attorney General. On June 27, the Senate confirmed Cole. The DOJ in return agreed to produce documents. The production of documents in no material way amounted to compliance. It was a sham, amounting to a small number of irrelevant documents that were already publicly available. Yet another lie by Eric Holder, and a deceitful fraud on the Brian Terry family and the American public.

Ironically, some of the documents produced, coupled with ATF Acting Director Melson's testimony on July 4, 2011, showed that James Cole "had been informed about [Fast and Furious] in March [2011] by Melson." Melson provided ATF documents, under subpoena to the ATF, to the Office of the Deputy Attorney General for DOJ's production to Congress. Cole refused to produce them to Congress after his confirmation. The Obama administration and the Attorney General's office continued their lies, deceit, and obstruction!

On one hand, Attorney General Holder stonewalled Congress' requests for documents, requests for interviews, and even subpoenas based on the fact that the DOJ IG was supposedly conducting an independent investigation and there were prosecutions of Fast and Furious defendants that would be compromised. On the other hand, the DOJ leaked extremely sensitive internal documents, like the Avila memo and the Dodson memo, to the press to advance their own self-serving agenda of denial, lies, and an aggressive program of retaliation against anyone who said anything that was deemed to be adverse to Attorney General Holder, his key deputies like Lanny Breuer, or President Obama and the White House staff. The targets of their retaliation included ATF whistleblowers, an Arizona Sherrif's organization, conservative media reporters like Sharyl Attkisson, and patriotic citizens like Andre Howard.

On July 11, 2011, Congress sent another letter to Attorney General Holder protesting his administration's overt campaign to obstruct the congressional investigation by influencing or ordering witnesses not to cooperate or testify, and attempting to improperly tamper with the actual testimony of those who did choose to cooperate with Congress.

Andre Howard was one such witness they attempted to keep from testifying, then attempted to influence his testimony, and then retaliated against him for cooperating. Andre gave truthful testimony to both Congress and the DOJ IG. Congress found that the testimony from Andre (and other FFLs) was corroborated by documents and other testimony. The DOJ IG, who had access to the same testimony and documents, largely dismissed the testimony of Andre and the other FFLs, choosing instead to cover-up and whitewash to protect Attorney General Holder, his key subordinates, and the Obama White House. The DOJ IG found that the ATF may have done things that gave the FFLs "the impression" that the ATF wanted them to sell firearms to the straw purchasers:

"[The] ATF's requests for cooperation […] created […] the appearance that sales to particular Operation Fast and Furious subjects were made with [the] ATF's approval and authorization."

"I'm sorry, DOJ IG Horwitz, but you and your report are just not credible."

In their July 11, 2011, letter, Congress further rebuked AG Holder for his blatant attempt to tamper with witness testimony. While the DOJ would not produce documents to Congress because it might interfere with the DOJ IG investigation or influence witness testimony, they secretly made their own computer system containing ATF and DOJ documents fully available to all ATF and DOJ witnesses subpoenaed to testify before Congress. Congress characterized this as an "egregious decision" and demanded that the Attorney General "promptly self-report this matter to the Office of Inspector General." Of course, AG Holder did not self-report his intentional misconduct to the DOJ IG.

This database included documents produced to Congress by their cooperating witnesses, which were "made available to AG Holder solely for in-camera (non-public) review." This violation of trust, and direct violation of Holder's agreement with Congress that he would not allow outside access to the documents, could only have one purpose — to taint their testimony.

On May 5, an Associate Deputy Attorney General asked Congress to "not show their witnesses new documents" or "orally convey facts to the witness of which the witness was previously unaware."

Congress pointed out that the "DOD did to witnesses in their [Congress'] investigation precisely what it asked [Congress] not to do in its [DOJ] investigation.

Congress asked Holder to "mitigate any harm that may have been caused" by identifying which witnesses accessed which information in "preparing" for their testimony. Of course, Holder refused to provide any information.

On July 11, 2011, Congress also sent DOJ another document request for all records relating to communications between and among twelve senior DOJ officials regarding Operation Fast and Furious. Congress said:

"As our investigation...has progressed, we have learned that senior officials at the Department of Justice (DOJ), including Senate-confirmed political appointees, were unquestionably aware of the implementation of this reckless program."

Holder's response was to maintain full cover-up mode and protect all of the Obama administration's political appointees at all costs — ethical or unethical, legal or illegal.

Between July 11 and July 15 of that year, Congress sent document requests to three other federal agencies that were part of the Organized Crime Drug Enforcement Task Force that coordinated with the ATF during Operation Fast and Furious.

On July 11, 2011, they sent FBI Director Robert Mueller a request that identified eight FBI agents who had involvement with "paid FBI informants, prospective informants assigned an informant number, or cooperating defendants" involved in Fast and Furious.

The FBI was also the lead agency involved in the investigation of Border Agent Brian Terry's murder on December 14, 2009, and the murder of Immigration and Customs Enforcement Special Agent Jaime Zapata. Agent Zapata's murder by cartel members also involved U.S. firearms that were walked to Mexico, and were seized at his crime scene in Mexico on June 14, 2011.

Both the Terry family and the Zapata family were kept in the dark by the FBI regarding the circumstances of the murders of their law enforcement family members. Despite abundant media coverage of the Obama administration's despicable and callous treatment of the families of these two brave law enforcement officers, who tragically lost their lives serving America, Obama and Holder had only one agenda that mattered — protecting themselves and their reputations.

The document request Congress sent to John Morton, Director of ICE (Department of Homeland Security), was somewhat broader and addressed similarities between Fast and Furious and an ICE-led Tampa operation, Operation Castaway. Reports to Congress indicated "that firearms [...] in that operation may have been provided to dangerous criminal gangs in Honduras, including MS-13."

That investigation was handled by Gus M. Bilirakis, Chairman of the House Subcommittee on Emergency Preparedness, Response, and Communications; Michael T. McCaul, Chairman of the House Subcommittee on Oversight, Investigations, and Management; and Candice S. Miller, Chairman of the House Subcommittee on Border and Maritime Security.

Finally, on July 15, 2011, Congress followed up on their March 15, 2011, request for information to Michele M. Leonhart, Administrator of U.S. Drug Enforcement Agency. AG Holder responded to the March 15, 2011, document request on April 12, 2011, with one sentence: "The DEA works cooperatively with other agencies in OCDETF investigations." He produced none of the information requested by Congress.

This obvious nonresponse, was designed to deflect direct inquiries to the DEA, and was coupled with instructions to DEA prohibiting any direct cooperation with Congress. Congress' original request in March said: "I understand from documents and other information that [...] (DEA) agents were aware of Operation Fast and Furious and possibly deeply involved in the operation. Reportedly, DEA funds were used to facilitate operations in ATF's Operation Fast and Furious."

Congress knew that the DEA and the ATF both targeted the same individual, Manuel Fabian Celis Acosta, at the same time.

By July 2011, Congress had multiple subpoenas outstanding to Obama administration agencies. The Obama administration did not comply with any of these subpoenas. Every major department and agency involved in the OCDETF Strike Force program Fast and Furious was involved: the Department of Justice, the Federal Bureau of Investigation, the Drug Enforcement Agency, and the Immigration and Customs Enforcement Agency were all on board with obstructing the congressional investigation.

There were also outstanding subpoenas and requests for information to non-DOJ Obama administration departments that were still unanswered — most notably the United States State Department and Hillary Clinton.

On March 4, 2011, Senator Grassley sent a document request to Secretary Clinton. It was a non-burdensome, straightforward request. He asked for all records relating to meetings between Assistant Attorney General Lanny Breuer and the U.S. Ambassador to Mexico between June 2010 and September 2010, regarding Project Gunrunner. Congress wanted "meeting minutes, briefing notes, emails, or cables."

Based on ATF Agent testimony to Congress, Congress had reason to believe that the government of Mexico had been kept in the dark about Operation Fast and Furious, and may have also been misled and lied to by the Obama administration. There is no way that the Obama administration and the DOJ could have, or would have, made a decision to treat a major United States ally like this without the full knowledge, input, and approval of the U.S. State Department. A policy like this would be one of the biggest betrayals of a key U.S. neighbor, trade partner, and diplomatic ally in modern history.

Secretary Clinton refused to even respond to Congress and did not produce any documents.

The Obama administration's denial strategy had to be approved by someone at the top of the Obama administration. AG Eric Holder had power over all the DOJ agencies, but not the State Department. Is it even conceivable that this level of defiance of Congress could be done without President Obama's knowledge and approval?

On March 29, 2011, Congress again wrote Secretary Hillary Clinton reminding her that she had not responded to Senator Grassley's request for "basic information." Chairman of the House of Oversight Committee Representative Issa expressed his concern that the Secretary of State would not even give Senator Grassley, the Ranking Member of the Senate Judiciary Committee the courtesy of a response. He also reminded her that her refusal to respond "stands in stark contradiction to the promise of transparency" President Obama repeatedly made to the American people. Less than two weeks earlier, President Obama "recommitted his administration to be the most open and honest ever." President Obama and his administration were already the most murderous administration of modern times and maybe ever. He was now well on the way to becoming the least transparent, least open, and least honest administration ever. Representative Issa said:

> "Given the gravity of this matter, this refusal is simply unacceptable. [...] Please explain in detail the reason behind your refusal to answer the Senator directly."

Representative Issa joined Senator Grassley's original simple request for limited information.

The "most transparent, open, honest administration ever" did not respond and did not produce any documents. They did continue to perpetuate their false statement, given to Congress on February 4, their denial strategy, and their obstruction of Congress.

Perhaps the most damning evidence of Obama's cover-up during the denial phase of his administration's attempt to obstruct the congressional investigation involved Acting ATF Director Kenneth Melson.

Although it was unclear exactly when Melson knew, or appreciated, exactly what the full breadth and details of the Fast and Furious Operation were, he certainly was aware of the red flags during the operation and certainly should have known more than he recalled, or was willing to admit, prior to Agent Terry's murder. He also clearly should have been more protective of, and supportive of, ATF whistleblowers in the period preceding and after the murder. Still, he deserves a great amount of credit for his personal actions in the period from February 2, 2011, to July 4, 2011.

Holder and Obama went into full protection mode when they received Senator Grassley's January 27, 2011, letter regarding intentional gun trafficking, the link to Agent Terry's murder, and the illegal abuse of regulatory threats to make FFLs sell weapons to illegal purchasers.

ATF Acting Director Melson voluntarily offered to testify before Congress on July 4, 2011. He refused to give advance notice to the DOJ, and did not want a DOJ attorney to be present.

When AG Holder found out that Melson testified before Congress, he immediately demanded a copy of the transcript. Congress refused, citing the agreement between the DOJ and Congress that the DOJ IG investigation and the congressional investigation would be independent and neither would share transcripts of their witnesses with the other.

On July 18 Congress sent Attorney General Holder another letter concerning his obstruction of the congressional investigation. That letter did include some damning excerpts from Melson's testimony, as well as other incontrovertible evidence of the DOJ and the Obama administration's obstruction.

Melson testified:

> "[After receiving Senator Grassley's] [initial] letter, our first instinct and intuition was to directly march over to Senator Grassley's office and brief him on what Fast and Furious was for purposes of explaining the concept and role it played and how it got there, and where ATF was going with it. And we expressed that desire to the Deputy Attorney General's office."

The Department of Justice prohibited Acting Director Melson from communicating with Congress. The Department of Justice also prohibited Acting Director Melson from communicating with his own staff at the ATF. Even though the Congress addressed their January 27, 2011, letter to Acting Director Melson, he was ordered not to respond. His request to respond was directly communicated to the number-two political appointee in the Department of Justice who reported directly to Attorney General Holder. Acting Deputy Attorney General Cole delivered the Holder gag order to Melson.

Senator Grassley put his objections succinctly in a letter to AG Holder on July 18, 2011:

> "The Department [of Justice] has blocked the flow of information from the Acting Director's office. [...] Instead, the Department devised a strategy to withhold information from the Senator. 'Instead of giving Congress the information the Department of Justice guaranteed would be provided, Holder sent officials with no personal knowledge of the facts to testify before Congress. They denied the whistleblower allegations in a widely attended briefing open to all Senate judiciary staff on February 10, 2011.' [...]

Instead of providing Congress answers from the individuals best positioned to provide them, Mr. Melson and his staff were muzzled.

"Instead of providing Congress answers [...] the decision to withhold information at the earliest sign of congressional interest [...] DOJ leadership chose to protect their own interests at the expense of exposing the DOJ leadership [...] to congressional scrutiny.

Acting Director Melson "desired to speak [to Congress] as far back as January 2010." Congress advised Holder that "the Department needs to move from spin mode to disclosure mode."

Main Justice took over the document production process purportedly because it 'wanted to ensure that the information being provided to Congress was accurate.' The real reason Main Justice took over the document production was to prevent [Congress] from gaining access to documents and information, by using the existence of the DOJ IG investigation to justify withholding evidence.

Congress also addressed AG Holder and the DOJ's efforts to lie about their direction of the firearms sales to illegal purchasers and the nature and content of Andre's December 2009 meeting with the DOJ and the ATF. Melson testified about AUSA Hurley's memo purporting to memorialize the meeting. Congress recognized that "creating such a record more than a year after the meeting" was a thinly veiled "attempt to paper the file with an after-the-fact rationalization rather than an honest attempt to record an accurate and contemporaneous account of the meeting." In other words, it was a false document.

Although Congress requested that the DOJ produce all documents relating to the December 17, 2009, meeting, the Department refused to produce them. Ultimately, after the DOJ IG investigation was over, the Department's only basis for withholding the meeting documents was a vague, and undefined assertion, that the records were 'law enforcement sensitive.'

In other words, their internal documents created at the time of the meeting would prove that Hurley's January 2010 memo was an intentionally false document designed to obstruct justice.

Chairman Issa followed up his document subpoena to the DOJ with letters to "[the] ATF and [the] DOJ dated April 8, April 11, April 20, May 3, May 5, and June 8. Congress received no non-public documents.

ATF Director Melson testified that after Grassley's letter in January 2010, he reviewed all ATF reports of investigation and found one particular ROI that caused him so much concern he immediately took it to the DOJ. He gave it to, and briefed, Associate Deputy Attorney General Siskel, "because to [him] that was a smoking gun." It was not in the sixty-nine pages of documents the DOJ produced on June 10, 2011.

On March 31, 2011, Congress sent FBI Director Mueller a subpoena about the FBI's involvement in Fast and Furious. FBI Director Mueller did not produce documents, so on July 18, Congress made the demand for documents directly to AG Holder, specifically asking again about the FBI's use of paid informants. Melson confirmed his understanding that "taxpayer's dollars [...] funded those helping to arm Mexican drug cartels. [...] It would also mean the ATF unwittingly targeted indictable defendants." Melson testified that he expressed those concerns to the DOJ IG and to Deputy Attorney General James Cole, who said: "We'll have to look into this." He never did.

Witnesses testified before Congress that "some of the very targets of Operation Fast and Furious — the high-level weapons suppliers to the cartels" — were paid FBI informants.

In fact, one document produced by ATF whistleblowers showed that three major purchasers of the firearms, Manuel Celis-Acosta, Sean Steward, and Juan Martinez-Gonzalez were registered FBI informants with FBI #6385360D1, #778479RB6, and #976785ED3.

Melson summed up his testimony: "The Department [of Justice] was more concerned with protecting its political appointees than with [...] sharing the truth."

After the March 11, 2011, meeting with the DOJ and the ATF at their offices in Phoenix, Andre left the meeting disgusted by the callous comments made by both DOJ attorneys and ATF agents about the Brian Terry murder. They made it abundantly clear that the fellow federal law enforcement agent's death meant nothing to them.

As Andre told Congress in a letter dated September 22, 2011:

> "Something horribly wrong had taken place [...] I and my attorneys were not being told the full truth [...] [The] DOJ [and the] ATF made numerous inconsistent statements and falsehoods that made me sick and angry.
>
> "I was left with the full belief and understanding that the ATF and the DOJ were orchestrating a massive cover-up and attempting to persuade me to go along with it.
>
> "In the absence of any further explanation, and in response to what appeared to me as an immediate danger to I and my family, I made the decision to tape record my conversations with the case agent [MacAllister] in an effort to obtain the truth by any and all means necessary no matter what. [...] The decision [...] to tape was mine alone.
>
> "After I retained Mr. Gaydos and we were preparing for our March 11, 2010, meeting with the DOJ and the ATF in Phoenix, ATF Special Agent John Dodson

appeared at my store and privately made several revelations and statements that contradicted the DOJ/ATF's asserted position in this entire matter. He alluded to evidence being deliberately suppressed and FBI involvement. [...] Agent MacAllister and [the] DOJ were not being truthful.

"He told me to 'watch my back.'

"I called Mr. Gaydos while ATF Agent Dodson was in my office, and put them on the phone together so my attorney could hear the truth before our meeting in Phoenix.

"[I]t was clear that I had been lied to, and in addition, they were attempting to try and involve me in a cover-up of the truth.

"After our meeting in Phoenix, Mr. Gaydos and I contacted Congress and agreed to cooperate with the investigation. At the interview we provided the congressional staff with a copy of the tape recordings I made with ATF Special Agent MacAllister.

"I apologized to Congress for the 'derogatory statements as well as the extremely offensive language I purposely used on the taped conversations to gain Agent MacAllister's confidence.' I believed that the tactics I used in taping Agent MacAllister were necessary and justified in getting out the truth.

"Mr. Gaydos and I understood from our meeting with congressional investigators that the tapes, and my interview, would both be kept confidential."

In June 2011, Congress produced a copy of Andre's taped recording of SA MacAllister to the DOJ IG because the DOJ argued that the tapes could be the subject of document discovery in the prosecution cases against straw purchasers. The DOJ spun the demand in terms of obstructing criminal cases. Nothing could have been further from the truth. The tapes were produced to Congress in their completely independent investigation. The DOJ had no right to the tapes, and more importantly, they did not have custody or control of the tapes, which were produced to Congress under a confidentiality agreement. The DOJ knew that none of the straw purchaser cases were likely to go to trial. In the tapes themselves, made on March 17, 2011, SA Hope MacAllister said that seventeen of the nineteen indicted straw purchasers had already agreed to plead guilty, the other two were in the process of negotiating a plea and there was only a possibility the one might go to trial.

The DOJ IG wanted the tapes for their own damage control. He knew that many officials at the highest levels of the DOJ lied to Congress in testimony, lied in writing on February 4, 2011, and again on May 2, 2011. AG Holder then gave false testimony to Congress on May 3. They also wanted to know what ATF Agent Dodson said to Andre and me during the week preceding our March 11, 2011, meeting with the DOJ and the ATF.

After the DOJ IG got Andre's tape recordings from Congress, the DOJ IG sent a copy of the tapes to the DOJ and ATF witnesses in Phoenix who were in line to testify before Congress. Congress protested this obvious attempt to tamper with witnesses.

The DOJ IG tried to cover up their obstruction and witness tampering. They demanded that Andre produce a copy of the tapes voluntarily, or they would issue a subpoena. We did not know that Congress already produced them. The DOJ IG investigative counsel, Allen Levy, used the same bogus rationale with us that they used with Congress — the tapes may have to be produced to the defendants in the straw purchaser trials. Levy said the DOJ would oppose production in any criminal discovery at trial, but they needed to access the content of the tapes to formulate their legal arguments.

This rationale was flawed in several ways. First, the tapes themselves demonstrate there was very little chance there would ever be a trial. In the tape recordings on March 17, 2011, SA MacAllister repeatedly said only one defendant might go to trial, but that was unlikely because they were already in guilty pleas negotiations. Second, the tapes were in no way exculpatory for any defense. The government's obligation to produce documents to the defense under the United States v. Brady applies only if the government has documents that help the defense's case, i.e. are exculpatory. The second grounds for the defense's discovery of prosecution documents is the Jencks Act. That act only applies if and when Andre is a witness at the trial, and it only applies to prior statements Andre gave the government. The defense is only entitled to pretrial statements after the witness testifies for the government. The taped conversations are arguably not a pretrial statement. Andre was not likely a witness. Any documents from Lone Wolf needed for trial could be admitted by the government as business records kept in the ordinary course of business with an affidavit from the document custodian. Any eyewitness evidence of the purchase could be covered by the ATF surveillance tapes, with the testimony of an ATF witness. Finally, in the unlikely event a judge would still order disclosure, the DOJ could fall back on the same argument they were using to keep documents from Congress: "They are part of an ongoing criminal investigation."

Despite their transparently weak justification for requesting the tapes, we decided to provide them to the DOJ IG under a confidentiality agreement.

On June 15, 2011, after our conversation, I sent the DOJ IG investigative counsel an email and a Federal Express package with the tapes.

My email was:

> "Enclosed per your request is a CD containing audio recordings. [...] We request that these documents be

afforded confidential treatment and that they not be publicly disclosed."

I had produced documents containing sensitive business information to the DOJ and the SEC on countless occasions using the exact same confidential treatment language and never had any problem.

I was shocked when I got an email from DOJ IG Investigative Counsel Levy:

"You agreed at my request to send us a CD containing the two recordings that Andre Howard made of conversations with Hope MacAllister. I also told you that we would be alerting the U.S. Attorney's Office of the existence of the recordings, and sharing a copy with them because they would need to review them to satisfy potential discovery obligations."

The last part of the email was absolutely false. They never said they were going to send a copy to the DOJ and the ATF in Phoenix. They told me the opposite: The tapes would be kept confidential, would not be disseminated, and they would legally resist any disclosure.

It soon became evident that the DOJ IG planned to try to counter any congressional inquiry into witness tampering by saying that I authorized distribution of the tapes to witnesses. Congress knew better, because I previously told them about my conversations with Investigator Levy.

On September 20, 2011, Congress sent a letter to Cynthia A. Schneider, the Acting Inspector General of the Department of Justice, addressing their concerns about the U.S. Attorney's office for the District of Arizona and their multiple attempts to obstruct their congressional investigation.

The first issue they wanted the Acting DOJ IG to address was their decision to provide Andre's tape recording of his March 2011 conversations with SA Hope MacAllister to the U.S. Attorney in Arizona.

"We wanted to reiterate our deep concerns that we have about your decision to turn over [...] audio recordings. [...] The recordings corroborate the cooperating FFL's allegation that personnel at the ATF and the USAAZ sought to recruit him in an effort to obstruct the congressional inquiry and obscure the truth about Operation Fast and Furious from public scrutiny [...] you decided to provide them to the USAAZ before you even obtained them [...] and you had not personally reviewed them before turning them over.

"This tape corroborates what both the FFL and his current attorney [Andre and I] have each told our committees about the USAAZ's initial denials of basic facts surrounding Operation Fast and Furious and the murder of Border Patrol Agent Brian Terry.

"There would have been considerable investigative advantages to questioning the USAAZ and ATF personnel about these issues directly before these recordings were released to them [...]. The Justice Department delayed Congress' access to these individuals, and you provided them with copies of the recordings before they testified. [...] Then they were leaked to the press.

"Your conclusion that discovery obligations [...] might be required at some point in the future [...] was premature [...] it seems unlikely that disclosure would be required."

The second issue was the attempt to get Andre to obstruct their investigation after our March 11, 2011, meeting, where they were put on notice that they were simply "not credible."

Chris Rapp got physically ill after hearing multiple high-ranking Obama administration DOJ and ATF officials change the story they previously told him, and he passed this on to Andre. AUSA Hurley "told Mr. Rapp to tell his client, the FFL, that the U.S. Attorney's office, the ATF, and the

FFL 'were all in the same boat.' ATF Group Supervisor David Voth [...] told the cooperating FFL [Andre] [...] we are all on the same sheet of music. [...] If we stay on the same sheet of music, we will be alright."

Congress wanted answers about:

(a) Why the DOJ IG gave the tapes to officials under investigation;

(b) What steps the DOJ IG took to prevent leaks of the tapes to the press;

(c) How potential discovery obligations could justify the DOJ's actions;

(d) How did the press get the tapes; and

(e) Would there be an investigation into witness tampering and obstruction?

Congress received no official answers from the DOJ IG. We all know the answers now:

(a) So they could craft false testimony;

(b) None, we did the leaking; and

(c) We made this up, and it sounded legal;

(d) See answer (b); and

(e) Sure. OK, we're done, didn't happen — any more questions?

By September 19, 2011, the press verified, documented, and reported extensively on specific details about the Obama administration's "gunwalking" and the tragic consequences of their illegal and immoral actions.

AG Holder's response — we stand by our February 4 and May 2 letters to Congress and the testimony of numerous high ranking DOJ officials — all the guns were interdicted.

President Obama's response — no one did anything wrong to his knowledge, no one would be held accountable, AG Holder still didn't know anything until April 2011.

How could President Obama and Attorney General Holder be "clueless in Washington" when Congress, Fox News,

CBS News, multiple prominent bloggers, and Andre and I all knew exactly what the DOJ and the ATF did, and we all knew it in March 2011?

The Obama administration would not even withdraw their false statement to Congress until December 2011! Shocking and reprehensible!

On September 19, 2011, William La Jeunesse of Fox News wrote an article, "Justice Officials in 'Panic Mode' as Hearing Nears on Failed Anti-Gun Trafficking Program":

"Officials at the Department of Justice are in 'panic mode', according to multiple sources, as word spreads that congressional testimony next week will paint a bleak and humiliating picture of Operation Fast and Furious, the botched undercover operation that left a trail of blood from Mexico to Washington, D.C. [...] Mexican officials estimate 150 of their people have been shot by Fast and Furious guns. Police have recovered roughly 700 guns at crime scenes.

"A high-powered sniper rifle was used to shoot down a Mexican military helicopter [...] two other AK-47s were found in a shootout that left 11 dead... The guns were traced to [the] Lone Wolf Gun Store [...] and were sold only after the store employees were told to do so by [the] ATF [...] Arizona gun store owners [...] were explicitly told by [the] ATF to sell the guns and those orders, from at least one ATF case agent, are on audio recording.

"[The] ATF allowed and encouraged five Arizona gun store owners to sell some 1,800 weapons to buyers known to them as gun smugglers.

"-It installed cameras inside the gun stores to record purchases made by those gun smugglers.

-It hid GPS trackers inside gun stocks and watched the weapons go south on computer screens.

-It obtained surveillance video from parking lots and helicopters showing straw buyers transferring their guns from one car to another.

-It learned guns sold in Phoenix were recovered only when Mexican police requested 'trace data'."

By October 2011, the Obama administration's denial strategy was on perilous ground. Congress kept investigating and publicly released a report on June 14, 2011, titled "The Department of Justice's Operation Fast and Furious: Accounts of ATF Agents." It focused on the testimony of ATF agents who strongly addressed the validity of the denial strategy and the representation the DOJ made in their February 4, 2011, and May 2, 2011, letters to Congress.

Congress pointed out that AG Eric Holder's first guidance to the DOJ about gunwalking didn't come until March 2011, "well after the congressional investigation of Operation Fast and Furious had begun." Congress then concludes:

"This installment focuses on ATF's misguided approach of letting guns walk. The report describes the agents' outrage [...] and the continued denials and stonewalling by DOJ and ATF leadership. [...] Who will be accountable and when? [...] Agents knew that given the large numbers of weapons being trafficked to Mexico, tragic results were a near certainty."

Congress described ATF Special Agent in Charge Newell's statements as "incredible and false." Their final words:

"We will persist in seeking documents and testimony from Justice Department officials and other sources to thoroughly examine all the key questions. The Department should avail itself of the opportunity to come clean and provide complete answers. It should also reverse its position and choose to fully cooperate with the investigation."

In July 2011, Congress issued its second report that explores the effect of Operation Fast and Furious on Mexico.

As the number of weapons recovered at Mexican crime scenes dramatically increased from September to December 2009, Darren Gil, the ATF's attaché to Mexico, and Carlos Camino, Deputy Attaché, raised concerns with leadership in Washington, D.C. "Senior leadership within both [the] ATF and […] [the] DOJ assured them […] that everything was 'under control'."

ATF and DOJ leadership told them the operation would be shut down in July 2010, but it continued. Carlos Camino's response:

"This is, I mean, this is the perfect storm of idiocy."

The ATF held a series of briefings about large firearm recoveries. One ATF SA wrote to SA Hope MacAllister: "The head of the Sinaloa Cartel is arming for a war." Another testified: "It was common knowledge that [the firearms from Fast and Furious] were going down there to be crime guns." When asked "so these guns, in a way, are murder weapons?" The reply: "Potentially."

When ATF Acting Director Melson visited ATF agents in Mexico in the spring of 2010 and was confronted about the program, agents said he knew about the violence, but Melson said: "It's providing some good intelligence."

Congress concluded that by the spring of 2010 "Assistant Attorney General Lanny Breuer clearly knew about the Operation Fast and Furious," as did Deputy Attorney General David Ogden, who was responsible for wiretap applications in the spring of 2010.

Congress concluded:

"These flaws in Operation Fast and Furious made tragic consequences (that did occur) inevitable."

Congress elevated their pressure on the Obama Administration on September 9, 2011, by sending a document request to the White House. The request was sent to Thomas E. Donilon, Assistant to the President and National Security Advisor.

Congress had obtained documents that clearly showed SA Newell was providing regular updates about Fast and Furious directly to Kevin O'Reilly, Director of North American Affairs on President Obama's National Security Council Staff, and that he in turn shared the information with Dan Restrepo, Special Assistant to President Obama and Senior Director for Western Hemisphere Affairs at the National Security Council; and Greg Gatjanis, Director for Terrorist Finance and Counternarcotics on President Obama's staff. Congress also called for testimony from Kevin O'Reilly.

President Obama refused to provide documents and had the State Department transfer O'Reilly to a post in the Middle East so he could avoid responding to a subpoena from Congress.

On October 7, 2011, Eric Holder broke his long silence and wrote a self-serving defensive letter to Congress, "notwithstanding the Inspector General's ongoing review."

"I simply cannot sit idly by as [Rep. Issa] suggests [...] that law enforcement [...] be considered accessories to murder [...] ensuring that weapons sold here is of paramount importance. [...] [The] ATF and our prosecutors struggle mightily to make cases against gun smugglers and do outstanding work on a daily basis in an effort to stop the flow of guns across our borders. [...] In 2011, after the controversy about this matter arose, I took decisive action to ensure that such operations are never again undertaken. [...] The flawed tactics employed by Fast and Furious [...] were actually employed in an investigation conducted during the prior administration. [...] Equally unacceptable [...] is the fact that many in Congress are opposed to [...] fixing our laws that facilitate the staggering flow of guns each year across our border to the south. […] It seems some in Congress are more interested in […] [scoring] political points."

In a word, "delusional." No acceptance of responsibility and no accountability for others. No apology to Mexico or the families of murdered Mexican children, men, and women, and no mention of his personal shameful treatment of the Terry family. It is all about how great and sanctimonious AG Eric Holder is. Disgusting!

Holder's October 7, 2011 letter was a clear sign that his defense strategy was unraveling. Disregarding the law was becoming difficult because Congress was relentless, Melson broke ranks and testified, and the spotlight was starting to focus on his boss in the White House. Denial was growing less credible as more and more evidence accrued. The clock was ticking on delay so Holder decided to speak out while the DOJ IG was still investigating. Discrediting ATF and FFL witnesses was not getting any traction in Congress. His response was to try to "deflect". Put the blame on the FFLs, Congress and the Bush administration.

On October 12, 2011, the House Oversight and Government Reform Committee issued yet another subpoena for documents. Chairman Issa said:

"Top Justice Department Officials, including Attorney General Holder, know more about Operation Fast and Furious than they have publicly acknowledged […] documents this subpoena demands will provide answers to questions that justice officials have tried to avoid since this investigation began eight months ago. It's time we know the whole truth."

1. The documents requested included all communications to and from sixteen top DOJ officials relating to Operation Fast and Furious;

2. Documents at the DOJ relating to communications with the White House relating to Fast and Furious

or President Obama's March 22, 2011, interview with Univision;

3. Documents relating to the FBI examination of firearms from the Agent Terry crime scene;

4. Agent reports of investigation; and

5. Weekly reports and memoranda for Attorney General Holder created between November 1, 2009, and September 20, 2011.

None of these documents would be provided to Congress.

On October 20, 2011, Congress followed up on their July 11, 2011, letter to FBI Director Robert Mueller:

"The murder of Border Patrol Agent Brian Terry [...] is what motivated brave law enforcement agents [...] to risk their careers and blow the whistle on Operation Fast and Furious. The Department of Justice's false denials to Congress are what motivated them to speak out and testify publicly. A growing collection of documents and credible testimony has put the lie to those denials."

Frustrated by the DOJ's "obstruction of [their] previous inquiries", Congress asked for "more than just conclusory statements [...] regarding the state of the evidence in the investigation of Agent Terry's murder."

Specifically, Congress wanted to know whether there were two or three weapons recovered at the crime scene. The FBI briefed Congress on October 5 that there were only two guns, however, ATF documents written immediately after the murder said there were three and identified them as two AK-47s and an SKS.

When Andre tape-recorded his conversation with lead Fast and Furious case agent Hope MacAllister, on March 17, 2011, she confirmed:

"There [were] actually three weapons. [...] They had the serial numbers for all three [...] and two of them came from this store. [...] There's an SKS. [...] The two AKs came from the store."

In addition, one defendant in custody stated "that he was traveling with four individuals" and that "all of the individuals were armed."

Second, Congress wanted to know whether either of the two AK-47s from Lone Wolf Trading Co. was the actual murder weapon. The Department of Justice repeatedly said that FBI ballistics tests excluded both from being the murder weapon. In the March 17, 2011, tape-recorded conversation, Agent MacAllister told Andre:

"They were not the guns, to the best of anybody's knowledge, that shot the Border Patrol Agent."

When the actual ballistics report was released by the FBI, it actually said the results of the forensic ballistic analysis were "inconclusive". There was no more analysis of any crime scene evidence ever released.

On November 1, 2011, Congress asked AG Holder for "records of all government surveillance of suspected straw purchasers of firearms" in Fast and Furious. On December 21, 2011, AG Holder refused, saying :"The FBI and DEA [...] do not conduct surveillance of straw purchasers in the ordinary course of their law enforcement activities. We are not aware of any other Department components that would be likely to conduct surveillance of straw purchases. We regret we have been unable to assist with your request." This was a pathetic lie that had long since been disproved by overwhelming evidence presented to Congress.

On December 5, 2011, Congress again wrote AG Holder about his upcoming testimony before Congress regarding Fast and Furious, raising the issue of money laundering to the Mexican cartels through a program called the Attorney General Exempt Operation. Congress concluded "[t]he existence of such a program again calls your leadership into question. [...] The consequences have been disastrous. [...]

The United States government had made itself an accomplice to the Mexican drug trade, which has thus far left more than 40,000 people dead in Mexico since December 2006." Congress was raising the stakes by investigating financial misconduct by the Attorney General. The noose was definitely starting to tighten.

Evidence emerged that there may have been another gun-trafficking operation from 2009 to 2010 called White Gun, run by ATF Agent MacAllister, Newell, and Voth, that targeted nine known Sinaloa drug cartel suspects.

In late August 2011, Acting ATF Director Melson was reassigned to a senior position within the Department of Justice.

In October 2011, Congress revealed documents that showed that Attorney General Holder had been briefed about Fast and Furious by AAG Lanny Breuer and the National Drug Intelligence Center at least as early as July 2010.

On October 31, 2011, Lanny Breuer testified that he found out about gunwalking in Operation Wide Receiver in April 2010, and that he "wished he had alerted the deputy or the attorney general at the time."

On November 8, 2011, Attorney General Holder testified that gunwalking was used in Fast and Furious, and that his office had inaccurately described the program unintentionally in previous letters to Congress.

On December 2, 2011, the Justice Department sent a one-sentence letter to Congress, withdrawing its February 4, 2011, letter.

Later in December 2011, the Obama administration discussed using Fast and Furious to provide anecdotal cases supporting Demand Letter 3, a new gun-control rule that would require firearms dealers in the southwest border states who had a significant number of crime scene gun traces in Mexico to report multiple rifle sales.

On December 16, 2011, the anniversary of Brian Terry's murder, the Terry family issued a statement calling for criminal charges against Obama administration officials:

> "We will continue to press for answers and accountability from our government. Those responsible for such a misguided and fundamentally flawed operation must be held fully responsible [...] and should be held criminally liable."

At the time, an illegal immigrant was in custody and was charged with Brian Terry's murder. The indictment was sealed. The identity of the accused was not released. When the House Judiciary Committee asked for the identity to be released to them in a closed executive session, Holder refused. Holder also opposed the Terry family's attempt to get victim's rights status in the straw purchasing prosecutions.

The Terry Family attorney, Patrick McGroder, said: "though the family still doesn't believe justice has been done [...] they have confidence it will be."

No second-in-command in any military, corporate, private business, or civic organization, who was not personally, civilly, and/or criminally corrupt, would fail to disclose matters this significant and potentially explosive to their boss. Any boss that was not corrupt would terminate their second-in-command if they did not inform, consult, and get approval for actions that predictably would cause further scrutiny and exposure to liability.

If there had been a special prosecutor appointed and they offered immunities to the first top DOJ officials and White House staffers to tell the truth, or be prosecuted for perjury, what would have happened? As a white-collar defense attorney, I know that I, and every other white-collar attorney worth their salt, who represented a senior attorney or other top officials, that had been labeled "untruthful" by the DOJ and/or Congress in their investigative reports, would have been fighting to get to the front of that line! The DOJ and White House Counsel who were representing the witnesses would also be fighting to get in that line assuming they were comfortable they would not violate attorney client privilege, and their state bar ethics rules would allow disclosure of client confidences under that situation.

Who had the power and authority to prohibit the ATF director from responding to Congress, cooperating with Congress, or even communicating with his own staff on such significant allegations?

Who, other than DOJ IG Horowitz, would believe the new Acting Deputy Attorney General James Cole, who assumed his position one month earlier, would not inform, consult with, or receive direction from his boss Attorney General Holder before issuing those prohibitions to the acting director of the ATF?

Who, other than DOJ IG Horowitz, would believe that Attorney General Holder, senior counsel to President Obama during his campaign and close personal friend of President Obama, would not inform his boss, friend, and confidant of this explosive political, national-level confrontation with Congress, and the even more explosive consequences of obstructing Congress' investigation, lying to the Terry family, and presenting false statements and false sworn testimony to Congress.

The answer to the first question is self-evident.

My answer to the second and third question is:

"Sorry, gentlemen (and DOJ IG Horowitz). You are just not credible."

Special Agent John Dodson, ATF Phoenix Field Division
and author of "The Unarmed Truth – My Fight to Blow the Whistle
and Expose Fast and Furious."

Senator Charles E. Grassley, Ranking Member, United States Senate,
Committee on the judiciary.

Representative Darrell E. Issa, Chairman, United States House of
Representatives, Committee on Oversight and Government Reform.

Representative Elijah E. Cummings, Ranking Minority Member, United
States House of Representatives, Committee on Oversight and
Government Reform.

William Newell, Special Agent in Charge, ATF Phoenix Field Division.

George Gillett, Assistant Special Agent in Charge,
ATF Phoenix Field Division.

Kenneth Melson, Acting Director, Bureau of Alcohol, Tobacco, Firearms And Explosives (ATF).

Dennis Burke, U.S Attorney for the District of Arizona.

Main Justice Building, Washington, D.C.

Michael E. Horowitz, Inspector General, United States
Department Of Justice.

Jason Weinstein, Deputy Assistant Attorney General
(Criminal Division)

Edward Siskel, Associate Deputy Attorney General; Deputy
White House Counsel and Deputy Assistant to President Obama.

James M. "Jim" Cole, Deputy Attorney General.

Attorney General Eric J. Holder, Jr, and Assistant Attorney General
(Criminal Division) Lanny Breuer.

Chapter Six

Thank You for Your Help - Have a Serving of Retaliation

After the March 11, 2011, meeting with the DOJ and the ATF in Phoenix, it was clear that the Department of Justice was corrupt and could not be trusted. We knew that the right course of action was to cooperate with Congress. It was the only path for the Terry family and the American public to learn the truth about the Obama administration's lies, deceit, and obstruction of justice. It was the right thing to do!

What we didn't know was how corrupt and vindictive AG Holder and the Obama regime were, or the extreme measures they would take to retaliate and continue pursuit of their gun control agenda by trying to turn their Fast and Furious fiasco into gun-control "lemonade".

We did not know that the Obama regime already had set their plans into effect with the February 4, 2011, letter of lies to Congress. When we left the meeting, the important issue of safety for Andre and his family was still a concern. The January indictments named Lone Wolf as the FFL dealer that cooperated with the DOJ in prosecuting cartel members and their affiliates. The media immediately picked up on the story and started harassing Andre to get information. He also started getting threatening phone calls and personal harassment from the public. At the meeting, the DOJ committed to "do the right thing" and provide Andre protection. They said that ATF Agent Needles, who was at the meeting, would contact me to make the necessary arrangements.

At the March 11, 2011, meeting with the DOJ and the ATF, I raised the immediate important issue of Andre Howard's exposure to the cartels. The exposure was created by the outrageous drafting of the straw purchaser indictments made public on January 25, 2011. The indictments specifically mentioned Lone Wolf Trading Company over ninety times as the source of most of the illegal sales to the cartels. They could have just said the purchases were made at an Arizona Federal Firearms Licensed dealer; used a convention common in cases where there is a confidential informant like FFL1, which is what they used in their own internal reports and email correspondence; or filed indictments under seal to protect Andre from negative harassment, adverse effects on his business, or cartel violence.

The government officials at the March 11, 2011, meeting all acknowledged the risk to Andre and his family and promised they would take immediate steps to protect Andre and his family, specifically mentioning the witness security program. They also said they would protect Andre from any subpoena from Congress by citing national security concerns. They told us that SA Needles would be the POC, and he would contact me the next week to get the process started.

Andre had been besieged by reporters, customers, potential customers, and anonymous harassers as soon as the media started reporting the indictments. The indictments gave no context, so on one hand the cartels could conclude that Andre had set them up and was either cooperating with the DOJ and the ATF, or turned them in on his own. Andre's law-abiding customers and vendors—past, present, and future—also had no context other than the December 2010 Grimaldi article published right before Brian Terry's murder, which listed Andre and Lone Wolf as the gun store that sold the most firearms to Mexican drug cartels that were traced to crime scenes in Mexico from 2009 to 2010. Finally, the Terry family had no context, and they were left to believe that when Andre sold the firearms found at Brian Terry's crime scene, he knew they were going to the cartels, or at least he negligently ignored clear signs they were going to the cartels, where they were likely going to be used in violent crimes, including crimes of violence against United States and Mexican law enforcement that policed the border.

The indictment, the DOJ press release, and the media didn't know Andre's status, motivations, or knowledge of what happened to the firearms after they were sold. The DOJ certainly made no attempt to set the record straight. At the March meeting, they said they would not "fight the adverse media reports in the press." They said: "The truth would come out at the trial [of the straw purchasers]." We did not know the actual status of those criminal cases or what the likely disposition would be. It really wasn't clear what position the DOJ would take regarding Andre's status. Was he a confidential informant, a witness, a victim, or an agent of the government who acted at their direction? Their signals at the meeting were mixed. Regarding protection, they talked about WITSEC, which is a program for cooperating witnesses, either confidential informants, undercover agents, or regular trial witnesses in danger of harm. Regarding compensation, they talked about some unspecified agency fund they could access to pay him for the financial loss incurred because of his cooperation in a criminal investigation. Regarding avoiding a subpoena from Congress, they spoke in terms of treating him like a national security asset bound by a nondisclosure agreement precluding testimony. I hoped that clarity would come from SA Needles the next week.

When the media contacted the DOJ and the ATF, their spokesman talked about the indictments and promoted their own great work in identifying, arresting, and prosecuting illegal gun traffickers in one of the largest gun trafficking cases ever filed. They did not comment about Lone Wolf Trading Company or provide Andre any cover. They also told Andre not to talk to any media, or try to protect his own reputation with customers or vendors, leading him to believe he could be charged with obstruction of justice for compromising an ongoing criminal investigation and interfering with the prosecution of the straw purchaser cases. Andre's attorney prior to March 11, 2011, did nothing to fix this unfair dilemma. He did repeatedly emphasize the message he received from AUSA Hurley, AUSA Morrissey, and his brother, AUSA Rapp: "Do what we say. We are all in the same boat and as long as we are on the same page, your client will be OK."

On March 14, I talked with SA Needles who said getting Andre protected in a WITSEC program would be "no big deal", noting "they do that all the time". He also said that if Andre would put something in writing about any financial loss he had already suffered, he would submit it to the "right people" to process the claim.

On March 15, SA Needles called me and said that the ATF would have to interview Andre and submit a threat/risk assessment to get the paperwork started with the WITSEC program. He said that in the interim, the ATF would install a security system with a camera at Andre's residence. He said that SA Hope MacAllister, who had been Andre's handler, would do the threat assessment because she already knew a lot about Andre, his business, and his family situation. He assured me that the threat assessment was a pro forma bureaucratic step in the process and would be no problem. On March 17, Andre, who had grown more and more distrustful of the DOJ and the ATF, tape-recorded some of his conversations with SA MacAllister:

> Andre: "I just asked Rapp to give me a copy of the [straw purchaser] indictment and oh, my God, I had no idea. That is why the media is so focused on me, 'cause you know I am the most prominent one […] Rapp's only concern, Hope, is the danger that I may be in.

"There are only [twenty] defendants listed in that [indictment], but you and I both know this could spider out to more and who's dangerous and who's not.

"You know doggone well that the cartel knows who I am. And I am scared to death about that […] I've got a family and sister […] and Mom I have to think about because I take care of them.

"Now the Justice Department, as you know, came out and denied that weapon was part of their […] investigation […] I was told by one of the agents that the gun that killed the agent [did come from my store].

"Every major news organization […] has contacted me […] Rapp said […] 'the cartel knows who you are. […] They know that you cooperated. […]They'll make an example out of you.'

"But look [Hope] they're killing people left and right […] and the media […] has catapulted me into the forefront."Andre went on to ask SA MacAllister what the US Attorney would be able to do to protect him and his family. She assured him the witness protection program would take care of them. He went on to express his financial concerns:

"It's hurt our business tremendously […] with the bad press we are getting. […] One of my main wholesalers […] faxed me [a seven-page letter he got] from Glock."

Glock, one of the largest manufacturers of handguns in the world, prohibited the wholesaler from supplying handguns to Lone Wolf Trading Company based solely on the negative media coverage that painted the business as the number-one supplier of illegal firearms to the Mexican drug cartels.

SA Hope MacAllister responded:

"[D]o not discuss […] [this case] with anybody but me.

"[U]ntil the actual results come out from [the FBI forensic] investigation [...] they probably aren't going to be able to confirm what [Agent Terry] was shot with.

"If anybody is going to get sued, it is going to be the FBI, in my opinion.

"As far as the threat assessment [...] we can officially do a threat assessment [...] and do the camera thing.

"I talked to Dave [Nettles] and he said that obviously there [are] funds [for protection and compensation]."

They talked about what Andre wanted from the WITSEC program. First, he wanted his family moved out of Arizona and relocated permanently to another location away from the southwest border, like Utah.

SA MacAllister responded:

"As far as your mom [...] just give me a heads up [...] then we'll [...] work out how we want to do it."

Second, Andre wanted to be moved to a safe location, possibly Montana, where a close friend lived, but he recognized he might have to come back to testify in trials or hearings in Arizona. He would leave the gun store in the hands of his manager, but he would have to travel back to Arizona from time to time to check on the operation. They mutually agreed to try to get everything done by May, before any trials were scheduled. Technically, he would not be in the full WITSEC program because in that program he could not return to Arizona.

SA MacAllister reassured Andre:

"There is a victim witness program. [...] It is not WITSEC . [...] [It] has [its] own funds. [...] You are being paid for your protection as a witness."

On March 18, the next day, I talked to SA MacAllister and she confirmed that the ATF was going to work with victim/witness program officials to protect Andre and his family, with a target date in May 2011.

On March 29, 2011, I received a telephone call from SA Needles. At that time he knew Congress was interested in talking to Andre. He said that the DOJ intended to block any subpoena to Andre, and that he would not have to testify before Congress. The DOJ was supposedly going to use some type of national security argument to block the subpoena. He also said that there would still be a need for a threat assessment to support the victim/witness referral, and the new point of contact would change from the ATF to the DOJ "to make it an independent assessment." Our new point of contact was AUSA Patrick Cunningham, the Chief of the Criminal Division of the U.S. Attorney's Office in Arizona. Cunningham was a former Army Judge Advocate officer who coincidentally was a student I taught as a criminal law instructor at the Army JAGC School in Charlottesville, Virginia. I interpreted the assignment of Cunningham as Andre's new "handler" as a shift of control from the ATF to the DOJ, and a possible attempt to get Andre to agree to join their obstruction/denial team. They brought on a new person that neither Andre nor I had ever dealt with. Cunningham was a person who arguably would have an opportunity to establish a rapport based on prior military experiences. The Department of Justice wanted to have more control so that they could manage their own damage control defense.

The first two weeks in April were filled with repeated attempts by the DOJ to find out what Andre would say to Congress. They sent an IRS Agent out of the blue to interrogate Andre about his business, and then followed that up with more requests for information supposedly needed for the sham threat assessment. When AUSA Patrick Cunningham was unable to get us to talk about our conversations with Congress, they said the U.S. Marshals Service needed to do a more formal, independent investigation and assessment. In the interim, we voluntarily accepted a subpoena from Congress on April 16, 2011, to testify in a closed interview to be held in Phoenix on May 18, 2011.

I agreed to do a threat assessment conducted over the phone with the Marshals Service. On the scheduled time for the interview (April 20, 2011), Patrick Cunningham was on the phone. When I refused to give him information, he said the threat assessment had to be rescheduled because the matter was so important they had to bring in "the pros from Dover" to conduct a "Cadillac-level threat assessment."

Unfortunately for Cunningham, I was a fan of the show M*A*S*H. The pros from Dover, was a con-artist term Hawkeye Pierce supposedly used to get free access to play on various golf courses before he was drafted into the military.

The DOJ obviously knew that we accepted service of the subpoena because the minority members (Democrats) on the House Oversight Committee were in constant communication, and collusion, with Attorney General Holder.

Coincidentally, I also got two other telephone calls on April 20, 2011. One from minority staff members of the House Oversight Committee, Ms. Grooms and Mr. Sherman, wanting to interview Andre. The second telephone call was from an AUSA prosecutor who said she urgently needed to prepare Andre for trial testimony in the impending straw purchaser trials. We already knew from SA MacAllister's recordings that there were no impending trials, and that nineteen of the twenty straw purchasers who were indicted had already agreed to plead guilty.

On April 27, 2011, Andre and I participated in the U.S. Marshals Office threat assessment conducted by three U.S. Marshals - Mr. Tracey, Mr. Lindsey, and Ms. Harkins. The DOJ and the US Marshals Service refused to give us a copy of their report, or provide any feedback about protection or compensation.

On May 3, 2011, I watched Attorney General Holder on C-Span commit perjury in his testimony before Congress, when he said he first heard of Fast and Furious in April 2011. AUSA prosecutors continued to harass Andre and me with multiple telephone calls and requests for documents for fake trials.

On May 25, 2011, Andre and I voluntarily cooperated in a sworn interview conducted by the Department of Justice IG in Phoenix. Andre answered all their questions fully and honestly. One day later, on May 26, the leading Hispanic newspaper in the United States, *La Opinion*, published an article stating: "Robbie Sherwood, spokesperson for the prosecutor's office in the state of Arizona, says that the vast majority of guns seized in crimes across the border come from a small number of retailers, including Lone Wolf Trading Company. Andre Howard, owner of Lone Wolf, declined to be interviewed."

The May 26, 2011, article by *La Opinion* was the first DOJ media attempt to retaliate against Andre for his cooperation with Congress. Andre had rebuffed multiple overt attempts by DOJ officials to get Andre to join their conspiracy to cover-up the illegal DOJ/ATF gunwalking strategy. I checked court docket sheets relating to straw purchaser prosecutions and verified there were no imminent trials, there were no significant discovery motions, and there was absolutely no need for any AUSA to interview Andre to prepare for trial. These contacts demanding cooperation with the government were obviously fabricated attempts to find out what Andre told Congress. It was extremely disappointing that DOJ prosecutors blatantly lied about their urgent need to prepare Andre to testify at trial. To make matters worse they tried to convince me Andre's refusal to be interviewed was possibly obstruction of justice. I knew this threat was absurd.

The *La Opinion* article was published the day after Andre testified before the DOJ IG, and eight days after his testimony before Congress. I immediately contacted AUSA Cunningham who was our point of contact to secure protection under the victim/witness protection program. SA Hope MacAllister and SA Needles were in charge of the witness protection initiative from March 2011 until AUSA Cunningham and U.S. Attorney Burke transferred supervision to the DOJ in mid-April 2011. The DOJ retained supervision but deferred to the U.S. Marshals office to conduct the alleged threat assessment at the end of April 2011. After Andre's interview with the U.S. Marshals Service, which is part of the DOJ, we got no further information about protection or the threat assessment.

When I confronted AUSA Cunningham about the May 26, 2011, article quoting defamatory statements by DOJ spokesman Robbie Sherwood, AUSA Cunningham said he would investigate and get back to me. First he denied that Sherwood ever spoke to *La Opinion*. Then he said that the reporter fabricated the statement. Finally he said that the reporter misquoted Sherwood. All were obviously false.

While Andre and I got the runaround about protection and threat assessments, the DOJ in Arizona started a parallel track. On April 8, 2011, Attorney Chris Rapp met with Ms. Kelly of the Arizona U.S. Attorney's Office to arrange Andre's trial preparation interviews. I declined their invitation. Andre terminated his attorney-client relationship with Chris Rapp regarding the Fast and Furious matter.

After Andre's May 2011 interviews by Congress and the DOJ IG, the lines were clearly drawn in the sand. Andre and I were committed to continuing our cooperation with Congress. The DOJ knew any future attempts to get us to obstruct Congress would be futile. What was the Obama administration's plan B? It was the same plan B they had already been using with the ATF whistleblowers, the media that wrote negative articles about AG Holder or President Obama, and any other United States citizen that criticized their corrupt administration — retaliation!

The DOJ still tried to get information from Andre and me about conversations with ATF whistleblowers, but they went silent regarding the threat assessment.

In September 2011, I was interviewed by William La Jeunesse on Fox News.

In the interview I explained how Andre was victimized by the Obama administration and their many lies. I also talked about how terribly affected Andre was by the news that one of the firearms from his gun store might have been used in the murder of Agent Brian Terry. He felt terrible for the Terry family and was disgusted by the way the Obama administration treated the Terry family.

Several days later I got a telephone call from Phoenix Attorney Patrick Magruder, who represented the Terry family. He was considering a civil lawsuit against the DOJ and the ATF. He wanted to talk about Andre and the Fox News interview, especially Andre's willingness to cooperate with the Terry family in pursuing a civil lawsuit. He asked if Andre had liability insurance that the plaintiff could look to in the event of a judgement or settlement against Lone Wolf. I did not know Andre's insurance coverage, but it was obvious that if he had potential coverage, he would be included as a defendant in any civil lawsuit. He would also be a witness against the DOJ and the ATF. He could testify that they swore all firearms were interdicted. He could also refute their story that they never encouraged, or even knew of, any illegal sales by cooperating FFLs.

Experienced plaintiff attorneys are skilled at crafting civil complaints that fit within the four concerns of an insurance policy and trigger potential coverage. They motivate insurers to settle cases rather than get bogged down with expensive defense costs in a protracted case.

Although I represented Andre in the congressional and DOJ IG investigation, Andre would need different counsel in any civil lawsuit. I would be a probable witness, especially in any cross-claim against the DOJ or the ATF.

After a review of Andre's insurance policies, we determined that he did have liability insurance the Terry family might be able to access. The Phoenix law firm of Jardine, Baker, Hickman & Houston was retained to address insurance issues and any civil lawsuit naming Andre or Lone Wolf as a defendant.

On February 1, 2012, the Terry family filed a $25,000,000 wrongful death lawsuit against the ATF and added two negligence claims against Lone Wolf Trading Company.

After the Terry family filed their lawsuit, the Obama administration lawyers went into full defense mode and got all counts against the Obama administration defendants dismissed, arguing they were immune from prosecution. They assured the Terry family they would be fully compensated because they would get a life insurance payment and death benefits from the government. Andre and Lone Wolf Trading Company were left as the lone defendant in the case. Not only did the Obama administration get a free pass, they also refused to produce any of the evidence that would prove Andre was kept in the dark about what they did, and that he was being directed (effectively coerced) to sell the firearms to known straw purchasers.

In cases like this, the insurance company hires their regular insurance defense law firm to defend Andre, their insured. The insurance defense company is paid by the insurance company and often has loyalty only to the client who pays their bill. In Andre's case, the law firm was concerned mainly with minimizing the insurance company's liability.

Andre insisted that the insurance company hire an investigator. They eventually agreed and hired an investigator who was a longtime friend of Andre. Within days the investigator discovered the evidence that showed the FBI had been approving sales from Lone Wolf during and after Fast and Furious, which were illegal. The FBI knew they were illegal purchases but approved the sales to known felons, illegal aliens, and others prohibited by federal law from purchasing firearms.

Every FFL has to rely on the FBI NICS background check system when submitting a customer for approval. Otherwise every FFL would either have to take the customers' word on its face, or conduct their own background check by searching courthouse records in federal, state, and local courts. Andre was in disbelief:

> "To my shock and horror, the FBI had deliberately approved people while ATF officials were on the phone with them, and they were watching the people while they were in my store. Not only was this illegal, but they were putting the safety of the general public at risk."

Andre immediately informed Congress, which acknowledged an awareness of the problem with the FBI.

Former and current government sources, who were friends of Andre's, informed him "that [the] ATF was determined to retaliate against him and his business, and to ruin him with the help of the FBI."

Nine months later, on November 7, 2012, the insurance defense lawyers settled the civil lawsuit filed by the Terry family. Andre was relieved that the legal ordeal was over, but he was also glad that the Terry family finally received some compensation. He was determined to stop the Obama administration's multifaceted retaliation against him and his business.

The FBI's involvement in Fast and Furious started early in the operation as part of the "keep Andre in the dark so he continues to cooperate" phase of the operation. Historically, FBI agents did not come into Lone Wolf Trading Company unless they had a personal transaction. During the Fast and Furious investigation by Congress, FBI agents started coming into his business with no apparent business purpose. The first instance was on July 28, 2011, during the time that the DOJ wanted to know what Andre told Congress and what ATF whistleblowers told Andre. FBI SA Kurt Hemphill, who had been an occasional customer for several years, showed up at his business. During Fast and Furious, he went to Lone Wolf to ask Andre if he would handle a personal firearm transfer. This visit, more than a year later, was not for a business transaction. Agent Hemphill wanted information, not guns. He told Andre he "felt sorry for all the negative publicity that Andre was receiving." He asked Andre if he was working directly with the DOJ IG's Office, and offered to assist. He then tried to get Andre to talk about his participation in Fast and Furious. Andre declined to have that discussion. FBI Agent Hemphill left.

Over the next couple of years, numerous other FBI agents came into Lone Wolf during active business hours. They were obviously agents who were not there for business or law enforcement reasons. They asked no questions and had no discussions. They just walked around as though they were scrutinizing his sales to customers, leaving the impression Andre was under some kind of investigation. Their presence naturally intimidated customers. Andre was concerned.

I called FBI Agent Hemphill to ask what was going on. He put me on speaker phone and said the FBI was launching its "own" investigation into Fast and Furious, and the officials involved, including Attorney General Holder and President Obama. I declined to comment. This was an obvious lie. Over the next several years FBI Agent Hemphill would periodically walk into Lone Wolf with his recording device attached to his ear. He walked around the store, stared at customers, did not speak a word, and then just walked out. A number of his FBI colleagues did the same thing. The only possible reason for this conduct was retaliation — intimidate customers and get the word out: "Don't buy firearms from Lone Wolf."

In the midst of the DOJ IG investigation and the congressional investigation of Fast and Furious, and before Holder retracted the false statement to Congress made February 4, President Obama attempted to take action against gun dealers in the border states (California, New Mexico, Texas, and Arizona). The new requirement for those gun dealers, under threat of loss of license and criminal prosecution, was to report any individual who made multiple semiautomatic weapon purchases within a five-day period.

The Obama administration immediately targeted Andre and Lone Wolf by having FBI informants and others make attempted purchases of semiautomatic weapons.

Representative Issa characterized the new targeting requirements as "an attempt to deflect attention from the Operation Fast and Furious scandal […] a political maneuver […] designed to protect the careers of political appointees in the Justice Department", and part of "continuing attempts to distract attention from clear wrongdoing."

Deputy Attorney General James Cole argued that "the new reporting requirements will help ATF officials detect and disrupt the illegal weapons-trafficking networks responsible for diverting firearms from lawful commerce to criminals and criminal organizations."

Senator Grassley pointed out that "many federal firearms dealers are already voluntarily reporting suspicious transactions. […] Nearly all of these sales […] associated with the ATF's Fast and Furious case […] were reported in real time by cooperating gun dealers. The ATF watched the guns be transported […] often across the border."

Representative Issa added: "In Operation Fast and Furious, gun dealers didn't need this regulation, as they voluntarily provided ATF agents with information. […] In return for this voluntary cooperation, the Justice Department 'betrayed' them by offering false assurances that they would closely monitor sales of weapons that dealers otherwise did not want to make, and they would interdict the weapons."

In May 2013, Mr. Jardine wrote a letter to DOJ IG Horwitz filing a formal complaint against former U.S. Attorney Dennis Burke, former AUSA Patrick Cunningham, and their spokesperson, Robbie Sherwood, for leaking the defamatory information about Andre and Lone Wolf that was published by Ms. Nunez in the Hispanic publication *La Opinion*.

Mr. Jardine filed a Bivens complaint in the District of Arizona against ATF and DOJ defendants, setting out the true facts about Andre's participation in Fast and Furious:

> "Mr. Howard agreed to sell weapons to unauthorized buyers at the request and with the approval/encouragement of those named ATF and DOJ defendants. Sworn testimony before congressional committees has confirmed that Mr. Howard suspected the illegality of those purchases; promptly reported those suspicions directly to Department of Justice and ATF personnel; and was directed by those same personnel to continue to allow such purchases, in effect acting as the agent of those ATF and DOJ personnel. [...] Mr. Burke, Mr. Cunningham, and Mr. Sherwood knew [the] statements [given to *La Opinion*] were false."

No one ever gave sworn testimony to Congress refuting, or challenging, Andre Howard's testimony. Mr. Burke, Mr. Cunningham, and Mr. Sherwood all refused to testify, and AG Holder refused to produce documents about this defamatory retaliation against Andre.

AG Holder's DOJ also executed a well-documented retaliation campaign against the brave ATF whistleblowers who came forward to tell the truth about Fast and Furious. Agent John Dodson detailed the injustices he and others at the ATF had to endure from the corrupt Obama administration in his testimony and his book, "The Unarmed Truth."

Congress repeatedly warned the Obama administration about retaliation. It is a federal felony offense. Once again, Congress repeatedly requested answers and documents from the DOJ, only to be repeatedly stonewalled.

There are two felony offenses the Obama administration apparently overlooked: 18 U.S.C. §1512, tampering with a witness, victim, or an informant; and 18 U.S.C. §1513, retaliating against a witness, victim, or an informant.

According to the DOJ, Andre was a witness. They repeatedly said so in numerous communications. Starting in March 2011, they talked about putting him in the WITSEC program, then the victim witness assistance program. These are witness protection programs. For months thereafter, they wanted to prepare him for trial testimony as a key witness in the straw purchaser cases. He also testified as a witness before Congress and the DOJ IG, where he was sworn in as a witness and questioned under oath.

According to the DOJ, Andre was also a victim. He cooperated in multiple threat assessments regarding the victim/witness assistance program. On February 8, 2012, the DOJ sent Andre a letter saying he was a "victim of a state or federal crime" and advised him of his rights as a victim, which included:

1. The right to confer with the attorney for the government in the case;
2. The right to full and timely restitution as provided by law; and
3. The right to be treated with fairness and respect for [his] dignity.

The letter did not address witness tampering or retaliation. Those were not in the DOJ letter, or the DOJ pamphlet that

Mary Palas, Victim/Witness Coordinator, Phoenix Field Division, sent him. They are included in the Federal Crime Code.

- 18 U.S.C. §1512 states:

(b)"whoever knowingly uses intimidation, threatens, or corruptly persuades another person, or attempts to do so, or engages in misleading conduct toward another person to —

> (2) Cause or induce any person to —
>> (A) Withhold testimony [...] from an official proceeding;
>> (B) Evade legal process summoning that person to appear as a witness [...] in an official proceeding
>> (C) Shall be fined under this title or imprisoned not more than [twenty] years.

- 18 U.S.C. §1513 states:

(e) Whoever knowingly, with the intent to retaliate, takes action harmful to any person, including interference with the livelihood of any person, for providing [...] any truthful information relating to the commission or possible commission of any federal offense, shall be fined under this title or imprisoned not more than [ten] years.

There is no question that DOJ officials and Democratic Party congressional officials tried to get Andre to withhold testimony and evade the subpoena Congress served on him. There is also no question that DOJ and FBI officials tried to harm Andre's livelihood, through false media leaks and intimidation of customers, because he gave truthful testimony to Congress about illegal DOJ and ATF conduct.

Other federal criminal statues implicated in the Obama administration conduct include 18 U.S.C. §1505 (obstruction of justice), 18 U.S.C. §1621 (perjury), and 18 U.S.C. §1622 (subornation of perjury).

On October 11, 2011, Congress again sent a letter to AG Eric Holder requesting all documents relating to the so-called "threat assessments" relating to Andre's security and protection. In the letter, Congress pointed out the DOJ's role in encouraging Andre to make the illegal sales, lying to Andre about the interdiction of the weapons, promoting false and misleading reports about Andre in the media linking him to cartel gun sales without disclosing the extensive role he played in cooperating, and exposing him to retaliation unnecessarily by including the name Lone Wolf Trading Company ninety-eight times in the indictment.

They specifically questioned the DOJ's promise that Andre "would be put in good hands" and the "possibility of putting Mr. Howard in a victim witness protection program, the witness protection program, and [the] DOJ buying his house and relocating him and his family."

On March 30, 2012, Senator Grassley's Office sent another letter to the DOJ requesting the results of Andre's threat assessment.

> "It has been over a year since the threat assessment has been performed and this is extremely concerning for Mr. Howard. Can the Department [of Justice] explain why the finding of the Threat Assessment have [...] never been communicated to Mr. Howard?"

The response? Crickets.

> After repeated attempts by Congress and me to get copies of Andre's threat assessment report, we eventually got a redacted copy on July 20, 2012. The Judicial Security Unit, District of Arizona, issued a report titled "ATF Cooperating Witness." The report, which was heavily redacted, was called a "protective intelligence briefing that was exempt from release to Congress or the witness as 'law-enforcement sensitive.'

So much of the twenty-one-page report was redacted that when it was eventually released the release was meaningless. What was unredacted demonstrated that the Marshals Service interpreted cooperation as merely providing information. They ignored the real facts. Guns were intentionally walked to the cartels, many ATF agents had already been threatened with violence, and the specific cartel in question had murdered five victims execution style in Texas and Arizona in August and October 2010.

The rest of the report discussing cartel crimes of violence was redacted. Andre and I both provided extensive information about over sixty incidents of extreme harassment and business disruption that Andre had suffered. At his threat assessment proceeding on April 27, 2011, Andre testified that we was "in an egregious position" and "at great risk."

The U.S. Marshals Service indicated that due to "intelligence gaps," which were redacted and not disclosed, they were unable to identify any specific imminent threat. They offered to put a security system in his home and concluded that "agencies responsible for the security of the cooperating witness (i.e. the agencies who were still lying to Congress, retaliating against ATF whistleblowers, and lying to Andre about promised protection) must be prepared to react quickly if/when the risk level escalates."

I informed the U.S. Marshals Service "that Mexico had hired an American law firm to file lawsuits against the FFLs who provided information to the ATF." I also told them the Attorney General for Mexico had "discussed plans for all who were involved in the gun runner/Operation Fast and Furious to be extradited to Mexico to be tried as war criminals."

I concluded by saying that Andre faces threats from all sides: the ATF, the DOJ, Mexico, Mexican cartels, and the general public, and that it is unknown where or when extreme retaliation may come in the future.

Retaliation continued from ATF, DOJ, and the general public. The only organizations that didn't retaliate were the Mexican cartels. The next organization to retaliate was the Obama White House.

In the spring of 2013, the Obama administration launched Operation Choke Point, supposedly to protect financial institutions from mass-market consumer fraud by blocking the perpetrator of fraud from using various banks for payment systems.

Like many Obama administration programs, Choke Point really had a different purpose. Obama's Operation Fast and Furious was supposedly an investigation to stop gun trafficking, but it was really an operation to let guns be trafficked to Mexican cartels so the resulting violent crimes could be traced to U.S. firearms dealers, and the Obama administration could use the deadly statistics to support gun control initiatives.

The real purpose of Choke Point was to financially strangle targeted industries, in particular targeted businesses within the industry that AG Eric Holder and President Obama did not like.

Thirty merchant categories were arbitrarily designated high-risk merchants. The Attorney General had the authority to seek civil money penalties against entities that commit a fraud affecting a federally insured financial institution. His powers also included the power to issue burdensome subpoenas for documents and testimony, without any judicial authorization, to any person or entity he deemed to have information relevant to his inquiry.

In Operation Choke Point, the DOJ used these powers to pressure banks to shut down the accounts of supposedly high-risk merchants, even if there was no indication, allegation, or charge that the merchant had done anything wrong. The rationale was that a high-risk merchant using normal banking services necessarily poses a variety of risks of fraud, and that these hypothetical risks "may affect" the financial institution. Obama and Holder were just "protecting" the financial institution from some inevitable future fraud. If the financial institution did not shut down a questionable account when directed to do so, the Department of Justice could penalize the financial institution. The merchant and the financial institution could both be punished even if neither had done anything wrong whatsoever!

Obama's Department of Justice, the holder of these powers, repeatedly assured Americans they "have no interest in pursuing or discouraging lawful conduct." Just like they had no interest in retaliating against, and ruining the lives, of ATF whistleblowers who testified truthfully under oath to Congress, exposing the Obama administration's crimes and corruption in Operation Fast and Furious.

The merchants who were targeted by the Obama administration and Holder on the list of thirty "high risk" merchants included:

Online Gambling
Pornography
Racist Materials
Escort Services
Drug Paraphernalia
Debt Collection Scams
Pyramid-Type Sales
Telemarketing
Ammunition Sales
Firearm Sales
Get-Rich Products
Ponzi Schemes

How did firearm sales and ammunition sales get included with Ponzi schemes, drug paraphernalia, escort services, pyramid schemes, collection scams, racist materials, and pornography? AG Holder and President Obama saw them as the same thing? Federal Firearms Licensees are among the most regulated merchants in the United States.

Financial institutions that: made loans to high-risk merchants, had bank accounts where they deposited money, and had checking accounts or mortgages became targets themselves. Banks were pressured to discontinue longstanding legal and profitable relationships with fully licensed legal firearms businesses, or face a potentially ruinous lawsuit by Obama's Justice Department.

On May 18, 2014, the *Washington Times* published an article about how a number of firearms merchants immediately had their bank accounts frozen or terminated. One of the first firearms merchants immediately singled out for targeting was Lone Wolf Trading Company. No surprise, since the Obama administration had already targeted Lone Wolf for illegal electronic surveillance after they began cooperating with Congress in Fast and Furious. Multiple reliable sources had informed Andre that the Obama administration was illegally intercepting our attorney-client communications.

During my representation of Andre, an intelligence operative, from some government agency, dressed as a building security guard, was in my office late at night going through my legal files, which included my Fast and Furious files. The next morning, an attorney who worked for me, reported that he confronted the intruder late at night in our office. I took the matter to building security. They did not employ any security officer that remotely fit the intruder's description. The intruder did not steal anything but was sophisticated enough to bypass the building and law firm security and surveillance systems. The building security cameras did not record the intruder entering, or exiting, our elevator or our stairwell on the thirtieth floor. Both were covered by full time surveillance. The only known motive — go through my legal files.

The U.S. House of Representatives Committee on Oversight and Government Reform investigated Operation Choke Point and issued two reports on May 29, 2014, and December 8, 2014. The first report was titled "Department of Justice's Operation Choke Point: Illegally Choking Off Legitimate Businesses"; the second addressed the "Federal Deposit Insurance Corporation's Involvement in Operation Choke Point"."

Among the findings and conclusions by Congress:

"-Operation Choke Point was created by the Justice Department to "choke out" companies the administration considered high-risk or otherwise objectionable despite the fact that they are legal businesses.

-The DOJ's internal documents confirm that Operation Choke Point is an inappropriate exercise of the Department's legal authorities, and is being executed in a manner that unfairly harms legitimate merchants and individuals.

-Documents produced to the committee call into question the accuracy of the DOJ's statements that the agency 'has no interest in pursuing or discouraging lawful conduct.'

-The FDIC and the DOJ provided no explanation for how or why a particular merchant was designated as high-risk.

-The experience of firearms and ammunition merchants — an industry far removed from consumer fraud — calls into question the sincerity of the Department's statements that individual lawful firearms merchants were not targeted based on individual vendettas or a gun-control 'hidden agenda.'

　　-The FDIC actively partnered with the Department of Justice to implement Operation Choke Point, and may have misled Congress about this partnership.

　　-The FDIC required banks to 'prohibit payment processing for firearms merchants, characterized loans to firearms dealers as 'undesirable', and generally subjected firearms and ammunitions merchants to significantly higher due diligence standards.'

　　-There remain serious questions as to the truthfulness of the FDIC's Acting General Counsel's testimony that Operation Choke Point did not single out any particular merchant.

　　-The experience of firearms and ammunition dealers — one of the most heavily regulated businesses in the United States — is a testament to the destructive and unacceptable impact of Operation Choke Point."

Confidential briefing documents produced to the committee revealed that "senior DOJ officials informed the Attorney General himself that, as a consequence of Operation Choke Point, banks are exiting lines of business deemed 'high-risk' — like firearms merchants."AG Holder took no action to address the issue.

The FDIC, in a training package, justified targeting firearms dealers because "arms and ammunition dealers are identified as higher risk businesses because they have a higher risk of being associated with terrorism and terrorist acts."

The Deputy Attorney General at the DOJ refused to cooperate with the House investigation, refusing to provide even basic information unrelated to specific investigations.

President Trump officially ended Operation Choke Point in August 2017, after five years of illegal financial assaults on firearms dealers like Andre Howard.

The Obama administration executed a shamefully illegal program against Andre and other "enemies" of the administration in what could only be characterized as an extreme, mean-spirited, illegal, massive abuse of power.

Operation Choke Point had a very insidious effect on its targeted business victims like Andre Howard and Lone Wolf. They only learned that they were an Obama administration target when they got a notice from their bank that their account was overdrawn, that their payment checks for the month were not put into their accounts, and that all their accounts were financially frozen. Andre was one of the very first businesses targeted when Operation Choke Point went into effect in 2013. Legitimate businesses like Lone Wolf had no real notice that Choke Point would affect them, because they were not doing anything wrong. On paper, Choke Point was an operation directed at financial institutions, and how they dealt with bank fraud. But it really was a program that had a secret agenda — attack the enemies or targets of the Obama administration.

Andre was blindsided. Even though he never did anything wrong, had a great relationship with his bank, and spent fifteen months cooperating with the Obama administration in Fast and Furious, he was still targeted by the Obama administration. Why? Because he refused to follow their demands to obstruct justice, risk contempt of Congress charges by refusing to comply with a subpoena, and lie to protect the criminal conduct of the Obama administration.

How did this impact Andre?

"From 2013 through 2015, until I switched banks, my existing bank, Wells Fargo, increased my fees on credit card purchases by [five percent] per month, held up pending checks written to my wholesalers until my account was low, then put them through, which caused me to go thousands of dollars into my overdraft account, which [then] charged a very high monthly fee."

Andre had a very good relationship with Wells Fargo and the local bank personnel. When he tried to discuss these abnormal practices, which were far different than his years and years of normal business dealings with them, they would only say they were "following orders from the Justice Department under Operation Choke Point."

Although President Trump terminated this illegal effort to drive Andre out of business, the banks were never fined, Andre received no restitution, and the Obama administration was never held accountable.

On October 7, 2013, Bradley Jardine, Andre's attorney in the Terry civil lawsuit, wrote DOJ IG Horowitz:

"Our firm has filed numerous complaints on behalf of our client Mr. Howard and Lone Wolf regarding misconduct of both Phoenix DOJ and ATF officials. [...] [That] was intended to deliberately target and harm Mr. Howard and his business.

"Yet, surprisingly, to date, not one single involved official referenced in your report has been held to account [...] paid informants, who possessed extensive criminal backgrounds which these officials intentionally concealed from Mr. Howard, were used to illegally purchase weapons. [...] [The] FBI/NCIS [...] directed Lone Wolf to approve what were otherwise illegal sales. [...] these same officials deliberately misled Mr. Howard [...] to believe that these weapons would be interdicted. [...] These same officials conspired to manipulate [trace] data [...] adversely against Mr. Howard. [...] These approvals continued well after Operation Fast and Furious was shut down."

Mr. Jardine reiterated his request to Mr. Horowitz on October 25, 2013, and November 22, 2013. The bottom line was that the corrupt DOJ and ATF officials who went unpunished for their misconduct, lies, obstruction, and murders during Fast and Furious were still in power. Some had more power through promotions—and the Obama administration gave them encouragement, and direction, to retaliate at will. They still continue to attack his business, which now faces ruin.

There were many other examples of the Obama administration's vengeful attacks.

When the Arizona Sheriff Association planned a meeting where their organization would publically call for AG Eric Holder to resign, the DOJ got advanced notice and executed a preemptive strike, attacking the reputation and credibility of all of the sheriffs involved. Holder ordered his deputies to collect intelligence from any possible source that they could use to attack the sheriffs.

They enlisted the Washington, D.C., Capitol Police to harass Andre in March 2017, to try to get copies of documents Andre sent to the House Oversight Committee related to the DOJ's continued approval of sales to illegal purchasers, even though the Capitol Police had no jurisdiction whatsoever to investigate or handle that issue. Andre sent copies to Congress. Representative Issa's staff replied: "We've been getting threats, and have been grumping around with them about doing little."

This book does not address the disgraceful retaliation campaign by the Obama administration directed against many ATF agents who were whistleblowers or cooperating witnesses. The Obama campaign against them can best be summarized in a statement issued by Scot Thomasson, ATF's Chief of the Public Affairs Division, when the DOJ received the January 27, 2011, letter from Senator Grassley: "We need to get whatever dirt we can on these guys [the whistleblowers] and take them down. […] [The] ATF needs to f—k these guys."

When Congress asked DOJ IG Horowitz to investigate those responsible for the despicable retaliation against the ATF agents who were true patriots, his response was to help get the perpetrators promoted.

Chapter Seven

Stonewalling, Fake Privilege, Retaliation, Gun Control

December 2011 was a benchmark for Operation Fast and Furious. After ten months of lying about the interdiction of firearms, Attorney General Holder withdrew his February 4, 2011, letter to Congress. When Attorney General Holder withdrew the February 4 letter, he did not address the equally false May 2 confirmation letter that reiterated the false statements from February 4. He also did not specify what was false and inaccurate in the February 4 letter, or when he actually knew it was false. Of course, that would be awkward because the DOJ knew it was false when they sent the letter, so providing details would be an admission to a federal criminal offense. It was clear that the Obama administration's denial strategy was not going to work. So what was the new strategy? It was to delay. The delay strategy was based on the mantra "the DOJ is still investigating." The Obama administration simply refused to meaningfully produce any documents, or respond to any congressional requests for information. But the strategy was more than just delay, it also involved retaliation and obstruction.

The first reaction of the Obama administration was "the best defense is a good offense", so they aggressively tried to use negative press, which they created, against Andre and the other FFLs, as a springboard to get gun-control legislation. That initiative went nowhere in Congress.

After Acting ATF Director Melson provided testimony adverse to the Obama administration on July 4, 2011, he was transferred to Main Justice. Congress found that "instead of owning up to its own shortcomings, the Department [of Justice] sought to put the blame on Ken Melson."

When U.S. Attorney Burke got caught leaking sensitive internal documents to the media twice and resigned on August 29, 2011, the DOJ later tried to spin these two events together. They argued that they did their own investigation and "cleaned house" by getting rid of the top two senior Obama officials responsible for the "flawed program." First, Melson was not terminated; he was transferred to a new position. Second, Burke resigned for leaking and lying about it to his superiors at the DOJ. They had two fall guys to "sell", but Congress was "not buying" their story.

When top officials at the DOJ got interviewed by Congress, Associate Deputy Attorney General Ed Siskel said he "did not recall" or "did not know" twenty-one times. Deputy AG Grindler invoked the amnesia defense twenty-eight times, Deputy Chief of Staff Monty Wilkinson invoked the amnesia defense thirty-eight times, and U.S. Attorney Dennis Burke, who was never at a loss for words in the dozens of Fast and Furious email opinions he sent to the DOJ, invoked the amnesia defense a total of 161 times.

Someone once said, "The worst trait a liar can have is a bad memory." At least the Obama administration witnesses recognized that, so they didn't have to remember their lies, other than "I don't know", "I can't recall."

On June 7, 2017, Congress released Part III of its joint staff report, titled "Fast and Furious: Obstruction of Congress by the Department of Justice." That report "describes the Justice Department's response, primarily between the period February 4, 2011 and October 11, 2011. They said they would later issue Part IV, which would cover the period October 11, 2011, to June 28, 2012, but that report had not yet been released at the time this book was published.

The 2017 report addressed four points that still lingered until the end of the Obama regime in January 2016:

1. "Failure to provide answers for the Terry family: The Department [of Justice] viewed the Terry family as a […] nuisance;

2. Failure to objectively gather the facts: The Department's internal investigation […] was deeply flawed;

3. Lack of respect for congressional oversight: The documents show senior Justice Department officials — including the Attorney General — had a disdain for the congressional oversight […] and […] [used] tactics […] to delay and withhold information from Congress; and

4. The Department's priority on politics and spin came from the Attorney General. […] To date, the Department has failed to provide internal documents responsive to the October 12, 2011, subpoena from Congress."

The most despicable of these findings is the way President Obama, and his corrupt administration, treated the Terry family. No one in the Obama government even told the Terry family that guns recovered at the crime scene came from Fast and Furious. In fact, when U.S. Attorney Dennis Burke finally contacted the family on March 10, 2011, almost three months after the murder, he lied to them and told them the weapons at the crime scene "were sold out of a gun store in Texas."

The Obama administration also denied the Terry family status as victims in the trial of Jaime Avila and the other gun traffickers. This refusal to acknowledge the possible connection between Fast and Furious and their son's murder deprived them of rights every citizen in their position should have had.

The Terry family asked Senator Grassley for help:

"It's hard to accept that our son was shot and murdered with a gun that was bought in the U.S. We have not had any contact from [the Obama administration]. Our calls are not returned. I truly feel that our son's death is a cover-up, and they hope that we will go away. We want to know who allowed the sale of that gun that murdered our son."

Attorney General Eric Holder and President Barack Obama did not respond even though they both knew the answer to that question on December 15, 2009. Not only did they never respond, they had the Arizona U.S. Attorney lie to the Terry family. Then they did everything within their power, and actually abused their power, to keep the truth from Congress.

During the denial phase of the Obama administration's cover-up and obstruction, some honest officials tried to get Breuer, Holder, and Obama to tell the truth. The head of the Department of Justice Public Affairs office pushed back on the May 2, 2011 false letter to Congress:

"I think people will accuse us of playing with semantics when we say that you did not authorize Fast and Furious, but they find out that [the Attorney General's Office] did authorize wiretaps" that contained detailed information about the entire gunwalking operation, the trafficking to the cartels, and the murderous crime scenes.

ATF Acting Director Kenneth Melson concluded that Holder was lying to Congress at least as soon as July 4, 2011. On August 4, 2011, Deputy Assistant Attorney General Weinstein notified top officials at the DOJ that the February 4 and May 2 letters to Congress were false, to no avail.

When some of his top senior DOJ officials pushed back on Holder's lies, his response was: "Hit back, HARD."

On April 15, 2011, the Attorney General wrote to his senior advisors: "Issa and his idiot cronies never gave a damn about this when all that was happening was that thousands of Mexicans were being killed." Odd that this was actually Holder and Obama's precise position for fifteen months during Fast and Furious: "They are just Mexicans being murdered." He also sent out other guidance to his senior advisors.

"Why don't we just answer this asshole [Representative Issa] by stating the facts and go on offense?

"[H]it back HARD. [...] [E]veryone get ready. This isn't about facts."

When ATF Acting Director Melson was transferred to Main Justice, Holder directed his senior advisors to "close the door [to Melson's] office so none of his staff or employees could see that it was empty."

When other U.S. Attorneys reacted to U.S. Attorney Burke's resignation, Holder replied to his Chief of Staff that "some people can kiss my ass."

The Obama administration also made a run at a deflection defense. On January 31, 2012, the minority (Democratic) members of the House Oversight and Government Reform Committee released their own report on Fast and Furious titled "Fatally Flawed: Five Years of Gunwalking in Arizona." They concluded that no senior officials in the Obama administration had any role in gunwalking, and that Fast and Furious was just the fourth phase of a five-year program started by President Bush. Of course, that attempt to tie operation Wide Receiver together with Operation Fast and Furious was a misguided attempt to compare apples to oranges. Fast and Furious was a completely different strategy created by the Obama administration between April 2009 and September 2009. The Bush administration strategy never contemplated letting U.S. guns be used in crimes in Mexico.

In May 2012, Representative Issa started the process to make Attorney General Holder the first cabinet officer in the history of the United States to be held in contempt of Congress. Representative Issa released a memorandum to the entire House Committee on Oversight. It included a draft resolution for the entire committee to consider. He targeted AG Holder as the DOJ leader who orchestrated, and ordered, the ATF, the DOJ, the DEA, the FBI, ICE, and the DHS to obstruct the joint Senate and House investigation.

This was an historic showdown between the Executive Branch and the Legislative Branch of the United States Government that had been growing since January 2011. The explosive nature of the allegations the ATF whistleblowers raised internally within the DOJ in December 2010, the congressional public exposure in January 2011, the major media coverage starting in February 2011, and the international relation implications with our neighbor Mexico, never got the attention of Attorney General Holder or President Obama?

All of their top officials had these on their radar, but Holder and Obama were not aware of anything? None of their high-paid personally selected advisors ever told them anything? They never watched TV? They didn't read newspapers? How is it even plausible that they were completely in the dark? Even Andre, who the government intentionally kept in the dark, knew the truth by March 2011.

I was able to figure out the truth in the one week between my retention as counsel on March 3, and my meeting with the DOJ and the ATF on March 11, 2011. How is it possible that over a year later AG Holder and the President of the United States would not admit the truth? Instead they did everything they could to keep the truth from the American people. The answer is that they definitely knew the truth from day one, but they had the power and influence to control the damage for years.

On June 12, 2012, AG Eric Holder testified before Congress and tried to advance the deflection defense initiated in the House minority report. Holder tried to portray himself as the one who stopped gunwalking, and his predecessor from the Bush administration, Attorney General Michael Mukasey, as the Attorney General who started "gunwalking by authorizing Operation Wide Receiver."

It was a last-minute attempt to persuade Congress to abandon, or defeat, a contempt-of-Congress vote. Holder argued:

"If you want to talk about Fast and Furious, I'm the Attorney General that put an end to the misguided tactics that were used in Fast and Furious." What evidence is there that AG Holder stopped gunwalking? The first time his office addressed gunwalking with DOJ and ATF was a memo in March 2011. Fast and Furious was over in January 2011. Between February 4, 2011, and December 2, 2011, AG Holder denied there ever was any gunwalking during Fast and Furious. AG Holder testified under oath that he never even heard of Fast and Furious until April 2011.

The fact is that gunwalking in Fast and Furious stopped in December 2010, when Brian Terry was murdered. AG Holder never testified or produced any evidence that he stopped the operation in December 2010 when he was notified by his deputy chief of staff, Monty Wilkinson, that Border Agent Terry had been murdered.

Holder went on to deflect:

"An Attorney General, who I suppose you hold in higher regard [Michael Mukasey], was briefed on these kinds of tactics in an operation called Wide Receiver and did nothing to stop them — nothing. 300 guns, at least, walked in that instance."

It is not clear why Holder started this deflection argument with the "hold in higher regard" statement. On one hand, you could argue it alludes to the impending vote on contempt, but that doesn't make sense because the contempt issue was only about Holder's refusal to produce documents in response to a legal subpoena. It is more likely a race card innuendo of some type, or it could be both. It is vague and ultimately not relevant to any pending issue before Congress. What is most troubling about his testimony is that it is totally false.

On June 25, 2012, Representative Issa (Chairman of the House Oversight Committee), Representative Cummings (Ranking Member of the Minority on the House Oversight Committee), Senator Leahy (Chairman of the Senate Judiciary Committee), and Senator Grassley (Ranking Member of the Minority on the Senate Judiciary Committee) met with Attorney General Holder to attempt to work out a last-minute agreement to resolve the document production issue, before the contempt vote that was scheduled for the next day. This was an extraordinary, and historic event. The top Democrat and Republican members of two of the most powerful Senate and House committees met with the Attorney General to work out a compromise to end the Executive branch seventeen month obstruction of Congress and avoid the first contempt vote against a Cabinet member in U.S. History.

The meeting did not result in any agreement. Attorney General Holder left the meeting and immediately presented President Obama with a written request asking that he assert executive privilege over all documents Holder was withholding from Congress.

The next day, June 26, Deputy Attorney General Cole presented Congress with a letter from President Obama claiming executive privilege. Minutes later, the House Oversight Committee voted to recommend that the House of Representatives hold the Attorney General in contempt.

A vote of the full House of Representatives was scheduled for June 28, 2012. There were two votes scheduled, one for criminal contempt and one for civil contempt. The House could vote to hold Holder in criminal contempt, but any prosecution of that criminal charge would have to be made by a special prosecutor or someone within the Department of Justice. It would normally be expected that AG Holder, and those officials within the DOJ who were involved in withholding the subpoenaed documents, would recuse themselves from making the decision whether or not to prosecute the case. The civil contempt could be prosecuted by Congress in a civil lawsuit filed in the Federal District Court in Washington, D.C. President Obama's assertion of executive privilege could also be challenged in the civil lawsuit.

On June 26, 2012, Senator Grassley sent a letter to President Obama trying to get an explanation about his assertion of executive privilege earlier that day:

"As you know, two guns that federal law enforcement allowed to be illegally purchased and trafficked to Mexico as part of Operation Fast and Furious were found at the murder scene of Border Patrol Agent Brian Terry on December 14, 2010. I have been seeking documents related to this matter from the Justice Department since January 2011. [...] After [eighteen] months of investigation and interaction with Justice Department officials on this matter, this was the first indication that anyone at the Department, or the White House, believed the documents being sought were subject to executive privilege claims."

Congress requested internal ATF documents, internal DOJ documents, internal State Department documents, internal FBI documents, and documents exchanged between those agencies. The Attorney General never argued any of those documents were covered by executive privilege. Attorney General Holder described them as part of a "deliberative process privilege" and documents that were "law-enforcement sensitive." Neither of these are actual privileges under the law that would prevent their disclosure to committees of Congress whose members have high-level security clearances.

Senator Grassley asked for "a more precise description of the scope of [the president's] executive privilege claim. [...] Are you asserting it only with regarding to documents [...]

that may have involved communication with you [as president]?"

The White House did not respond.

June 20, 2012, was also the day that Immigration and Customs Enforcement Agent Jaime Zapata's family filed a wrongful death claim against the Obama administration regarding Zapata's February 2011, murder in Mexico by the Los Zetas Mexican drug cartel using firearms from another separate gunwalking operation in Texas.

Zapata was a Homeland Security Investigations Special Agent stationed in Laredo, Texas. On duty in Texas, he stopped a vehicle carrying between thirty and forty Fast and Furious weapons. They were travelling east towards Texas from Arizona, not south. He called in the stop and was ordered by superiors to allow the vehicle to proceed. On February 15, 2011, he and another agent, Victor Avila, were driving from Laredo, Texas, to Mexico City, where Zapata was assigned to the ICE attaché office. They were stopped at a fake checkpoint set up by the cartel. Fifteen cartel members dressed as Mexican military personnel surrounded the car. The car had diplomatic license plates and they identified themselves as Americans going to Mexico City on a diplomatic mission. They were both shot, but managed to drive away. Zapata, who was driving, died in the car after they escaped the ambush site. The companion agent, Avila, was able to be medivaced by a Mexican police helicopter. He got emergency medical care and survived. Neither agent was armed because Mexico did not allow United States agents to carry firearms into the country, even for self-defense.

When the *Brownsville Herald* reporter tried to interview Agent Avila, U.S. officials said he was not authorized to talk about the case. Mexican officials also said they were not authorized to talk about the case. Brownsville was Agent Zapata's hometown.

The Zapata family, like the Terry family, demanded to know the source of the weapons used in the attack. The gun that killed Zapata was a semiautomatic WASR-10 purchased by a known straw purchaser, Ofilio Osorio, in Dallas, and trafficked to Mexico along with nine other assault rifles.

President Obama's response: "The United States will work with Mexico to bring the assailants to justice."

Mexican President Felipe Calderon's response in an interview by Univision on May 15, 2011:

"His death must urge us to work together to ensure a prosperous and peaceful future for our region. […] One of those weapons [of Operation Fast and Furious] was the one that killed Officer Zapata, an American agent in Mexico. […] The American agencies should stop the criminal flow of arms into Mexico."

Brownsville mayor Pat M. Ahumada expressed his frustration:

"I am angered […] and frustrated […] criminals have the firepower in Mexico." In April 2010 Brownsville police stopped going into Mexico for any purpose because of the cartel violence across the Texas-Mexico border.

Texas State Representative Eddie Lucio III supported the Zapata family:

"As in all events as tragic as this, it is not uncommon to seek answers and to demand explanations. […] Please rest assured that Jaime's passing will not be so quickly overlooked."

Representative Lucio apparently did not know how the Obama administration treated victims' families, or denied transparency to the American public.

On the same day, June 20, 2012, the Terry family issued a statement:

"Attorney General Eric Holder's refusal to fully disclose the documents associated with Operation Fast and Furious and Obama's assertion of executive privilege serves to compound this tragedy. [...] For more than [eighteen] months, we have been asking our federal government for justice and accountability. [...] It is very disappointing that we are now faced with an administration that seems more concerned with protecting themselves rather than releasing the truth behind Operation Fast and Furious."

One reporter covered the June 20 events and Obama administration stonewalling in an article titled "Is Fast and Furious Becoming Obama's Watergate?"

To his credit, Representative Issa made one more attempt to resolve the Obama administration's stonewalling of Congress' investigation. On June 25, 2012, three days before the contempt vote by the United States House of Representatives, he sent a seven-page letter to President Obama.

He started by pointing out the legal limitations on a claim of executive privilege:

"Courts have consistently held that [...] the constitutionally based executive privilege —the only privilege that even can justify the withholding of documents from a congressional committee — is only applicable with respect to documents and communications that implicate the confidentiality of the president's decision-making process."

Since President Obama himself claimed to have no knowledge of Fast and Furious and no involvement in either the DOJ IG or congressional investigations, the only decision he made regarding Fast and Furious was to assert executive privilege the same day it was requested by Attorney General Holder.

Representative Issa reminded the President: "To date, the White House has steadfastly maintained that it has not had any role in advising the Department." Issa concludes: "If that is true, you are asserting a presidential power that you know to be unjustified solely for the purpose of further obstructing a congressional investigation."

The Department of Justice took eight months to identify over 140,000 pages of documents that were responsive to Congress' October 12, 2011, subpoena. They only produced 7,600 of those pages and almost all of those were documents that were already publicly available.

On June 15, 2011, the Terry family appeared before Congress and asked for answers about the program that put guns in the hands of the men who killed their son and brother. Over a year later there were no answers from the Obama administration. President Obama didn't care.

Representative Issa met with Holder on June 19, 2011, to try to prioritize what documents were most important, and structure a process for production of the rest of the 140,000 pages, to avoid the contempt vote. Holder and Obama had already decided on their strategy. Holder showed up with a take-it-or-leave-it nonnegotiable position, backed up by Obama's fake, vaguely worded, assertion of executive privilege.

Holder's counteroffer was the DOJ would produce a "small compilation" of internal documents, all created after the false February 4, 2011, letter that was withdrawn in December 2011. The DOJ said it would be a "fair compilation" of a small number of representative documents. Holder's conditions to producing this "small compilation"?

First, Congress had to permanently cancel the contempt vote. Second, Congress had to agree the compilation, which would not include a single document from the fifteen-month period of Operation Fast and Furious, the Terry murder, or the two-month period after the murder, would be accepted by Congress as full compliance with the October 2011 subpoena, and Congress would never ask for any other documents. Third, Congress had to accept these terms without having any idea what the DOJ would put in the compilation. They had to accept the fair compilation selected by DOJ sight unseen.

Attorney General Holder said the Obama administration wanted to "buy peace."

This offer by the Obama administration was absurd on its face. The last time Congress trusted the good faith of the Obama administration was when they told Senator Grassley they would produce the documents if he and the Senate Judiciary Committee would officially vote to confirm Acting Deputy Attorney General James Cole as the Deputy Attorney General. Congress agreed and confirmed Cole. The Obama administration produced a very small number of documents. Most of the documents actually produced were completely blacked out or redacted based on deliberative privilege or a made-up "law-enforcement sensitive" claim.

Congress would not be fooled again, but the Obama administration was so arrogant and emboldened, they thought there was no harm in trying. It was definitely not done in good faith. No white-collar lawyer in the United States would have accepted it. Thankfully, Congress applied the adage "Fool me once [...] Fool me twice [...]".

In the Holder letter requesting assertion of executive privilege, he represented that producing any document, including the sham offer of the documents that would have been included in the small compilation settlement offer, would have "significant, damaging consequences."

There is no way that President Obama, or his staff, reviewed the documents he claimed were privileged. AG Holder and his Department of Justice attorneys, who drafted the eight-page letter to the president, did not know what documents they were asking to be covered by executive privilege. They also ignored their ethical obligations under the rules of professional conduct.

Although Holder, and his other senior white-collar criminal attorneys, cited legal authorities, they thought supported a broad assertion of executive privilege covering all internal agency documents, they failed to follow ethical rules that prohibit attorneys from failing to disclose known controlling legal authority in an ex parte setting like this. They also failed to make a privilege log of the documents alleged to be privileged so that a court could review the validity of the privilege claims. The DOJ did not even mention the U.S. Court of Appeals for the District of Columbia opinion, which was the controlling case on point in the controlling jurisdiction, *In re: sealed cases* (Espy). That case held that executive privilege only covers communications with "members of an immediate White House advisor's staff who have broad and significant responsibility for investigating and formulating the advice to be given the President on the particular matter."

To be covered, communications with the White House must pass an operational proximity test, and then they only get a qualified privilege. Documents must still be produced if Congress can show they need the documents to perform their oversight responsibility.

Courts recognize a deliberative privilege for other executive branch communications involving executive branch decision-making, but that is a lower level qualified privilege that gives way to a much lesser showing of need by Congress, and, more importantly, it does not apply at all if there is any reason to believe government misconduct has occurred.

Issa's letter to the President posed an unsolvable dilemma for the Obama administration. On one hand, they had a long history of insisting that President Obama had absolutely nothing to do with Fast and Furious. He said he only heard about it when he happened to read an article about it in a newspaper. He also said that if anyone did anything wrong, he wanted them held accountable. Congress asked AG Holder when he first talked to the President about Fast and Furious. His response: "I don't know."

225

On the other hand, Obama and his administration claimed a broad privilege over every document about Fast and Furious written in the past two-and-a-half years because they were all related to high-level executive branch decision-making. The Obama response: "No comment."

The response from Congress? The criminal contempt vote passed in a House of Representative vote of 255-67. Civil contempt passed by a vote of 258-95. On June 27, 2012, Holder became the first attorney general in U.S. history to be held in criminal and civil contempt of Congress.

The stalemated chess match between Congress and the Obama administration still continued. Who would blink first?

The Obama/Holder delay strategy was centered around the DOJ IG investigation. The DOJ IG would supposedly conduct a comprehensive, independent investigation of Wide Receiver and Fast and Furious and issue a report. This was the Obama administration's primary justification for stonewalling the congressional investigation. Congress, the Judiciary, and the Executive Branch are equal branches of government in one sense, but under our constitutional system of checks and balances, they each have their own duties and responsibilities. The Executive Branch controls the criminal process checked by the Judicial Branch and by the Legislative Branch. Congress has an oversight responsibility. There is no constitutional guidance on the situation where they both want to investigate the same matter and it falls within both branches' area of responsibilities. Fast and Furious was an operation that clearly fell within both branches' areas of responsibility. The DOJ refused to cooperate with Congress and wanted to control the investigation. The problem was that Fast and Furious implicated the highest levels of the Executive Branch in both criminal and civil issues. Congress started their investigation first, because ATF whistleblower claims were ignored and dismissed by Executive Branch officials in their chain of command who should have investigated. Then, when the whistleblowers came to Congress, Congress started their legitimate oversight investigation.

The Obama administration's delay strategy, designed to pre-empt Congress' investigation, hit a big hurdle with the DAG Cole confirmation debacle. The Obama administration embarrassed Congress, all because they trusted their equal branch counterparts. Strike one. The contempt vote settlement discussions were a good faith attempt by Congress to reach a compromise resolution. Once again, their counterparts at the DOJ rejected any reasonable negotiation and instead issued a demand in place of a discussion. Strike two.

Congress responded with an overwhelming contempt of Congress vote that included many Democratic votes. The DOJ thought they had the upper hand with their obstruct Congress strategy, so they now had no choice but to use a wait-for-the-DOJ-IG-report strategy.

Wrong! Congress instead issued Part I of their report on July 31, 2012.

Part I of the three-part report from Congress was titled "Fast and Furious: The Anatomy of a Failed Operation." The executive summary and preface set the tone of the congressional response to President Obama and Attorney General Holder:

"Soon, the U.S. House of Representatives will commence legal proceedings to enforce its prerogatives following the June 27, 2012, vote holding Attorney General Eric H. Holder, Jr. in criminal and civil contempt. […] Extensive evidence informs this review despite hurdles and stonewallings. […] The Justice Department has withheld tens of thousands of pages of documents, and denied access to numerous witnesses, including ATF Case Agent Hope

MacAllister, ATF Co-Case Agent Tonya English, and AUSA Emory Hurley — the central individuals running the case."

Congress interviewed seventy-four witnesses and reviewed the 7,000 pages of documents the DOJ produced. Congress said "of the small number of documents the Justice Department produced [...] a substantial portion were heavily redacted [...] and 1,200 pages [...] related to investigations other than Fast and Furious."

Even with these limitations on documents, the witness testimony by ATF agents, FFLs, and others provided enough evidence for Congress to reach important conclusions:

> The operation was conceived in the summer of 2009 by the Deputy Attorney General at the Department of Justice;

> ATF agents in Phoenix had no intention of interdicting these firearms even though they often received contemporaneous, or advance, notice of the illegal firearms purchases;

> The ATF would alert the FFLs in advance that straw purchasers were heading to their stores, and requested that the FFLs stock up on certain models of assault weapons;

> FFLs depended on the ATF's regulatory arm for their livelihood, so they agreed to make the sales; and

> The top officials at the ATF all had knowledge and culpability, but no one had been held accountable.

Parts II and III of their report would address the culpability of the DOJ and the entire Obama administration, including Attorney General Holder and President Obama.

It was very clear from Part I of the Congress report that many of the top Obama administration officials who did testify were not credible.

The House of Representatives did file a lawsuit against Attorney General Holder in the United States District Court for the District of Columbia on August 12, 2012.

The lawsuit filed by the General Counsel of the U.S. House of Representatives asked for the court to enforce their subpoenas and reject, or in the alternative, limit the scope of President Obama's assertion of executive privilege. The case was assigned to Judge Amy Berman Jackson, who was appointed by President Obama. On August 20, 2014, Judge Berman ruled on the Obama executive privilege claim. She ruled that the Obama administration "has not cited any authority that would justify this sort of blanket approach." She ordered the Obama administration to comply with normal judicial procedures when a party to the litigation claims any privilege. They must create a privilege log that lists each document and the specific basis for the claim of privilege. If the document contains facts, that part is not privileged. Only the parts of the document that are created prior to the decision and are deliberative, i.e. part of the decision-making thought process, are even potentially protected and these can still be required to be turned over based on the other side's showing of need for the disclosure. The burden is always on the owner of the document to first show that it falls within a legal privilege, in whole or in part. The required privilege log was never produced. However, Judicial Watch filed a Freedom of Information Act request for the same types of documents in June 2012, and followed up with their own lawsuit, *Judicial Watch v. Department of Justice* in September 2012. In that lawsuit, the court required the Obama administration to create a similar index of privilege documents that were withheld. The Vaughn index listing the documents withheld showed that President Obama and Attorney Holder claimed executive privilege over 15,662 documents, including emails that Holder sent to his wife and to his mother, neither of whom even worked for the United States government. Tom Fitton, President of Judicial Watch, said: "Few of the records seem to even implicate presidential decision-making. [...] Obama's executive privilege claims over these records are a fraud and an abuse of office." It took Tom Fitton's determined efforts over the course of sixteen months to get an index of documents so that Obama's fake assertion of executive privilege could be challenged in court.

Fitton said: "Finally we may get some accountability for Border Patrol Agent Brian Terry, and the countless others murdered as a result of the insanely reckless Obama administration program."

In March 2018, the Trump administration Department of Justice, under Attorney General Sessions, settled the Holder lawsuit brought by the U.S. House of Representatives. President Trump waived the executive privilege. Six months later, none of the documents have yet been produced. The settlement was apparently conditioned on the District Court vacating one or more decisions it made during the litigation regarding executive privilege. On October 23, 2018, Judge Amy Berman Jackson denied a joint DOJ and House of Representatives motion to vacate her prior orders. The bottom line is the American public, and the Terry family, may never see the documents, or know the complete truth.

After the House of Representatives contempt vote against Attorney General Holder, and after Congress released Part I of their Fast and Furious investigation report, the Department of Justice Inspector General, Michael Horowitz, finally released his report on September 19, 2012. Before the report was released, the DOJ IG sent multiple drafts to the very people he was investigating so they could comment on, and edit, the drafts. That does not sound like an independent investigation, especially when the people you are investigating are your bosses. The day before the report was released, Deputy Attorney General James Cole sent independent Inspector General Horowitz a nine-page letter:

"This letter conveys final comments of the United States Department of Justice (the Department) on the office of the

Inspector General's (OIG) report titled 'A Review of ATF's Operation Fast and Furious and Related Matters.' These 'final comments' were attached to the report as Appendix A." No one knows how many drafts and pre-final comments were exchanged, or what they said, before these "final comments" were incorporated in the "independent" DOJ IG report.

The American public and Congress were put on hold, and kept in the dark by Obama and Holder's stonewalling, from February 2011 until September 2012. They finally received a supposedly independent investigative report that the people being investigated reviewed and edited.

The title of the DOJ IG report tells you all you need to know, before you even read the first sentence of the report itself. The operation was the "ATF's" operation. Congress' reports said it was a DOJ operation, and the facts of both investigations clearly show it was a President Obama/Attorney General Holder operation.

The DOJ's final comments are a laughable charade. Their first comment is that Attorney General Holder "concurs" and "agrees" that Fast and Furious was "field-driven" [i.e. low-level Phoenix level operation] and had its genesis in operations and prosecutions dating back to 2006 [the Bush Administration]. Who could possibly take this report seriously? Equally important, who would have the audacity to promote this charade so late in the game when the cat was already out of the bag? Answer: Arrogant politicians who believed that they were bulletproof.

The Department of Justice Inspector General Report, issued September 20, 2012, described the ATF operations genesis as follows:

"On October 31, 2009, special agents working in the Phoenix office of the Bureau of Alcohol, Tobacco, Firearms, and Explosives (ATF) received information from a local gun store about the recent purchases of multiple AK-47-style rifles by four individuals. Agents began investigating the purchases, and soon came to believe that the individuals were so-called 'straw purchasers' involved in a large-scale gun trafficking organization responsible for buying guns for transport to violent Mexican drug-trafficking organizations. This investigation was later named 'Operation Fast and Furious.'"

This is absurd. The DOJ IG didn't even acknowledge that a program like this existed when two of the top known straw purchasers made their first multiple assault weapon purchases from Lone Wolf while being under ATF surveillance.

According to the DOJ IG, gunwalking started out of some kind of magic pixie dust on October 31, 2009. The ATF actually gave Andre the names of about twenty known straw purchasers who would potentially purchase firearms under Fast and Furious before October 31, 2009.

If the DOJ and the ATF did not plan to let guns walk, why didn't they arrest the straw purchasers on October 31, 2009? There is no ATF Report of Investigation saying "they got away," "we got the information too late," or that otherwise explains how Fast and Furious actually started.

The top Obama administration officials who refused to testify before the DOJ IG, or the congressional investigation, included:

Deputy Assistant Attorney General Barry Sabin; the ICE Agent assigned to Fast and Furious; Darrin Gil, former ATF Attaché to Mexico; AUSA Patrick Cunningham (the Criminal Chief in Phoenix); U.S. Attorney Dennis Burke; Kevin O'Reilly (White House National Security Staff); and Charles Highman, ATF Resident Agent in Charge (Tucson). The White House refused to produce any internal White House communications to the Department of Justice Inspector General or to Congress.

The DOJ IG had access to all the internal Department of Defense documents, but Congress did not. The DOJ IG only had the ability to compel testimony from current DOJ employees. Former DOJ employees could voluntarily testify or submit to an interview. Non-DOJ employees, like Andre, were not required to cooperate, but Andre did voluntarily cooperate and gave testimony under oath.

There are no legal checks or balances on what the DOJ IG puts in his reports, or how he characterizes the testimony of witnesses. In Andre's case, the DOJ IG totally misrepresented his testimony, and mischaracterized the role the DOJ and the ATF played in his cooperation. They did not release a transcript of what he actually said. Fortunately, Congress did accurately record, and report, the testimony he gave to them the week before he met with the DOJ IG investigators.

The DOJ IG did report many facts accurately. The problems with his report are: (1) They did not interview many people with relevant knowledge, like Holder, Obama, and many DOJ and ATF witnesses; (2) their findings and conclusions were grossly understated based on the real facts that they did report; (3) they totally whitewashed, or ignored, anything negative about top DOJ or other Obama administration officials; and (4) they held no one from the entire Obama administration accountable for anything. No one!

The DOJ IG investigative approach was flawed. They criticized the ATF for not using the time-honored investigative technique of pressuring low-level wrongdoers into providing evidence against the higher-level wrongdoers. The DOJ IG did the exact same thing for a different reason: They did not want to get any evidence about the wrongdoing of high-level DOJ, or Obama administration, officials.

They also ignored the fact that many high-level Obama officials blatantly lied under oath. If the witness didn't know, didn't recall, or gave what the DOJ IG said was "not credible testimony", "testimony contradicted by the other evidence", or "testimony contradicted by totally impartial, non-interested evidence", they concluded they could not make any findings because the evidence was simply "inconclusive." Part of every white-collar internal investigation is weighing inconsistent testimony and examining the totality of the objective available evidence to determine whether someone is clearly lying, or just not credible. Your job as an attorney in those investigations is to determine and report the facts. On some occasions, after a full investigation, you may have to report the facts, pros and cons, and give an opinion or advice. The DOJ IG called everything a "jump ball" regardless of how the actual evidence favored one side over the other. Eventually, every baseball umpire has to say "ball or strike." Every football referee has to say "catch or no catch", "penalty or no penalty." The DOJ IG took the position that if a DOJ witness said "X", and the overwhelming objective evidence said "Y", the evidence is "inconclusive."

This approach allowed the DOJ IG to make findings and conclusions that were seriously "flawed", to use their own term. Fast and Furious was "flawed. To use my words: "Gentlemen, you are just not credible."

Throughout the DOJ IG report they say government witnesses lied, were culpable, were negligent, or used poor judgment. The key question is where was their accountability? The DOJ IG's 471-page report was filled with hundreds of facts any prosecutor could have used to bring felony criminal charges against dozens of high-level Obama administration officials. The last paragraph on the last page of the report said:

"[W]e recommend that the Department [of Justice] review the conduct and performance of the Department personnel as described in this report and determine whether discipline, or other administrative action, with regard to each of them is appropriate."

Shockingly, there was no review, and there was no disciplinary or administrative action. Attorney General Holder got to decide whether there was any wrongdoing. That was most likely a three-minute deliberation, because nothing was ever done. Eric Holder wants to run for President in 2020. Let's take a closer look at his conduct in Fast and Furious before we vote!

Chapter Eight

Attorney General Holder — Perjury? Incompetence? Bad Memory? Or All of the Above?

I do not personally know Eric Holder. I have never met him. We are the same age and have both been involved with the criminal justice system for over forty years. Although our paths have never directly crossed, I have had many dozens of cases with the law firm and government agencies where he worked during his career. We have both been involved in the prosecution and defense functions. In my experience within the white-collar criminal bar, everyone has always been professional and collegial, even in the heat of adversarial representations, disagreements on legal issues, and despite political affiliations. Prior to March 22, 2011, my thirty-plus years of practice only involved one negative incident with an opposing counsel, and several years later that counsel apologized for his conduct. My lifelong career experience in the criminal justice system changed, and has continued to change, since March 11, 2011. As previously documented in earlier chapters, the meeting Andre and I had with the DOJ and the ATF that day had a significant impact on both of us. Neither of us had ever had an experience that caused us to distrust the honesty or integrity of senior high-level government officials. Like most Americans, we had lived our lives in a generation that trusted our President, their top political appointees, and the Department of Justice. The March 11 meeting was the first time senior DOJ officials had clearly, and irrefutably, lied to my face. It was an event that was beyond disappointing. They had been lying to Andre since September 2009. The question we had, and Congress had, was: "How far up in our government did these lies and deceit go?"

We already knew that the senior leadership at the ATF and the DOJ in Phoenix knew about, and were involved in, lying about Fast and Furious. AG Holder had asked the DOJ IG to conduct an investigation and had denied any knowledge about any guns crossing into Mexico or being recovered at the Brian Terry crime scene.

I wanted to give Holder the benefit of the doubt but the March 11 meeting, the January 27 letter from Senator Grassley (with documents), our conversations with ATF whistleblower Dodson, DOJ's February 4 letter to Congress, and growing evidence in the media gave us pause.

On April 15, 2009, four months after President Obama's inauguration, new Attorney General Eric Holder gave a speech at the grand opening of West Point's Center for the Rule of Law. He began by pointing out that:

> "West Point is perhaps the only institution of [a] higher level where undergraduate students are required to take a class in constitutional law."

Although I can't speak to the curriculum of all undergraduate institutions, West Point did require all students to take courses in the Department of Law. When I graduated from West Point I was honored to receive the award for graduating first in our class in Law. The American Bar Association presented me with the four volume book set "The Adams Papers". Those Papers, and the writings of Thomas Jefferson, provide a great historical perspective on our Founding Fathers' commitment to a democracy based on the rule of law.

In his West Point speech, Holder said:

> "That fact may seem unusual to some, but it is in keeping with the revered traditions of our military. From its earliest days, the rule of law has been its code of honor. [...] At the beginning of a new presidency

> [...] we must once again chart a course rooted in the rule of law and grounded in both the powers and the limitations it prescribes [...] as we usher in a new period of openness and transparency."

The rule of law is an essential keystone to our constitutional democracy. It should be a common centerpiece that governs the respectful relationships opposing criminal prosecutors and defense counsel have for each other. In law school, at the University of Virginia School of Law, I was privileged to study criminal law under Professor John Jeffries, who is widely recognized as one of the foremost legal scholars in the area of criminal law. He later served as the dean of the Law School from 2001 to 2008. I was also privileged to study constitutional law under Professor J. Harvey Wilkinson III, one of the foremost legal scholars in the area of constitutional law. He currently serves as the Chief Judge of the United States Court of Appeals for the Fourth Circuit. They both clerked for Supreme Court Justice Lewis Powell, and they shared an abiding respect and dedication to the rule of law.

In his April 2009 speech, AG Holder also recognized the U.S. Army Judge Advocate General's Corps for its dedication to the rule of law:

> "The JAG Corps had proven time and again that their commitment to duty [and the rule of law] never waivers."

During my years in the Army JAG Corps, the fidelity of the JAG Corps attorneys to the rule of law never wavered. Prosecutors and defense counsel represented their clients zealously, they aggressively opposed each other as advocates on issues, but always respected each other. In my first JAG assignment at the 3rd Armored Division in Germany, I served first as a chief prosecutor, then as a senior defense counsel, in what was then the most active criminal jurisdiction in the United States military. The prosecutors and defense counsel positions changed during our tour there, but no one ever lied to the other, no one lied to the court, no one hid evidence, and no one tarnished or ignored the rule of law. The military justice system required that both sides have equal access to all of the facts and all of the witnesses. The rule of law was honored. Forty years later, JAG attorneys who regularly opposed each other in court still have the upmost respect for each other and many are lifelong friends.

When I was the chief prosecutor in Germany, the first extremely high-profile case I had involved the alleged rape of a deaf/mute German young lady. The two accused soldiers raised an alibi defense through their counsel — they didn't know the victim and were somewhere else at the time of the crime. The evidence disproving their defense was overwhelming. The commanding general appropriately ordered a general court martial. They were certainly going to be convicted and probably receive life sentences. The week before the trial, they changed defense counsel. The day before the trial, he came to me and said, "They lied." They were with her the night of the alleged crime, but they didn't rape her. I could have gone to trial the next day and easily gotten a conviction, but their lawyer came to me and asked if I would delay the trial so he could persuade me they were innocent. I delayed the trial, and he was able to persuade me they may be innocent. I did some follow-up investigation with the assistance of ex-Scotland Yard experts. The physical evidence of the rape appeared to be fabricated. I convinced my Staff Judge Advocate Colonel William Eckhardt, who was also a Virginia Law graduate, that we should drop the charges. He advised the commanding general of our recommendation, and a potential injustice was avoided. There were international political repercussions that had to be dealt with, but justice and the rule of law were upheld.

During my thirty years practicing white-collar criminal law at Haynes and Boone, Republicans and Democrats seamlessly practiced together representing clients of every political, ethnic, religious, international, or sexual persuasion. We advocated based on facts and law but never crossed the line into dishonesty or deceit, even when a large client occasionally hinted we should. If a client's founding CEO committed fraud, we honestly reported it to the board of directors, government law enforcement, and outside auditors.

When the Attorney General of the United States and his senior officials in the Department of Justice are being investigated by committees of Congress, who are constitutionally charged with oversight responsibilities, the American public should be able to expect the same commitment to the rule of law, honesty, and justice that thousands of government and private practice attorneys have expected from each other for decades.

Unfortunately, that did not happen in Operation Fast and Furious. Starting in January 2011, Congress tried to get AG Holder and the DOJ to voluntarily cooperate in their oversight investigation. AG Holder and the alleged "transparency-driven" Obama administration steadfastly refused. Instead, they made false representations to Congress then they delayed compliance by deferring to the DOJ IG's ongoing independent criminal investigation. The DOJ IG eventually issued his report in September 2012, one-and-a-half years later. Before the report was issued, Congress moved forward with no cooperation from the Obama administration. In October 2011, they issued AG Holder a subpoena. There was no compliance. Congress repeatedly tried to negotiate, compromise, and make accommodations to get the Obama administration to be transparent to the American public. Nothing worked. Why?

When AG Holder started his deny-and-delay strategy in February 2011, the DOJ's only substantive response to Congress was the February 4, 2011, letter to Senator Grassley. At the end of February when Holder asked the independent DOJ IG to conduct an investigation, the DOJ IG was actually Acting DOJ Inspector General, Cynthia Schnedar. She worked at the Department of Justice for twenty-two years in various positions, starting in 1989, later becoming the Acting Inspector General on January 29, 2011, two days after the DOJ received Senator Grassley's letter. She was replaced on April 12, 2012, by Michael Horowitz, who was a white-collar attorney at the Washington, D.C., law firm Cadwalader, Wickersham & Taft LLP. Holder and Horowitz had previously worked at the DOJ and were colleagues in the Washington, D.C., white-collar bar association group. In today's terms, they were both part of the "swamp". For people like Andre and me in Texas and Arizona, any investigation by swamp attorneys of other swamp attorneys required a critical and skeptical review. Whenever the swamp insiders tell the rest of America to trust the great integrity and independence of other swamp insiders, red flags should be raised and their reports demand scrutiny.

The long-anticipated DOJ IG report was eventually released in September 2012, after AG Holder was held in civil and criminal contempt, and after Congress filed a civil lawsuit against him to obtain documents they needed, and deserved, to perform their oversight duties. The Obama administration was clearly not the most transparent presidency in history. It did not care about public disclosure. It did everything possible to thwart public access to information through the Freedom of Information Act. Its campaign promises, and the hollow words AG Holder spoke at West Point, betrayed the American public. AG Holder's alleged allegiance to the rule of law proved to be false.

The Department of Justice Inspector General's Report on Fast and Furious concluded that Attorney General Holder did not know about Operation Fast and Furious until sometime in February 2011. In order to reach that surprising conclusion, the DOJ IG made two equally surprising and incredible sub-conclusions.

First, they concluded that the Attorney General's most senior advisors, including his Deputy Attorney General, his Chief of Staff, the leadership of the criminal division, and the leadership of the ATF all "failed to alert the Attorney General to significant information about the flaws in Operation Wide Receiver and Operation Fast and Furious."

Second, they concluded, based on Holder's own testimony, that he never read any of the weekly reports the ATF, his personal staff, or the National Drug Intelligence Center sent him.

The DOJ IG also believed that the five different Deputy Assistant Attorney Generals, who signed fourteen different wiretap applications, never read any of the applications they signed and presented to federal judges for approval. All of the applications contained detailed information about the firearms being walked to the Mexican cartels. These five deputies, who reported to Attorney General Holder, were required by law to read and analyze these applications before telling the court that the application was legally correct and was necessary based on the facts of the particular case. They had to represent to the court that other attempts to investigate, which were less invasive to individual privacy rights, had all been tried and failed. If the applications were not true, Attorney General Holder was complicit in committing fraud upon the court. Are we to believe that Holder's top deputies were willing to neglect their own duties, which were required by law, and were willing to put the Attorney General at risk? If they did that, why didn't

Holder or Obama take any action against them after their misconduct was reported by both Congress and the DOJ IG?

Everyone can now take a reasonable, common-sense look at the undisputed evidence that was reported in Part II of the congressional investigative report titled "Fast and Furious: The Anatomy of a Failed Operation", released on October 29, 2012, and Part III of their report titled "Fast and Furious: Obstruction of Congress by the Department of Justice", released on June 7, 2017.

Congress found that shortly after he took office, Attorney General Eric H. Holder, Jr. delivered a series of speeches about combating violence along the southwest border. He focused specifically on fighting Mexico's Sinaloa Cartel, and in the fall of 2009, the Justice Department released a document crystallizing the Attorney General's vision titled 'Department of Justice Strategy for Combating the Mexican Cartels.'

We know that this strategy involved not arresting or prosecuting low-level straw purchasers, and instead was about getting intelligence about the cartel behind the purchases. So how do you take down a cartel in Mexico? If you don't arrest the straw purchaser when he buys the guns, what is going to happen to the guns? Obviously, the guns are going to be trafficked to the Mexican border. If you arrest the trafficker at the border, are they going to tell you where they were destined to go? No, because they were going to someone they probably didn't know in Mexico. If you have no tracking device in the gun, and have not coordinated with Mexican law enforcement to interdict, or at least follow the guns across the border, what information can you get? The only information you could get from Mexico is a crime scene report after the guns are used in a crime of violence in Mexico.

In April 2009, Attorney General Holder amended the mission of OCDETF to include firearms trafficking. This meant more money, and assets from multiple DOJ agencies could be dedicated to the Fast and Furious OCDETF Strike Forces. That same month, Lanny Breuer was confirmed as Assistant Attorney General (Criminal Division), a role in which he served as Holder's third highest in command. Holder and Breuer were partners together at the Washington, D.C., law firm Covington and Burling. Holder created the Southwest Firearms Trafficking Strategy Group. Holder made Breuer the head of the Group, which included members from the ATF and the FBI.

The mission of the SFTS group was to dismantle the Sinaloa Cartel. As group leader, Breuer was required to regularly report to the Attorney General about the group's progress in their new mission. Deputy Attorney General Ogden, Holder's number two within the DOJ, worked with Breuer, and they unveiled their new OCDETF arms trafficking initiative in Phoenix on September 22, 2009. That same month, they recruited Andre as their primary cooperating FFL. On October 26, 2009, Ogden, Breuer, Mueller, and Melson finalized the new strategy during a Washington. D.C., teleconference, and five days later, the first two batches of multiple illegal assault weapons were purchased at Lone Wolf by two known straw purchasers. Those guns were allowed to walk to Mexico.

Holder, Breuer, and Ogden all denied any knowledge of the program or how the new mission was going to be accomplished. Why don't we know what their real plan was if gunwalking wasn't the real plan? SA William Newell testified that senior leadership at the DOJ knew about the gunwalking strategy. It defies logic that the top officials at the DOJ would spend a huge amount of time, effort, and travel their first eight months in office after President Obama's inauguration creating this new organized structure for OCDETF, creating a multi-agency group headed by one of Holder's longtime colleagues and law firm partner, and defining a totally new firearms trafficking strategy with a totally new mission, yet they never presented documents to Congress about any details of how any of this was actually going to be implemented, and they never released any information about Breuer's required regular reports to the Attorney General.

Instead, Holder denied, then deflected, then blamed "rogue low-level officials at the ATF in Phoenix." Five days after the top leaders at the DOJ, the ATF, the FBI, and top border state prosecutors finalized their new strategy, gunwalking began. When the new Holder strategy was finalized, what guidance did the ATF in Phoenix and elsewhere on the border receive about executing the new strategy? Does it make any sense that five days after the leadership at the DOJ, the FBI and ATF headquarters finalized a national strategy, low-level ATF agents developed their own secret gunwalking operation? When the Bush administration enacted Project Gunrunner in 2006, every FFL was given information and training. Every FFL understood the mission, and their role in accomplishing the mission. When Operation Wide Receiver was conducted, there was full transparency with the government of Mexico and the FFLs who cooperated in the Operation.

Dozens of ATF agents were transferred to Phoenix, and millions of newly appropriated funds were given to the new Phoenix OCDETF Strike Force to support the new Phoenix ATF operation. Is it believable that this allocation of resources was made without any leadership within the DOJ in Washington, D.C., knowing about, or approving, these allocations? Once made, who in leadership tracked the use of this investment of resources?

It is noteworthy that a government program like Fast and Furious crossed over several budget cycles: the 2009 budget, the 2010 budget, and possibly carried over into the 2011 budget.

All government agencies have financial accounting and reporting requirements. Every government agency has to track and report on major projects. No one investigated this aspect of Fast and Furious from the angle of who knew what, when.

By the time Congress released Part II of their three-part report, on October 29, 2012, they had already held Holder in civil and criminal contempt of Congress and filed a civil lawsuit against him.

Congress had also heard testimony from ATF Director Melson that was quite shocking. Attorney General Holder obviously gave the order to silence Melson. He had his brand-new Deputy Attorney General do the dirty work and deliver the message, even though James Cole had only been on the job a short time. Holder did not even have the decency to discuss it with Melson. The first official Fast and Furious hearings were held by Congress the week of June 13, 2011. Congress had already conducted extensive interviews with ATF agents and issued a report on their testimony. They had already interviewed Andre Howard and reviewed his tape recordings of SA Hope MacAllister. When Congress contacted Melson through an intermediary (because Holder ordered him not to talk to Congress) on June 16, 2011, to see if he would testify, he responded:

> "I can't do that. They [Holder, Cole, and Breuer] would slaughter me."

Holder's method of operating was clearly emerging — he controlled everything going on in the DOJ during Fast and Furious and the follow-up investigation by Congress.

He controlled everything from behind the scenes. He kept most of his subordinates in lockstep. Some complied out of loyalty, some because of political biases or other reasons. He tried to control people outside of the DOJ through threats of retaliation. If threats failed, he aggressively attacked through various forms of illegal surveillance and actual retaliation.

When things blew up, he took cover, and those loyal to him, or who feared retaliation themselves, protected him. He tried to create a persona of aloofness. His story was always: "I'm so important and powerful. I only deal with the highest level of national issues." His excuse in Fast and Furious? "No one in the DOJ even thought it was important enough to inform me." The truly amazing part of this fabricated persona was he said all of his senior officials were right not to bother him with these trivial matters.

He never said: "I wish they had told me about thousands of guns provided to the cartels in Mexico; I wish they had told me about the murder of the children at a birthday party; or the murder of the Mexican beauty queen, or the other 300 murders in Mexico." He also never said: "I wish they had told me about the ATF whistleblowers; I wish they had told me about the January 27 letter to Congress and the February 4 false statement to Congress; or I wish they had told me about Border Agent Brian Terry's murder and the fact no one did anything for the Terry family." All of these were so unimportant and beneath him that he applauded his senior officials for not wasting his super valuable time. He operated right out of the playbook of his mentor, Barack Obama.

The truth is he knew all of the above, and micromanaged the DOJ from the shadow of plausible deniability. The problem is, it wasn't plausible.

In April 2009, Attorney General Holder met with Mexican President Calderon and other Mexican officials in Mexico. His briefing paper stated "weapons trafficking into Mexico has emerged as a central area of concern for both countries."

At the meeting, Holder and DHS Secretary Napolitano committed to form a working group led by the Criminal Division to reduce firearms trafficking.

Also in April 2009, during a joint press conference with Mexican President Calderon, President Barack Obama asked

Attorney General Holder to personally review firearms enforcement efforts.

In August 2009, AAG Breuer wrote a memorandum to Holder recommending "high-level talks with Mexican authorities about cross border-controlled deliveries of firearms." Attorney General Holder told the DOJ IG he "did not recall" any such discussions with Breuer.

On February 4, 2011, the day the DOJ and the ATF responded to Senator Grassley's January 27, 2011, letter denying any gunwalking, AAG Breuer was in Mexico meeting with Mexican law enforcement, where he suggested "allowing straw purchasers to cross into Mexico." The proposal was flatly rejected by the Mexican government. In March 2011, Attorney General Holder issued a Department policy to require interdiction of firearms in the United States.

There are two theories about the role of the Mexican government during Fast and Furious. Both are plausible. Both required lies, deceit, and a lack of transparency by the Obama administration. The Mexican government's official position was that it was "betrayed" by the Obama administration. They had no idea that the United States was allowing guns to be transported across the border to the drug cartels. On the surface, there is evidence to support this theory. After the truth about Operation Fast and Furious became public in 2011, the Mexican government hired an American law firm to bring a lawsuit against those responsible in the United States. They expressed outrage, even threatening to request extradition of the FFLs like Andre, to Mexico where they would be criminally prosecuted for war crimes. That certainly would be an expected and justified response from a neighboring government. Their outrage would especially be justified based on the fact that there were still over 1,000 assault weapons in their country that were unaccounted for. The Mexican government takes the transportation of firearms across the border into their country very seriously. In March 2014, an ex-United States Marine sergeant, who suffered from PTSD, accidentally got lost and mistakenly wound up at a border crossing in Tijuana, Mexico. He had three firearms that he legally owned in his car. He was immediately arrested and jailed in Tijuana's La Mesa Penitentiary, where he was held without bail. He never intended to leave the country. He had recently moved from Florida to San Diego. He was driving to a small town on the U.S. side of the border to have dinner with friends. He missed an exit and could not turn around before arriving at the border. At the border, he told Mexican authorities he had the guns and asked if he could turn around. They said no. He called 911. The operator said they could not help him because he was already on foreign soil. His plight was highlighted on national news. Over 100,000 Americans signed petitions to the Obama White House urging the President to intercede with the Mexican government. United States politicians and veterans' groups demanded his release. The movement grew after reports about his physical abuse in prison came to light. My law firm had a large office in Mexico City with attorneys from some of the most powerful families in Mexico. I asked them to help. There was nothing anyone could do. He spent eight months in a Mexican prison.

When you examine the facts about Fast and Furious more closely, some aspects about the Mexican-government-was-kept-in-the-dark theory don't really seem to make sense. The second plausible theory is that the Mexican government did know about Operation Fast and Furious. If that theory is true, it was the Mexican citizens who were betrayed by both the Obama administration and their own Calderon administration.

The first troubling fact is that, during the eight-month period that the top Obama administration officials were meeting to develop their new firearm-trafficking strategy,

AG Holder, AAG Breuer, and President Obama all met with top Mexican government officials and discussed firearm trafficking. Second, during Fast and Furious, Mexican law enforcement authorities cooperated in submitting data for crime scene firearm traces of recovered Fast and Furious firearms. Before Fast and Furious ATF officials frequently complained that access to recovered weapons and trace data in Mexico was difficult. Third, ATF Attaché Darren Gil and his Deputy Attaché assigned to Mexico City were purposely kept in the dark about the operation and thus could not share any information about it with their lower level Mexican counterparts. After Fast and Furious, the protestations of the high-level Mexican political leaders seemed like they were obligatory and political. The Mexican government never followed up, and never took any known action. They never sought reparations or apologies. Finally, the Obama administration never officially responded to the government of Mexico, or apologized to the citizens who lost family members at the hands of cartel members using Fast and Furious weapons. President Obama did a staged interview with Univision during which he denied that he and AG Holder had anything to do with the Operation. The interview, conducted at the end of March 2011, was the first time President Obama publicly addressed Fast and Furious.

> "Well, first of all, I did not authorize it. Eric Holder, the Attorney General, did not authorize it."

The reporter asked:

"You were not even informed about it?"

President Obama responded:

> "Absolutely not. There may be a situation here which, if that is the case, we'll find out and will hold somebody accountable."

ATF Agent Gil questioned Lanny Breuer and several of his deputies about Fast and Furious when they visited Mexico in the summer of 2010. He also questioned ATF Director

Melson when he visited Mexico City in 2010. They both said: "It was a big trafficking case [...] getting good results. [...] It's a good case, still going on. [...] We'll close it down as soon as we possibly can."

ATF Agent Gil was appalled that guns were being walked. He had to figure it out himself based on the number of gun traces, and then he was ordered not to talk about it or notify his Mexican counterparts. Of course, it was not closed down until after Agent Terry's murder in December 2010. In January 2010, Agent Gil sent an email to his staff that "no firearms would be allowed to cross into Mexico [...] without his approval" and approval would only be given "on a case-by-case basis when the weapons could be stopped on the Mexican side of the border." He was betrayed by the Obama administration. He retired in December 2010 amidst "threats of some Mexican politicians to prosecute ATF agents in Mexico [...] for acts of war."

Those threats did not materialize. Perhaps because the government of Mexico was complicit?

In all of this high-level international controversy, where was Secretary of State Clinton? On a least two occasions Congress requested documents and answers. They got neither.

On August 20, 2009, the DOJ did hold a press conference about some Sinaloa Cartel indictments, and on October 22, 2009, a press conference about some arrests about Project Coronado, which targeted the La Familia cartel, but neither had anything to do with Fast and Furious.

As previously discussed, Attorney General Holder was responsible for the false letter to Senator Grassley sent on February 4, 2011, and the false affirmation of that letter sent to Congress on May 2, 2011.

By May 2, 2011, there had been extensive coverage of Fast and Furious. AG Holder asked the Acting DOJ Inspector General to conduct an investigation at the end of February

2011. He ordered his senior DOJ officials to not wait for the DOJ IG investigative report, but to be proactive to get "out in front" of both the congressional and DOJ IG investigations. "Getting out in front" of a known, or anticipated investigation, is a term of art used by experienced white-collar defense counsel. When used by ethical members of the white-collar defense bar, it means gathering and reviewing the relevant documents before the government investigators. The first step is always to preserve all documents so there can be no destruction or tampering of evidence. Every corporation under investigation will have some problem documents that may or may not really be a problem. Often the creator of the document used vague or ambiguous language that can easily be explained. Sometimes it is a document that does implicate wrongdoing. Either way, the defense counsel usually wants to know about it, get the facts nailed down, and take the issue to the government before they raise the issue. The defense counsel wants the witnesses to be well prepared to testify truthfully. The documents are usually essential to refresh memories, and prevent a witness from making inadvertent misrepresentations under oath.

As in any practice, there are attorneys who are less than ethical, who view "getting out in front" as hiding bad documents and using documents to influence or "fabricate testimony, or undertake a strategy of amnesia.

On March 10, 2011, James Grimaldi of the *Washington Post* wrote an article titled "ATF Accused of Allowing U.S. Firearms to Flow into Mexico":

> "Agent Dodson and other sources say the gunwalking strategy was approved all the way up to the Justice Department. The idea was to see where the guns ended up, build a big case, and take down a cartel. And it was all kept secret from Mexico. [...] Documents show the

inevitable result: The guns that [the] ATF let go began showing up at crime scenes in Mexico."

In March 2011, Sharyl Atkinson did a series of investigative reports about Fast and Furious that aired on CBS News. She interviewed ATF Agent Dodson and Agent Darren Gil, who was the lead ATF official in Mexico, about Fast and Furious. In a March 25, 2011, posting titled "ATF Gunwalking: Who Knew and How High Up?", she reported that Gil confirmed the DOJ was aware of Fast and Furious.

> "Is the Director [of ATF] aware of this?" Gil asked his superior when he learned about Fast and Furious in the spring of 2010. His superior in Washington, D.C., at ATF headquarters "told him point-blank the Operation was approved higher than ATF Director Melson" at the DOJ.

The evidence developed during the DOJ IG investigation strongly indicated that ATF headquarters and Holder's most senior officials within the Attorney General's office knew about the gunwalking in Fast and Furious. They were all extensively prepared for their testimony by the internal DOJ attorneys who had access to all the key documents needed to refresh their memories, or to collaborate on an amnesia defense. When the witnesses testified that they did not recall documents or briefings, or did not read important documents like wiretap applications, and memos about an exit strategy for Fast and Furious, the DOJ IG did not push back. He simply concluded they had no knowledge about the facts.

Attorney General Holder testified under oath before Congress on May 3 and May 4. Representative Issa asked the Attorney General, who was under oath: "When did you first know about the program, officially, I believe, known as Fast and Furious? Best of your knowledge, what date?"

The Attorney General responded: "I'm not sure of the exact date, but I probably heard about Fast and Furious for the first time over the last few weeks."

I watched that testimony live on C-SPAN. I was shocked that the United States Attorney General, who undoubtedly was prepared by his staff for his appearance before Congress, would blatantly lie. At the time, I did not know that the previous day the Department of Justice collectively lied to Congress in a letter saying no firearms were ever allowed to "walk" to Mexico; they were interdicted. Unbelievable!

The next day, May 4, 2011, Senator Grassley asked Attorney General Holder, who was testifying before the Senate Judiciary Committee, how guns were allowed to walk and ended up at the murder scene of Agent Terry. His response: "I frankly don't know." He did not disclose that he had dozens of DOJ/ATF officials involved in a comprehensive internal "get out in front of it" investigation for over two months. Is it believable that no one who prepared the Attorney General for his congressional testimony ever reported on the status, or findings, of their internal investigation?

On May 26, 2011, Congress followed up on Attorney General Holder's sworn testimony with a list of specific questions for the record. Assistant Attorney General Ronald Weich provided answers to sixteen of those questions on July 22, 2011. The answers to those sixteen questions were concerned with the recovery of guns in connection with violent crimes and accountability of DOJ and ATF leaders. The responses were incomplete, misleading, and false.

The DOJ denied that the ATF was aware of the majority of Fast and Furious purchases at the time they actually occurred. They refused to answer thirteen questions because there was an ongoing DOJ IG investigation and/or the "question seeks information regarding sensitive law enforcement operations."

AG Holder's professed "ignorance" at the hearings. His total lack of candor, that began on February 4, 2010, prompted calls for his resignation from a Bellevue-based gun rights group, the National Rifle Association, for which Wayne LaPierre is executive vice president, and the Citizens Committee for the Right to Keep and Bear Arms. The chairman of CCRKBA said:

> "Holder is either monumentally stupid, or he is telling a monumental lie."

Representative Issa stressed that Congress was not investigating crimes by gunrunners, but at the cover-up of an operations gone bad:

> "We're not looking at straw buyers, Mr. Attorney General. We're looking at you."

Senator Grassley added:

> "[I am] extremely disappointed [in the Justice Department]. [...] Congress should not allow its fact-finding efforts to be stonewalled just because the details might be embarrassing to certain officials in the Department."

Representative Issa asked:

> "The president said on March 22 that you didn't authorize it. Did your deputy attorney general, James Cole, authorize it?"

Holder answered:

> "I don't think he was in the department at the time."

Representative Issa asked:

> "How about the head of the criminal division, Lanny Breuer?"

Holder responded:

> "I'm not sure."

AG Holder's next false statements to Congress occurred when Attorney General Holder testified during a June 7, 2011, House Judiciary Committee hearing. Investigative reporter Matthew Boyle wrote a September 19, 2012, article titled "Quayle on Fast and Furious Report: Holder 'Lied to My Face' During House Testimony."

During his testimony, AG Holder said that after he learned about Fast and Furious, he personally reviewed all of the wiretap applications and summaries from Fast and Furious. He testified that there were no references to gunwalking, and nothing that would have "raised the concerns of senior Justice Department officials who signed and approved the wiretap."

Arizona Representative Ben Quayle called the testimony "a blatant lie" after he read the DOJ IG report that clearly reached a far different conclusion: "the affidavits [...] included information that would have caused a prosecutor [...] to have questions about ATF's conduct" relating to "the issue of 'gunwalking.'" DOJ spokeswoman Tracy Schmaler would not "comment about the Inspector General contradicting Holder's testimony before the House Judiciary Committee." One of AG Holder's key deputies, Jason Weinstein, who was involved in the approval of the wiretap application, resigned the day the DOJ IG report was released.

In its October 29, 2012, report, Congress found that "had the [DOJ] criminal division officials [...] read the initial wiretap applications in Fast and Furious, they would have discovered in the spring of 2010 that gunwalking was occurring during Fast and Furious." [This] "represents a major failure of criminal division leadership." Did AG Holder read the same wiretap applications that the DOJ IG and Congress read?

The Attorney General and Deputy Attorney General received [eleven] weekly reports in 2010 from the ATF, the DOJ Criminal Division, and the National Drug Intelligence Center that referred to Operation Fast and Furious by name.

An example of one report said: "From July 6 through July 9 2010, NDIC supported the Phoenix OCDETF Strike Force investigation of Manuel Celis-Acosta as part of Operation Fast and Furious.

"Celis-Acosta and [twenty-five] straw purchasers are responsible for the purchase of 1,500 firearms that were then supplied to Mexican drug-trafficking cartels. They also have direct ties to the Sinaloa Cartel, which is suspected of providing $1 million for the purchase of firearms in the greater Phoenix area."

Both claimed they never read any of the reports.

On February 9, 2011, Senator Grassley sent Attorney General Holder a letter challenging the DOJ February 4 letter they sent, denying gunwalking, and he enclosed an email he received from the Terry family saying they had no contact from anyone in the government since Agent Terry's murder. He closed his letter with: "The Terry family deserves answers."

On March 10, 2011, U.S. Attorney Burke finally met finally with the Terry family. He told them "that the weapons found at Agent Terry's crime scene were sold out of a Texas shop, not an Arizona shop." Once Congress and the DOJ IG started questioning top DOJ and ATF officials about Fast and Furious, Holder's "amnesia virus" travelled through DOJ faster than the Asian flu on a crowded bus.

Holder's amnesia strategy was also used by the senior DOJ officials when questioned about the murder of Border Agent Terry.

Attorney General Holder and Deputy Attorney General Grindler received notification of Agent Terry's murder at approximately 10:00 a.m. on December 15, 2010, the morning after the murder.

At 11:00 a.m. that morning, Holder emailed Grindler, Wilkerson, and three other staff members to ask for more details about the shooting.

Wilkerson learned the evening of December 15 that the guns found at the crime scene were from a "gun store in Phoenix" that was part of ATF Operation Fast and Furious. "That day, Wilkerson forwarded three emails from U.S.

Attorney Burke to Holder with more details. Melson found out about the connection at 4:00 a.m. on December 16."

Senior Counsel to the Deputy Attorney General Brad Smith received detailed information about Avila, the purchases, and two detailed briefing papers from the ATF. The briefing papers were written on December 3 and supplemented December 16. Smith received the detailed papers about Fast and Furious on December 16, and forwarded all the information to Deputy Attorney General Grindler and three members of his staff on December 17. "Holder told the DOJ IG that he did not recall receiving any more information other than the basic fact of the shooting. Attorney General Holder told the OIG that he did not learn of the link between the firearms recovered at the scene [...] until February 2011, after he received Senator Grassley's January 27, 2011, letter."

The OIG found "no evidence that Holder or Grindler asked specific questions about the circumstances surrounding Agent Terry's murder until February 10, 2011"after Holder received a third letter from Senator Grassley on February 9, 2011, reiterating requests sent on January 27. Kevin Ohlson, Holder's chief of staff, did not recall being told about details of the murder, but said that "the Attorney General should have been informed [...] because it was significant."

On May 2, 2011, after extensive preparation, AG Eric Holder testified under oath before Congress. He testified that he first heard of Operation Fast and Furious "a few weeks before the hearing."

In November 2011, AG Holder, after being confronted with evidence that belied this testimony, finally conceded that he "probably should have said a few months." Of course Holder never explained why he waited six months to correct his May 2 testimony. That is especially strange since Holder was prepared by his staff for testimony in June 2011 and they identified the need to correct his May 3 testimony.

Maybe he waited until November to make the correction because the best excuse his staff could come up with to explain his obvious "misstatement" was to say "time flies".

On January 27, 2012, the DOJ produced 486 new documents to Congress that clearly indicated that AG Holder was told about the murder of Border Agent Terry on December 15, 2010.

On January 31, 2012, Representative Lamar Smith, Chairman of the House of Representatives Committee on the Judiciary, sent a letter to the Attorney General Holder about the DOJ and AG Holder's "disturbing pattern" of obstruction in the Fast and Furious investigation:

> "Far from being forthright, the Department has been slow to produce responsive documents and has continuously conceded only what Congress has already been able to prove."

The newly produced DOJ documents showed, among other things, that AG Holder knew the February 4, 2011, letter to Congress was false.

Even after Melson's damaging July 4, 2011, testimony, Holder stood by his two denial letters and his obviously false testimony to Representative Issa on May 3, 2011.

The Attorney General continued to repeatedly ignore legitimate requests for information from Congress, refused to provide witnesses subpoenaed to testify, and generally obstructed Congress from carrying out its lawful government oversight responsibilities.

On October 4, 2011, Representative Lamar Smith, Chairman of the Committee on the Judiciary, wrote a letter to President Obama urging him to instruct the Department of Justice to appoint a special counsel to investigate Holder's potential perjury.

Chairman Smith pointed out that documents provided to his committee "raise significant questions about the truthfulness of the Attorney General's testimony."

Weekly updates from the National Drug Intelligence Center briefed the Attorney General on Fast and Furious with specific details about guns being trafficked to Mexico as early as July 5, 2010. In addition, Lanny Breuer sent a detailed memo to the Attorney General on October 18, 2010, which described Fast and Furious.

Smith concluded by urging President Obama to appoint an independent special counsel to investigate the "extremely troubling" allegations that "senior Justice Department may have intentionally misled [...] Congress."

Although Attorney General Eric Holder would produce no meaningful documents in response to multiple congressional requests and subpoenas "because of the DOJ IG investigation" and refused to produce DOJ witnesses for testimony, Representative Lamar Smith's call for the appointment of a special counsel to investigate Holder's May 2011 suspected perjury did not elicit any response from the Attorney General, or from President Obama.

On October 7, 2011, Attorney General Holder wrote a letter to Congress to address issues about Fast and Furious that he considered "so base and so harmful."

In his five-page, self-serving letter, Holder totally ignored the facts which were already publicly available. He starts by characterizing Congress' rebuke of putting assault weapons in the hands of dangerous drug cartels that resulted in the foreseeable murder of Mexican citizens and U.S. Border Agent Brian Terry as "irresponsible and inflammatory rhetoric [that] must be repudiated in the strongest possible terms."

He then starts his indignant defense of the DOJ and the ATF by incredulously arguing that "protecting American citizens from the devastating effects of gun violence is among the most important responsibilities of the Department of Justice." Really? Wasn't Border Agent Brian Terry an American citizen? What did you do for his family besides lie to them and call them derogatory names because they wanted to know the truth about Brian's murder? The DOJ lied repeatedly.

His next sentence is particularly appalling: "Likewise, ensuring that weapons sold here do not flow south to Mexico is of paramount importance." Really? Why did you allow 2,000 firearms to go to Mexico over a fifteen-month period? Why didn't it stop until ATF agents had no recourse within the DOJ to stop it other than become whistleblowers to Congress? By the way, what did you personally do to stop retaliation against the whistleblowers, the media that truthfully reported DOJ misconduct, the Arizona sheriffs who did nothing wrong in calling for your resignation, and Andre Howard, who the DOJ lied to and then tried to ruin through false leaks to the media and other retaliatory conduct? Oh, that's right. You ordered retaliations against anyone who spoke negatively about you or the Obama administration.

Holder then goes on to say that the DOJ's "desire to bring cartel leaders to justice does not and cannot justify losing track of dangerous weapons." The DOJ did not "lose track of them." There was no accident, mistake, or lack of ability to interdict all of the 2,000 weapons that you and the Obama administration intentionally put into the hands of the Sinaloa Cartel. How do you explain the fact that the two key officers in the Sinaloa Cartel, who were the targets of Fast and Furious, were actually paid FBI informants? Is it the same explanation as why another FBI undercover agent was going to allow ISIS terrorists to kill innocent Americans with Fast and Furious weapons in Garland, Texas?

The third prong of Holder's repudiation tirade was that the Fast and Furious tactics "were actually employed in an investigation conducted during the prior [Republican] administration." Oops, another lie! Project Gunrunner was an attempted controlled delivery program where the guns failed to be tracked due to tracking equipment problems, and the plan coordinated with Mexican law enforcement didn't work. That project was stopped when the ATF realized these deficiencies. At the time of Holder's letter, the DOJ official position with congressional investigators was "no guns were allowed to walk, [the] ATF made best efforts to interdict all weapons, no Fast and Furious weapons were traced to the Brian Terry murder scene, and no FFLs were told, or even encouraged, to sell assault weapons to known straw purchasers."

The final three arguments in the letter are so lame they fit in the my-dog-ate-my-homework category.

(a) The U.S. Attorney in Phoenix said he didn't know about the tactics (complete lie);

(b) Congress was only interested in Project Gunrunner (Fast and Furious was actually part of Project Gunrunner); and

(c) It all happened because "Congress [is] opposed to fixing loopholes in our laws that facilitate the staggering flow of guns each year across our border to the south" and "the lack of reporting requirements for multiple long gun purchases in a short period of time hindered law enforcement efforts to combat gun trafficking." You could watch the actual sales that your employees directed to be made to known straw purchasers on your personal laptop in real time!

On December 16, 2011, following the one-year anniversary of Border Agent Brian Terry's murder, Matthew Boyle, investigative reporter for the *Daily Caller*, wrote an article titled "Terry Family Wants Criminal Charges Against Officials Responsible for Fast and Furious." In the article, he cites statements from the family and an interview he conducted with the family's attorney, Pat McGroder.

"Terry's family wants Obama administration officials held accountable with criminal charges. The family said in a statement: 'Our priority continues to be the successful arrest and prosecution of all individuals involved in Brian's murder. [...] However, we will continue to press for answers and accountability from our government. [...] We now believe that if it can be shown that laws were broken, then all those responsible for Fast and Furious should be held criminally liable.

"At least 300 people in Mexico were killed with Fast and Furious weapons.

"McGroder added that another track the family is considering is civil litigation [...] under the umbrella of the Federal Tort Claims Act."

One individual, an illegal immigrant, was charged with Terry's murder, but his name was not released and the case file was sealed. When Holder was asked to release the name of the illegal immigrant who was charged with Terry's murder, he said he would not.

When Iowa Republican Representative Steve King asked Holder if he would release the name of the individual charged [...] to House Judiciary Committee members in executive session, which would have been a private conversation between certain committee members and Holder, Holder still refused.

The Terry family requested victim's status in the twenty straw purchaser trials. Holder and the DOJ opposed their motion, and they were denied victim's rights in those prosecutions. The Terry family issued a statement:

"The family [...] doesn't believe justice has been done. The government initially provided the family with inaccurate and misleading information. That was followed by the testimony of numerous ATF whistleblowers who came forward and expressed their disgust at the Fast and Furious Operation."

On April 16, 2010, Attorney General Holder gave a speech at the National Crime Victims' Rights Week National

Observance and Candlelight Ceremony, in Washington, D.C., where he hypocritically said:

"[This is an] important opportunity for us to come together in support of victims. [...] I understand how these crimes [of violence] can devastate lives, families, and communities. I [...] will do everything to help victims overcome its effects."

Well, Andre was a victim. He got official notice from DOJ Victim Assistance that he was put into the Victim Assistance Program. He got retaliation when he refused to obstruct the congressional investigation. The Terry family were certainly victims, but instead, AG Holder considered them a nuisance, so he denied them victim status. Finally, the families of over 300 murdered Mexican were clearly victims, but they never received any victim assistance.

A year after Brian Terry's murder, the government still would not provide the Terry family the information surrounding the circumstances around Fast and Furious: "how the two guns were found at the murder scene, whether these guns were involved, and the results of the ballistics reports."

Many reliable sources within the ATF and the DOJ have anonymously said that AG Holder may have ordered the FBI not to do a full ballistics report of the evidence retrieved from the Agent Terry crime scene.

On February 2, 2012, the Terry family filed a $25,000,000 wrongful death claim against the ATF regarding the death of their son.

Terry's mother emotionally explained: "I just can't believe our own government came out with a program like this that [let] innocent people get killed."

"Attorney General 'My People' Holder, whose Department of Justice oversees the ATF, has claimed for over a year that he knew nothing about the logic-defying, deadly, and secretive program known as Fast and Furious. President

Obama had shielded Holder from charges of perjury, obstruction, and conspiracy. Obama stated that he has 'complete confidence' in his Attorney General."

The government had six months to respond to the Terry family claim before the Terry family could file their civil lawsuit for $25,000,000. On February 1, 2012, the Terry family also filed a separate lawsuit against Andre Howard.

The Terry claim stated that U.S. Attorney Dennis Burke, who resigned due to leaks and lies related to the Fast and Furious investigation, met with the family in March 2011 and told them that the "guns at the scene were from a store in Texas and that the fatal bullet would never be found."

Holder knew for a fact on December 15, 2010, that the guns from the crime scene were positively traced to Avila's purchases in January 2010 from Lone Wolf during Fast and Furious. He also knew that the bullet was recovered during the autopsy and that either no ballistic tests were done, or that they were inconclusive.

On June 7, 2012, Attorney General Holder testified before the House Judiciary Committee that "former Attorney General Mukasey [in President Bush's administration] was briefed on the transmission of guns to Mexico and 'did far less than what I did.'"

Five days later, on June 12, 2012, Attorney General Holder testified before the Senate Judiciary Committee stating, "An Attorney General, who I suppose you would hold in higher regard, was briefed on these kind of tactics in an operation called Wide Receiver and did nothing to stop them — nothing. 300 guns, at least, walked in that instance."

Following his June 12, 2012, testimony, Senator Grassley sent a letter to Holder challenging the Department to produce evidence that Attorney General Mukasey was briefed on Wide Receiver.

In response to this challenge by Congress, the Department [of Justice] indicated that Holder's statement was "inadvertent."

Several days later, Senator Cornyn called for Attorney General Holder's resignation. Senator Grassley called for AAG Lanny Breuer's resignation for lying to Congress and authorizing, or at least allowing, gunwalking.

Holder later testified to the DOJ IG that his congressional testimony was meant to relate to to a briefing Attorney General Mukasey received on November 16, 2007, eight days after he was sworn in as Attorney General. The briefing was not about Wide Receiver, which had already been completed and officially ended early December 2007. It was about a past controlled delivery attempted jointly with the government of Mexico. The DOJ IG concluded that the November 16, 2007, briefing of Attorney General Mukasey did not in any way put the Attorney General "or others in his office on notice of gunwalking."

Eric Holder's string of lie after lie continued. Two more lies under oath to Congress with one cover-up lie to the DOJ IG added on.

On June 18, 2012, the Terry family filed an amended complaint in the separate lawsuit against Andre Howard and Lone Wolf Trading Company, eliminating the count alleging aiding and abetting tortious conduct. They still pursued a negligence claim for the primary purpose of trying to get some compensation from Andre's insurance carriers.

On December 14, 2012, one day before the second anniversary of Agent Terry's murder, the Terry family filed a civil wrongful death lawsuit against federal officials claiming defendants "should have known [Fast and Furious] created a risk to law enforcement authorities." The lawsuit named seven federal officials as defendants: Bill Newell, George Gillett, David Voth, Hope MacAllister, Tonya English, William McMahon, and Emory Hurley. The family also alleged that defendants engaged in a cover-up to conceal material facts linking Agent Terry's murder to firearms from Fast and Furious.

The lawsuit was consolidated with the prior lawsuit against Lone Wolf Trading Company. Andre was represented by Bradley Jardine of Jardine, Baker, Hickman & Houston, PLLC in Phoenix. I did not represent Andre in the civil lawsuit because I was a potential witness against the federal official defendants regarding the cover-up allegation, and I was also a witness in the defense case for Andre.

At the time of the lawsuit, one person involved in the Terry murder pled guilty to first-degree murder, two others were in custody, and three others remained fugitives.

Ironically, on the second anniversary of Agent Terry's death, Attorney General Holder gave a speech in Tulsa, Oklahoma, saying, "Americans need to ask 'hard questions' about constitutional rights, such as the right to keep and bear arms."

Representative Louis Gohmert, from Texas, commented about Holder's speech on Fox News:
> "[C]oming from a man who's over a department that forced the sale of guns to people that would bring about the death of people like Brian Terry, there should be national outrage about Mexicans — our neighbors — 200 or more that have been killed by the guns that his department forcibly forced to be sold."

The ATF defendants in the Terry family lawsuit denied any wrongdoing. Newell and Gillett said Fast and Furious was sanctioned at high levels at ATF and Justice Department headquarters. Howard, the gun shop owner, told CBS News that he acted under the direction of ATF agents who convinced him to cooperate and complete gun sales to suspicious purchasers.

The lawsuit claimed that "more ATF agents could be liable, as well as other Justice Department attorneys, [...] but because of 'actions to cover up their wrongdoing and hide their misconduct' their names are not currently known, and could be added later."

CBS News "repeatedly [over a two-year period] requested directly, or through [the] ATF and the Justice Department, on-camera interviews with the defendants. [...] No interviews were granted."

On May 17, 2013, Andre and Lone Wolf filed an answer to the Terry family's lawsuit pointing out that "at all pertinent times they were acting pursuant to directives and instruction" from the federal official defendants and their agencies.

"[The] ATF solicited and encouraged Lone Wolf and went so far as to install video monitoring devises on the premises of Lone Wolf [...] for the purpose of monitoring these sales and monitoring both the weapons and/or the individuals who purchased the weapons."

Andre Howard and Lone Wolf also filed a cross-claim against the federal official defendants who:

- Contacted Andre in the second half of 2009 and specifically advised him that certain individuals would be coming to his store to purchase arms, and told him ATF wanted guns sold to those purchasers as part of an ongoing criminal investigation;
- Specifically requested and encouraged Andre to continue to make sales after he met with them, and voiced his concerns about the legality of these sales;
- Told Andre Howard that his cooperation was "important" to their "investigation of the firearms-trafficking conspiracy" and assured Andre that the "ATF was tracking the weapons and intercepting them before they could be used to harm innocent civilians or law enforcement officers; and
- Continued thereafter, until January 2011, to tell Andre to continue the sales and reassured him they were tracking all illegal sales to straw purchasers.

Andre wanted the federal government to reimburse him for his legal expenses and damage to his business. They refused.

On June 14, 2013, the DOJ and the ATF defendant attorneys, with the assistance and guidance of the Obama administration, filed a motion to dismiss the Terry lawsuit based on technical legal grounds. Their effort to dismiss was greatly assisted by Obama's assertion of fake executive privilege at Holder's request so that neither Congress, the Terry family plaintiffs, nor Andre Howard could get any meaningful discovery of key documents in their investigations or civil lawsuits.

On October 29, 2012, reporter Tim Brown posted an article on *Freedom Outpost* about Congress' second report "Fast and Furious: The Anatomy of a Failed Operation." The report put responsibility for the failed operation on six senior

DOJ officials: Assistant Attorney General Lanny Breuer, Acting Deputy Attorney General Gary Grindler, Deputy Assistant Attorney General Jason Weinstein, Associate Deputy Attorney General Ed Siskel, and Deputy Chief of Staff Robert "Monty" Wilkinson.

In their testimony, "did not recall" or "did not know" was a popular answer: Wilkinson, thirty-eight times; Grindler, twenty-nine times; and Siskel, twenty-one times. They were way behind Dennis Burke, U.S. Attorney in Phoenix, who claimed amnesia 161 times.

Senator Grassley observed:

"The Attorney General appears to be letting his employees slide by with little to   no accountability."

In January 2013, right after his inauguration for his second term, Obama and Holder took twenty-three actions ordered by Obama to tackle gun violence. This wide sweeping group of proposed regulations validated his first term's true motive in Fast and Furious — gun control.

In November 2013, a federal judge dismissed the DOJ and ATF defendants from the Terry lawsuit on the grounds that the Terry family had other ways to get relief through government employee benefits and grievance processes, which included death benefits for survivors of federal officers killed in the line of duty. The court did recognize in his decision that "any financial remedy is likely insufficient to redress their injury."

The Terry family said the judge "ruled strictly on a technicality" and did not consider "the basis of the claim that said that ATF [and the DOJ] had created a danger in their pursuit of this gun-trafficking operation. [...] This has never been about a financial amount, this is about gaining justice and holding those individuals accountable for their actions."

In June 2016, the 9th Circuit Court of Appeals upheld the lower court ruling, thus leaving Andre Howard as the one and only individual in the entire Fast and Furious Operation with any legal liability, financial burden (legal and business), and continued government harassment and retaliation.

During President Obama's re-election campaign in 2012 for a second term as president, Republican presidential running mate Paul Ryan joined other Republicans — including Mitt Romney — calling for Attorney General Holder's resignation.

"Holder should step down or President Obama should ask him to do so."

After Eric Holder resigned as Attorney General in September 2014, the Brian Terry Foundation released a statement on September 25, 2014, through contact Mike Scarbo. "The Family of Slain U.S. Border Agent Brian Terry Issues Statement on Resignation of Attorney General Eric Holder:"

> "Despite Holder's aggressive pursuit of the Mexican nationals directly involved in Brian's murder, the Attorney General has repeatedly failed to accept responsibility for the ill-fated gun-trafficking investigation, and has most regrettably failed to hold those DOJ and ATF officials responsible for the many mistakes made in the operation.
> "Despite repeated pleas by Brian Terry's family, Holder has chosen to not discipline those individuals found at fault by the DOJ's own Inspector General.

"Despite the clear and present danger that exists even today to law enforcement and the general public on both sides of the border, Holder has repeatedly refused to hold government officials responsible for the deadly mistakes made in Operation Fast and Furious.

"Holder's resignation is welcomed by the Terry family and should have occurred immediately after Brian Terry's death."

On June 7, 2017, Congress issued a press release about Part III of their investigative report. Key findings from the report were:

1. "[The] DOJ viewed the Terry family as a public relations nuisance and failed to provide the family with answers regarding Brian's murder.
2. According to the DOJ, "the Terry family is not a victim. [...] There are [no] documents to demonstrate the Attorney General coordinated assistance for the Terry family.
3. "The Justice Department's internal probe was largely a sham, and it prioritized politics and spin over public safety.
4. "[The] DOJ demonstrated a complete disregard for proper congressional oversight. [...] Senior Justice Department officials, including the Attorney General, [had] disdain for [Congress]" and "consistently deployed tactics to delay and withhold information from Congress."

Chapter Nine

What? Obama's in the Loop?

The government investigations into Fast and Furious by Congress and the DOJ started in January 2011. The last report from Congress was released in July 2017. That is six-and-a-half years that included six years during the Obama administration. The congressional investigators worked their way up the government chain of command. They started by focusing on the ATF in Phoenix because that was where the whistleblowers came from. The Obama administration immediately denied that there was any gunwalking. They tried to preempt any investigation by sending a flat denial to Congress coupled with an aggressive campaign to discredit the first couple of whistleblowers, and prevent any other witnesses from cooperating with Congress. Then they said it was a program dreamed up by some field agents at the ATF in Phoenix. Then they said it was just a repeat of a Bush administration operation. Then they said, "Let us investigate ourselves. While we do, we can't cooperate with Congress." Then they said, "We found the problem in our internal DOJ investigation and 'cleaned house' by reassigning Acting ATF Director Melson and letting U.S. Attorney Burke in Phoenix resign." They followed up in September 2012 with: "We were exonerated by the DOJ IG report."

The questions that mattered were always still on the table. Who knew what, when? Who would be held accountable for the operation everyone agreed was at least flawed, with more probably thinking it was criminal?

The Obama administration thought they would get away with "Burke and Melson were the ones who lost control of their subordinates and now we replaced them." Unfortunately for the Obama administration, they underestimated Congress. There were too many holes in the dike for Obama and Holder to fill. The Obama administration could obstruct and delay, but Congress pressed on.

During President Obama's first presidential campaign, he and his senior advisor, Eric Holder, repeatedly stressed the theme of transparency. If elected, they promised the Obama administration would be the "most transparent presidential administration in history."

The first real public test of their transparency ironically came in October 2009, the first month of Operation Fast and Furious, but it did not involve Fast and Furious because that operation was not yet public. The Obama administration had been sued in civil litigation in a case styled *Shubert v. Obama*. During discovery in that case, the Obama administration wanted to withhold certain documents under the state secrets privilege. Attorney General Holder gave a speech on October 30, 2009, titled "Assertion of State Secrets Privilege in Shubert v. Obama." "The Department [of Justice] invokes the privilege only to the extent it is absolutely necessary to protect national security."

He described the decision-making process, which included a process of high-level DOJ document review that included the most senior Department officials, the Deputy Attorney General, Assistant Attorney General Lanny Breuer, "as well as my own personal review." They all concluded there was no other alternative but to extend a limited privilege. He went on to defend their decision:

"We are not invoking this privilege to conceal government misconduct or avoid embarrassment, nor are we invoking it to preserve Executive [Branch] power.

"Making the government more transparent and accountable is one of this administration's top priorities, which is why my Department has issued reformed guidelines to govern

Freedom of Information Act practices, released previously undisclosed Office of Legal Counsel memoranda [...] allows for appropriate oversight by the Courts and Congress."

The Obama administration passed new guidelines for invocation of the state secret privilege in September 2009. The Shubert case was a class action lawsuit alleging U.S. citizens were the subject of illegal warrantless surveillance.

The irony of this speech cannot be overstated. First, it was delivered on the day before the first Fast and Furious multiple assault weapon purchases were made at Lone Wolf.

Second, unlike the Bush administration Operation Wide Receiver, where the cooperating FFL was told the entire truth about the operation, the Obama administration and the Holder DOJ totally lied to Andre Howard and the other FFLs about Fast and Furious, telling them all firearms were being interdicted and that none crossed the border.

Third, the speech goes to great lengths to highlight the hands-on involvement of senior DOJ officials, including AG Holder's personal involvement, in making a document discovery decision in a civil litigation lawsuit. In Fast and Furious, they were all "me no Alamo" during the longest secret operation, and largest document obstruction of discovery dispute, in modern government history.

Fourth, Holder touts his reforms to FOIA to streamline access (to Bush administration documents) when media and public interest groups like Judicial Watch had to file expensive lawsuits and fight in courts for years to get Obama administration documents under FOIA.

Fifth, Holder highlights the Obama administration respect for oversight by Congress, on the first day of an operation where his complete disdain for oversight by Congress will result in him being the only Attorney General in history to be held in civil and criminal contempt of Congress.

These points don't even include the three most importation issues: invocation of privilege, transparency, and accountability.

On March 15, 2010, Attorney General Holder gave another speech at the Department of Justice's open government event, during which he reflected on President Obama's inauguration day:

"They gathered to witness a new administration make a historic pledge — a commitment to restore the sacred bond of trust that should exist between our nation's government and its citizens. [...] The president delivered. With bold executive orders on his first full day in office, he solidified this administration's unprecedented commitment to transparency and accountability. President Obama called on the Justice Department to guide the release of information about how our government operates. And he directed our Department to take the lead on fulfilling the promise of the Freedom of Information Act."

He quotes the president:

> "I require that we apply a presumption of disclosure to all FOIA requests. Put   simply, I asked that we make openness the default, not the exception."

How open, transparent, and accountable were President Obama and Attorney General Holder to Congress and, more importantly, the family of Border Agent Brian Terry?

The first public statement President Obama made about Fast and Furious was on March 22, 2011, to Univision reporter Jorge Ramos. He said:

"Well, first of all, I did not authorize it. Eric Holder, the Attorney General, did not authorize it. He's been very clear that our policy is to catch gun runners and put them into jail."

The House Oversight Committee wondered about the President's statement, as Attorney General Holder testified under oath on May 3, 2011, that the first time he heard of Fast and Furious was in April 2011. Representatives Tray Gowdy and Jason Chaffetz wrote President Obama a letter on October 14, 2011, requesting information. They wanted to know how the President knew Holder did not authorize Fast and Furious before Holder even heard of it.

"To that end, if you knew the Attorney General did not authorize Fast and Furious, how did you learn that and when did you learn it? If you knew Attorney General Holder did not authorize it, inherent of that response is knowledge of who did authorize it. That information would be most helpful to the committee as we seek answers to this tragically ill-conceived and tragically ill-executed investigation."

The President's response? Crickets!

In November, Attorney General Holder finally corrected his testimony, which stood uncorrected for six months, saying he should have said he first heard of Fast and Furious "a few months ago." That would still mean he never heard of Fast and Furious until sometime in 2011. Congress found otherwise.

On the issue of how Fast and Furious started, some interesting evidence surfaced during the investigation. When the discussions about "a new firearm strategy" started in April 2009, Attorney General Holder's top senior official was Deputy Attorney General David Ogden, who President Obama nominated on January 5, 2009, and Congress confirmed on March 12, 2009.

DAG Ogden was the highest-ranking DOJ official at all of the OCDETF and other gun-enforcement policy meetings during 2009 leading up to and including the October 26, 2009, teleconference where he announced the new finalized firearm-trafficking strategy. Ogden resigned after serving less than a year.

In his statement announcing his resignation, he listed establishing a border working group to combat Mexican cartels as one of his main accomplishments during his short tenure in the administration. He finalized the new firearms strategy, then resigned thirty-eight days later.

On July 8, 2011, a C-SPAN video of Ogden from March 24, 2009, resurfaced. In the video Ogden says:

"The President has directed us to take action to fight these cartels, and Attorney General Holder and I are taking several new and aggressive steps as a part of the Administration's comprehensive plan. [...] [The] DOJ's using $10,000,000 in Recovery Act funds and redeploying 100 personnel to the southwest border [...] to fortify its Project Gunrunner, which is aimed at disrupting arms trafficking between the United States and Mexico. [...] [The] ATF is doubling its presence in Mexico itself [...] specifically to facilitate gun-tracing activity, which targets the illegal weapons and their sources in the United States."

There are several things to note about this video statement. First, he made it twelve days after he was confirmed by Congress. Clearly this was a very high Obama priority. Second, the Obama administration had already decided on a new aggressive policy, and had already decided to dedicate money and 100 personnel to the southwest border initiative. We know for sure the decision to add those resources was not to arrest and prosecute straw purchasers. Third, doubling personnel to facilitate crime scene traces had to mean they anticipated more crime scene traces of U.S. guns in Mexico. This program was definitely conceived before March 24, 2009. The next seven months were spent getting other DOJ and non-DOJ entities on board and ironing out the details.

There are a few more interesting, but less substantiated takeaways. First, Lanny Breuer, AAG (Criminal Division), reported directly to DAG Ogden. He was apparently earmarked to run the program because the Deputy Attorney General has a wider range of ultimate responsibilities. Breuer accompanied Ogden at all the key 2009 meetings and was appointed the head of the Southwest Border group. Second, it was never clear why Ogden resigned so soon after the operation started. At the time of the resignation, Ogden said he "always intended to step down once [the] DOJ was on the right path." Some reporters attributed his resignation to management differences within the Obama administration. However, at the time of the resignation, political correspondents did not know that 1,000 weapons had been walked to Mexico and over 100 had been recovered at crime scenes in Mexico. When the video was released, at least one reporter suggested he resigned because he did not want to be the "fall guy" when the misguided operation fell apart.

The last point about the re-release of this video on July 8, 2011, is that President Obama had a press conference that day. He was asked about the unfolding gunwalking scandal. His reply:

> "My attorney general has made clear that he certainly would not have ordered gun running to be able to pass through into Mexico. [...] I'm not going to comment on

[the] current investigation. [...] As soon as the investigation is completed, I think appropriate actions will be taken."

So, between the March 22, 2011, Univision interview and the July 2011 press conference, President Obama changed his statement. He said, "There may be a situation here which a serious mistake was made, and if that's the case, then we will find out and we will hold somebody accountable." The new statement sounds like an admission that there was gun-running, but Holder, when confronted, denied he ordered it. It also changed from "we will hold somebody accountable" to "I think appropriate actions will be taken."

President Obama also joined his wingman, Eric Holder, under the blanket cover of "we can't comment because there is an ongoing investigation."

July 8, 2011, was also a significant time because reporters, and others including Senator Grassley, started challenging Acting DOJ IG Schnedar's competence and ability to conduct a thorough, unbiased investigation, and generally challenged whether any DOJ IG had too many conflicts to conduct a fair investigation.

The next problem for the Obama administration was that, on July 26, 2011, SAC William Newell testified before Congress that he regularly reported the progress of Fast and Furious directly to the White House. His contact on the

White House staff was Kevin O'Reilly, who was the White House National Security Director for North America. It was the first time anyone had publicly stated that a White House official had any familiarity with Fast and Furious. That same day, a White House spokesman responded saying their email exchanges were not about Fast and Furious. They were about some other, unspecified, gun-trafficking efforts.

Unfortunately for the Obama administration, the most transparent in history, that press release, which they never officially retracted or corrected, was a lie. Congress got some of the emails, which were heavily redacted. The unredacted portions that started in July 2010 talked exclusively about Fast and Furious. Newell repeatedly referred to "the large OCDETF case they talked about", showed pictures of many weapons "headed for Sinaloa drug-trafficking cartel", talked about straw purchasers on financial assistance and food stamps who purchased many thousands of dollars of assault weapons, and projected possible indictments in October. Newell also told O'Reilly not to let ATF headquarters know about their communications and said things like "you didn't get this from me." O'Reilly did confirm that the information was shared with other senior White House staff, including Dan Restrepo, Special Assistant to the President and Senior Director for Western Hemisphere Affairs at the National Security Council, and Greg Gutjanis, Director for Terrorist Finance, Internal ATF and Counternarcotics. Newell also sent O'Reilly reports about the Fast and Furious statistics.

On September 9, 2011, Senator Grassley and Representative Issa sent a request for information to Thomas Donilon, Assistant to the President and National Security Advisor at the White House. They asked for documents relating to Fast and Furious, and requested an interview with Kevin O'Reilly. When the most open and transparent administration in history chose not to to respond to the oversight efforts of Congress, Congress sent another request on March 28, 2012. This request was sent to Kathryn Ruemmler, Counsel to the President:

"To date, the White House has not complied with multiple congressional requests to interview O'Reilly. [...] O'Reilly's personal lawyer has represented to the Committee that he would permit his client to speak with the Committee in the absence of any objections from the White House. [...] We strongly urge you to reverse your position."

The White House had O'Reilly transferred to Iraq. Congress offered to do a telephone interview. The White House refused to produce him for an interview and refused to produce requested documents. I thought the Obama default was disclosure. Transparently not!

The DOJ IG also requested documents from the White House in their investigation. The DOJ IG reported:

"The White House did not produce to us any internal White House communications, noting that 'the White House is beyond the purview of the Inspector General's office.' [...] We were unable to further investigate the communications between Newell and O'Reilly because O'Reilly declined our request for an interview."

The White House was not the only Obama administration entity that refused to produce documents. Secretary Clinton and the State Department refused to cooperate; FBI Director Mueller and the FBI refused to cooperate; and the DEA and ICE also refused to cooperate.

On June 19, 2012, Attorney General Holder met with Congress regarding their scheduled vote the next day on June 20, 2012, to recommend that the full House of Representatives hold the Attorney General in contempt of Congress for refusing to comply with his subpoena.

AG Holder wrote President Obama to request that he immediately assert executive privilege with respect to all Fast and Furious documents being withheld from Congress. Minutes before the vote, Obama granted Holder's emergency request and asserted blanket executive over all subpoenaed documents.

On June 25, 2012, Congress sent President Obama a lengthy letter objecting to this obviously overbroad assertion of executive privilege. He signed the executive order without even knowing what the documents were; who authorized, received, or used the documents; whether any of the documents were publicly available; or if the documents contained evidence of federal felony offenses by ATF, DOJ, or FBI officials.

Given the limited scope of executive privilege, which only covers communications between the president and his most senior advisors, which implicates confidentiality issues regarding the president's decision-making process, Congress was rightly critical of this purely political move by the Obama administration.

President Obama publically stated he had no knowledge about Fast and Furious, and that he played no role in the operation. He also publicly disavowed "any role in advising the Department of Justice with respect to the congressional investigation."

According to Congress, Obama's surprising assertion of executive privilege raised questions about his actual involvement in Fast and Furious:

"[Your] privilege assertion means one of two things. Either you or your most senior advisors were involved in managing Operation Fast and Furious and the fallout from it, including the false February 4, 2011, letter provided by the Attorney General to [Congress] [...] or you are asserting a presidential power that you know to be unjustified solely for the purpose of further obstructing a congressional investigation."

Congress asked President Obama to define the universe of documents the White House believed were covered by a legitimate assertion of executive privilege. The Obama administration refused to do so.

Congress tried to avoid a contempt hearing at the meeting with Attorney General Holder on July 19. During the eight months of the investigation, after Congress served the October 12, 2011, subpoena, the DOJ identified over 140,000 pages of documents in response to the subpoena but only produced 7,600 pages, most of which were documents that were already available from third parties, such as the ATF whistleblowers. Congress offered to suspend the contempt vote and receive documents on a rolling basis, with a small production of the most important documents necessary to answer the Terry family questions raised to Congress on June 15, 2011. Who were the people who put guns in the hands of the men who killed Agent Terry, their son and brother, and why? One year after the Terry family plea to Congress, and eighteen months after the murder of their loved one, President Obama and Attorney General Holder not only refused to answer their questions, they treated the family with the utmost disdain and heartless contempt.

Attorney General Holder's counteroffer was: (1) Congress must permanently cancel any contempt hearing; (2) accept a small compilation of documents selected "sight unseen" and put together by the very DOJ officials who lied to the DOJ IG, lied to Congress, and violated numerous federal statutes that carried federal felony criminal penalties; and (3) Congress must agree by receiving this pig-in-a-poke compilation that the DOJ would be forever deemed to be in full compliance of any current or future obligation to provide Congress information about Fast and Furious. This was a bad faith counteroffer no one would ever accept.

When AG Holder testified under oath at a hearing before Congress in early June 2012, Representative Lamar Smith asked Holder when he first informed the White House about Fast and Furious, he responded. "I don't know. [...] I was not awfully concerned about what the knowledge was in the White House."

Congress reminded President Obama: "Members of [Congress] from both sides of the aisle agree that the Terry family deserves answers, so do Agent Terry's brothers-in-arms in the border patrol, the Mexican government, and the American people." President Obama, Secretary Clinton, and Attorney General Holder only cared about themselves. President Obama never responded.

The Obama administration's treatment of the Terry family was deplorable at best. President Obama was up for re-election in 2012. In May 2012, President Obama honored American law enforcement officers who were killed in the line of duty. John Carlson, a columnist for the *Des Moines*

Register wrote an article about the week of ceremonies on May 20, 2012, titled "Obama Wants This Dead Cop to Go Away."

That week, the Senate and House of Representatives both unanimously passed the Brian Terry Memorial Act. President Obama did sign the Act, which named a U.S. border patrol station in Arizona after the murdered agent. What is telling about Obama's character is that he signed the Act without inviting the Terry family to attend. There was no ceremony, no statement by President Obama, no mention of Brian Terry the entire week. Why? A contempt of Congress charge against his wingman Eric Holder was looming on the near horizon, and evidence was overwhelming that his administration had some responsibility for Agent Terry's murder. As Carlson reported:

"President Obama honored America's law officers killed in the line of duty. [...] Then there's Brian Terry, a cop who didn't get much attention last week. [...] Some allege the stunningly stupid operation [Fast and Furious] was implemented to intentionally increase violence in order to bolster the Obama administration's efforts to enact tougher gun control laws. [...] What has been proven is that Lanny Breuer lied about the operation [to Congress]. [...]Breuer's boss, Attorney General Eric Holder, testified under oath he had no knowledge of Fast and Furious, but Grassley proved he knew about it long before.

"A total of 127 members of the House [...] have demanded that Holder resign or be fired. [...] Obama's re-election campaign operatives desperately want the issue to go away. It won't. Fast and Furious was a catastrophe that is certain to bring deaths in Mexico and the United States for many years. The administration's refusal to explain itself is shameful."

On July 13, 2014, a federal judge ruled that the DOJ must release a Vaughn index, listing specific information about Fast and Furious documents withheld from production pursuant to a Judicial Watch FOIA Request filed in June 2012. The documents, also withheld from Congress since June 2012, were not produced in response to a congressional subpoena when Attorney General Eric Holder asked President Obama to make a last-minute blanket assertion of executive privilege over all the documents on the eve of their production deadline. It took the determined efforts of Tom Fitton, Judicial Watch President, over a sixteen-month legal battle to get an index of documents so that the exercise of executive privilege, which was highly questionable on its face, could be challenged in Court. Fitton said, "Finally, we may get some accountability for Border Patrol Agent Brian Terry and the countless others murdered as a result of the insanely reckless Obama administration program."

Judicial Watch filed the FOIA Request in June 2012. Obama refused to provide any documents. It took a court order, after sixteen months of litigation, to get a list of the documents supposedly covered by executive privilege.

I thought President Obama and Attorney General Holder promised America FOIA requests would be honored in the spirit of transparency and openness. In fact, Holder said President Obama signed executive orders his very first day as president to ensure and guarantee Americans would have access to all documents so they could see how the government was operating. Was that a fake campaign promise, or was it a lie?

On October 23, 2014, three months after the court order, the Obama administration did finally release a list of documents allegedly protected by executive privilege. They did not release any documents, but the list itself was shocking. The President of the United States claimed, for over two years, that emails his wingman Eric Holder sent to his wife and mother were essential documents he used as President of the United States to make executive decisions about our country. The 1,307-page list of 15,662 documents actually did not comply with the normal requirements of a Vaughn index, but the Obama administration did label it a draft. A couple takeaways from the limited information on the index are: (1) AG Holder was extremely involved in managing the DOJ response to the congressional inquiry; and (2) AG Holder had numerous communications with the White House about Fast and Furious.

After reviewing the Vaughn index, Judicial Watch President Tom Fitton criticized President Obama and his disgraced Attorney General:

"Obama's executive privilege claims over these records are a fraud and abuse of power. [...] Americans will be astonished that Obama asserted executive privilege over [twenty] Eric Holder e-mails he sent to his wife about Fast and Furious."

His wife was not even a government employee.

The FOIA legal debate before Washington, D.C., District Judge John D. Bates, a President George W. Bush appointee, was highly contested. Holder's DOJ wanted the judge to delay his rulings to produce documents until November 3, the day before the election. On September 23, 2014, he issued an order rejecting the continuance. Eric Holder announced his resignation two days later.

After the Vaughn list, which contained fake executive privilege documents, was released, the Terry family, who had waited almost four years for answers to their questions about their loved one's murder, spoke out. The family reiterated their grief and disappointment that the Obama administration had not lived up to its promises of transparency, and urged President Obama to rethink his claims of executive privilege and release the documents. President Obama refused to give them any information about their family member's murder. The Terry family responded through Ralph Terry, Brian's uncle, who was also President of the Brian Terry Charitable Foundation:

"We are shocked [...] that Attorney General Holder was personally involved in responding to and managing the congressional inquiry. [...] The administration continues to show no remorse, and the Department continues to engage in deceptive measures that are designed to cover up. [...] Americans deserve the truth and deserve transparency from the government."

On May 21, 2016, a federal judge under the Trump administration finally ordered the release of the 20,000 pages of the executive privilege documents.

The released documents showed several things:

(1) The most transparent administration in history flat-out lied to Congress, denying that Fast and Furious ever even existed;

(2) The Obama administration, led by Eric Holder, conspired to obstruct the congressional investigation. Representative Chaffetz said, "The degree of

obstruction was more than previously understood. [...] Brian Terry's family should not have to wait six years for answers; and

(3) President Obama's trusted Senior advisor, Valerie Janett, was brought in to help cover-up the fact that AG Holder lied to Congress in his May 3, 2011, testimony.

Was President Obama knowledgeable, complicit, and responsible for Fast and Furious?

Chapter Ten

Hope for Justice Fades, But Prayers Continue

As the Obama administration's second term got into full swing, "transparency and accountability" were still a mantra, but were they illusory?

At least in one respect there was some level of transparency. In January 2013, President Obama bypassed the legislative branch and used executive orders to take twenty-three actions to address gun controls. Fast and Furious was still on the congressional agenda. They had not released Part III of their investigative report, yet.

The DOJ IG report, released a couple months before the election, in September 2012, found that President Obama and Attorney General Holder had no knowledge about Fast and Furious, and that they had no gun control agenda. While the report was disappointing, it was not surprising. The Department of Justice was not an independent, unbiased agency. Eric Holder was President Obama's campaign advisor in his first campaign and his self-proclaimed "wingman" during the first term. They were close friends. Their families socialized frequently. They shared a box at performing arts events. While some in the media questioned the propriety of this Justice Department-President relationship, it was transparent. It was not independent, but it was transparent. Neither were apologetic or defensive despite the criticism. The arrogance of the administration was on full display when Obama made his blanket assertion of executive privilege the day it was requested. There was no independent White House document review and no time for independent legal analysis. It was simply a matter of "I've got my wingman's back."

What about accountability? The Department of Justice IG never actually addressed how Fast and Furious started, or how it was able to continue for fifteen months. He never interviewed the whistleblowers. He also never addressed the issue of obstruction of Congress or Holder's civil and criminal contempt. On the issue of accountability, he simply said that he would recommend that Attorney General Holder determine whether anyone deserved administrative or disciplinary action. He did not mention, or even hint at, potential criminal prosecution, even though it was completely obvious numerous witnesses who were interviewed, or testified under oath, lied to the DOJ IG, Congress, or both.

When the DOJ IG put the accountability issue in AG Holder's hands, what did the Attorney General of the United States do? The answer is: nothing. He already replaced Melson, who was reassigned to a position at the DOJ, and he replaced U.S. Attorney Burke, who resigned after he admitted to two counts of illegally leaking documents to the press. There were no other known reprimands or any other disciplinary actions. There were promotions and some job transfers to better positions.

After President Obama was re-elected, he felt emboldened to make the end around and address gun control through executive orders. Congress did file a lawsuit against Attorney General Holder, but they had to file it in Washington, D.C. ,where the case was assigned to the U.S. District Judge Amy Berman Jackson, an Obama appointee.

The Obama administration ramped up their gun-control agenda. Secretary Clinton was openly pushing gun control in speeches after Fast and Furious using a false statistic: that ninety percent of the weapons used by the Mexican drug cartels came from the United States. Part of the Obama Fast and Furious narrative promoted through the media was the implication that ninety percent was from a small number of FFLs in border states, including Lone Wolf.

The ninety percent statistic has been discredited by many critics, who have pointed out that only about twenty percent of guns recovered in Mexico were actually traced. Of course, all of the Fast and Furious guns were traced, so the numbers from Arizona gun shops were padded, especially the trace numbers attributed to Lone Wolf Trading Company. The other variable affecting gun statistics is that the United States government has programs that send guns to the Mexican military and to Central American countries. Many of those weapons end up in the hands of the cartels.

On August 20, 2014, Judge Berman ruled on cross-motions for summary judgment in the lawsuit Congress brought against Attorney General Eric Holder. She denied both motions but did address the broad assertion of executive privilege by President Obama. Almost all of the documents Congress subpoenaed were not covered by executive privilege, but were potentially covered by a deliberative process privilege which the D.C. Circuit recognized as a form of executive privilege. This issue is different than the Freedom of Information Act issue Judicial Watch litigated because the public is not entitled to the same level of access to DOJ documents as Congress.

Judge Berman recognized that the classic definition of executive privilege is limited. She called it the presidential communications privilege. It is not clear how many, if any, documents withheld from Congress are covered by the presidential communications privilege. Judge Berman also recognized that the deliberative privilege is limited. The privilege only applies to communications made prior to, and leading up to, an Executive Branch decision. It is not generally applicable to purely factual information. It can still be disclosed if Congress can demonstrate a need for the records, and the documents usually should be disclosed if they would shed light on government misconduct. She ordered the DOJ to conduct a "document-by-document" analysis of all withheld documents to determine if they met the definition of deliberative privilege, and to create a privilege log with details supporting the application of the privilege. She would then rule on whether each document should be produced to Congress.

This ruling "split the baby" between the motions for summary judgment, and both were dismissed. There was an opening for some documents to be released, but none were released during the Obama administration.

After Attorney General Holder announced his resignation in 2014, he listed the "inability to enact more stringent gun control regulations among the biggest failures" of his tenure, saying the matter "weighed heavily" on his mind.

When President Obama was re-elected, he announced universal background checks and a ban on the sale of assault weapons were a top priority. Both failed to pass in Congress.

In July 2015, President Obama was interviewed by BBC. He also said: "The issue of guns [...] has been the one area where I feel that I've been most frustrated and most stymied. [...] For us not to be able to resolve that issue has been something that is distressing."

Finally, there was some transparency by Obama and Holder. Fast and Furious was always about gun control. They were willing to do almost anything to achieve that objective. In their minds, the murder of Mexicans by the drug cartels was a non-factor. Fast and Furious was justified. In fact, after President Trump was elected, former President Obama famously bragged that the eight years of his administration were "scandal-free."

At the end of his presidency he still spoke about the need for gun control, often in extremely outlandish terms totally unsupported by the facts. In March 2015, he gave a speech to students at Benedict College saying:

> "What we [...] have to recognize is that our homicide rates are so much higher than other industrialized countries. I mean, by a mile. And most of that is attributable to the easy, ready availability of firearms. [...] It is easier to buy a firearm than it is [...] .to buy a book. There are neighborhoods where it's easier [...] to buy a handgun and clips than [...] to buy a fresh vegetable. People say we should have firearms in kindergarten and machine guns in bars. [...] You think I'm exaggerating?"

The *Washington Post* gave him "three Pinocchios" for his "exaggerated claims and faux statistics."

On March 7, 2018, after six years of litigation, Attorney General Sessions reached a settlement with Congress and agreed to produce the withheld documents. Sessions announced the settlement:

> "The Department of Justice under my watch is committed to transparency and the rule of law. This

settlement agreement is an important step to make sure that the public finally receives all the facts related to Operation Fast and Furious."

At last: there was hope!

The Terry family called on the Trump administration to reopen the Fast and Furious investigation, unseal the documents, reverse the executive privilege claims, and produce the withheld documents so that the people responsible for Fast and Furious could be held accountable.

There was only one hurdle left: Judge Berman had to approve the settlement. The settlement had one condition: The judge had to vacate her two previous rulings regarding privilege issues. Congress and the DOJ filed a joint motion agreeing to vacate the two rulings and settle the case.

On October 23, 2018, Judge Berman denied their motion. For reasons that ring hollow, she refused to vacate her rulings even though they were now moot. Why? Could it be that the Obama-appointed judge decided to protect the Obama administration by preventing the public from finding out the truth? That certainly appears to be the case.

For the Terry family, there still has not been complete justice. They received some insurance money when Andre's insurance company settled the civil lawsuit they had against Andre. Andre did nothing wrong, was glad to have the matter settled, and was glad for the Terry family to receive some compensation for the death of their loved one. No one in the government was ever held liable or accountable. A Justice Department official said that AAG Lanny Breuer had been "admonished, but will not be disciplined", and Eric

Holder "will not be taking any [...] disciplinary actions against any Department employees."

Eric Holder unexpectedly resigned two days after a federal court ruled that the government had to provide documents to Judicial Watch pursuant to their FOIA request.

"Eric Holder admitted [...] that Fast and Furious guns would continue to be used for crimes for years to come."

The Terry family issued a statement:

"It is our hope that the next Attorney General will do a far better job at protecting the American public and guarding the many rights guaranteed in the constitution."

In February 2016, the DOJ Office of the Inspector General issued a twenty-six-page report titled "A Review of the Department of Justice's and ATF's Implementation of Recommendations Contained in the OIG's Report on Operations Fast and Furious and Wide Receiver." In a footnote, they noted that DAG James Cole sent out an email in March 2011 to five U.S. Attorneys in southwest border states instructing them "not to [...] conduct [...] operations, which include guns crossing the border." There was never any follow-up or wider distribution, and the policy statement in the email was not made part of the U.S. Attorney's manual, or any other Department reference or training materials.

There was no mention whatsoever of any actions regarding the accountability of individuals who allowed firearms to go to the cartels, or those individuals who blatantly lied to the DOJ IG or Congress.

The Terry family had some level of justice regarding the actual perpetrators of the murder. One of the criminals was wounded and captured on December 14, 2010, the night of the murder. Several others were captured between 2010 and April 2017. On April 12, 2017, a joint U.S.-Mexico task force captured Agent Terry's suspected killer, Heraclio Osorio-Arellanes, at a ranch in northwestern Mexico. He was the last of seven suspects involved in the murder. All were in the United States illegally, and all were charged with first-degree murder, which carried a maximum sentence of life in prison. Osorio-Arellanes was extradited to the United States on July 31, 2018, to stand trial. Three of the suspects pled guilty, two were convicted by a jury, and a sixth was awaiting trial. Only five of the seven were actually at the crime scene. One person at the crime scene was sentenced to thirty years, and two received life sentences. Two, including the alleged killer, are awaiting trial. Two organizers, who were not physically at the crime scene, received eight-year and twenty-seven-year sentences.

Agent Terry's mother issued a statement:

> "If I had to give a report card grade to Eric Holder, he would get an A with respect to his department's prosecution of Brian's killers; but I would give him an F for his efforts in holding those [at] [the] ATF and [the] DOJ accountable."

In June 2017, Congress released Part III of their report at a hearing where Senator Grassley and the Terry family testified. Representative Chaffetz was the Chairman of the House Oversight Committee.

In his prepared statement, Senator Grassley was critical of the Obama administration:

"[The] DOJ and [the] ATF had no intention of looking for honest answers and being transparent. [...] [They] employed shameless delay tactics to obstruct the investigation. [...] [They] kept the truth hidden. [...] Obama refused to present the contempt citation [of Holder] to a grand jury as required by statute. [...] The [...] claims of privilege were deceptive and unfounded. [...] Documents show a highly politicized climate at the Obama Administration's Main Justice."

He closed with:

"The American people, including the Terry family, deserve a complete accounting."

Brian Terry's mother, Josephine Terry, made a moving statement:

"[The] ATF, [the] DOJ, and possibly people even higher up in the government knowingly intended to provide thousands of guns to Mexican drug cartels. [...] From the moment that bullet entered Brian's body and ended his life — Brian's government, my government, your government — began to hide the truth. [...] No one was punished or prosecuted. [...] Only one possible motivation remains for all those who have covered up. [...] To conceal their own shame and disgrace, and [...] their crimes."

Brian Terry's cousin, Robert Heyer, also issued a powerful statement:

"Assistant Attorney General Lanny Breuer arrogantly stated that if Brian Terry had not been killed with an operation Fast and Furious gun, he would have been killed by some other gun. I was sickened by Mr. Breuer's comments. [...] The most disappointing and demoralizing act of all was [...] President Obama asserted executive privilege [...] effectively [ending] the hope of the Terry family to fully understand why [the] DOJ denied gunwalking. [...] How many people besides Brian Terry have been killed or wounded by individuals carrying operation Fast and Furious weapons?"

Brian Terry's cousin hit on the question that has haunted Andre Howard every single day since December 15, 2009. When will the next firearm from Lone Wolf be recovered at a crime scene? There are over 1,000 unaccounted-for Fast and Furious weapons.

The other problem with the Obama administration is that it created a corrupt deep state that continues to retaliate against those that they deemed enemies during the Fast and Furious investigation.

During the Fast and Furious investigation, Andre and I were told by multiple reliable sources that the Obama administration targeted us for illegal surveillance and that our attorney-client communications were intercepted. During the investigation, one of the junior partners who worked for me in our law firm had to go to the office late at night and discovered an individual disguised in a fake building security guard uniform in my office, going through my files. The building management confirmed the next morning that the individual was not a security guard and the building security cameras did not show anyone exiting the elevator on our floor.

Obama-era FBI and ATF agents repeatedly entered Lone Wolf during business hours for no official business purpose. They did not communicate with Andre or anyone in Lone Wolf. The only explanation was they wanted to intimidate Lone Wolf customers. The FBI continued to approve sales to illegal aliens and convicted felons. The FBI started denying sales to Andre's regular customers, who had previously been approved, for no apparent reason.

Andre reported all of these issues to Congress and provided supporting documents. After President Trump's election, he sent detailed letters to Attorney General Sessions with supporting documents on April 3, 2017, and again on November 28, 2017, asking the DOJ to stop the harassment by the Fast and Furious holdovers. They continued.

For almost eight years Andre has had to wake up every morning praying that no new crime scene trace will arrive. He knows that there will inevitably be more. He doesn't know when. The vast majority of the many dozens that he processed after Fast and Furious ended in January 2011 only contain raw details about the weapon so that he can provide the government with purchaser information. They don't provide any information about the crime, the crime scene, or the victims. What he knows is that the gun was recovered at a crime scene, and the original purchaser was a straw purchaser from Fast and Furious. He assumes it was a crime of violence. He does not know how many victims were wounded or killed. He does not know how many lives have been destroyed. Living with this terrible uncertainty every day takes a toll.

This legacy of the Obama administration unfortunately has an even worse side. Some of the Fast and Furious crime scenes involve high-profile recoveries that do get media coverage. The victims are known. The details are often disturbing. Andre now knows the original purchasers were really the Mexican cartels — primarily the Sinaloa Cartel, but also La Familia.

Any reported violence by these cartels could involve Fast and Furious weapons from Lone Wolf. The thousand unrecovered guns undoubtedly were used in many crimes and murders since 2009. No one knows how many people were murdered. If the weapons recovered involved crimes where 300 people were killed, how many people were killed by those same guns before law enforcement got control of the weapon and traced it? How many are being used in murders every day?

We now also know that some of these Fast and Furious guns from Lone Wolf made their way to radical terrorists in the United States and abroad.

The Fast and Furious documents show that the Obama administration naively acted like the guns walked to the Sinaloa Cartel would primarily be used in turf wars between competing cartels. That is like thinking weapons given to the mafia will only be used against other mafia families in territorial disputes.

The list of known crime scenes where Fast and Furious weapons from Lone Wolf were recovered is horrific. We only have a partial list, and it only includes crime scenes where the firearms were recovered and traced from high-profile crime scenes. In previous chapters, we highlighted some of the worst. There were horrific mass murders at a children's birthday party and a young mens' rehabilitation center. There were also murders of high-profile Mexican judges, lawyers, politicians, and a beauty queen. Many of the firearms were recovered at the scene of cartel shootouts with the Mexican military. A .50 caliber weapon from Fast and Furious was used to shoot down a Mexican Army helicopter. Twenty-nine cartel members were killed in that incident.

The Obama administration stopped reporting crime scene information, and then asserted executive privilege to prevent disclosure of documents that reported crimes.

When the Sinaloa Cartel kingpin, "El Chapo" Guzman, was captured on January 8, 2016, after a gunfight in Sinaloa, he was armed with a Fast and Furious handgun from Lone Wolf. He also had a .50 caliber rifle from another Fast and Furious FFL. Congress requested information about these weapons from Attorney General Loretta Lynch. None was provided.

On May 3, 2015, two terrorists living in Phoenix with ISIS affiliations attempted a terrorist attack against the First Annual Muhammed Art Exhibit and Contest in Garland, Texas. The FBI had an embedded agent in that terrorist cell who knew about the planned attack, followed the terrorists to the attack scene, and took pictures of the terrorists exiting their car wearing body armor and carrying assault weapons. The FBI agent did not alert law enforcement in Texas and did not intervene. He drove away. The Garland police engaged the terrorists in a shootout. One was wounded. The terrorists were killed. They had at least one assault rifle purchased from Lone Wolf during Fast and Furious.

The FBI agent's involvement was only discovered when the undercover FBI agent was stopped at gunpoint at a roadblock set up by the Garland police. Why would the FBI director allow a terrorist attack to proceed? Only the fortunate reaction of Garland security and law enforcement prevented a potential massacre.

Again, Congress wanted answers from the Attorney General Loretta Lynch. Andre provided Congress a copy of the emergency crime scene trace he received the next day. AG Lynch refused to respond.

This was the first time the Islamic State of Iraq and Syria took credit for an attack on U.S. soil. Nadif Hamid Soofi purchased one of the weapons from Lone Wolf on February 24, 2010, during Fast and Furious. The FBI initially delayed the purchase. The next day, they told Andre to proceed. Congress wanted details about the FBI NICS approval process regarding Soofi because of the ISIS connection. The request for information came from Senator Ron Johnson, Chairman of the Committee on Homeland Security and Governmental Affairs. At the time, Congress did not know about the undercover FBI agent.

On March 26, 2017, CBS 60 Minutes aired a segment revealing that "an undercover FBI agent who had been communicating with one of the terrorists [...] travelled to Garland, was present at the scene of the attack, and took photos of the terrorists' moments before the attack." When FBI Director Comey responded to Senator Johnson in 2015, he said the FBI did not travel to Garland and did not know about any planned attack. The FBI refused to provide any information to Senator Johnson.

On April 27, 2017, Senator Grassley sent another request for information to FBI Director Comey asking for details about the FBI's involvement in the terrorist attack. Congress already knew that the terrorists wanted the undercover FBI agent to participate in the attack. The agent declined but told the terrorists to "tear up Texas." One of the terrorists cautioned the undercover agent:

> "Bro, you don't have to say that. [...] You know what happened in Paris. [...] I think. [...] Yes or no? So that goes without saying. [...] No need to be direct."

FBI Director Comey did not respond.

It is odd that the Garland, Texas, terrorist mentioned the Paris terrorist attack. Or is it?

On November 13, 2015, there was a horrific terrorist attack in Paris, France. Islamic terrorists murdered 130 people, including eighty-nine at the Bataclan theatre. It was a terrible atrocity. At least one of the AK-47 weapons used in that massacre was part of Fast and Furious, according to an ATF report of investigation obtained by Judicial Watch. ATF spokesman Corey Ray told Judicial Watch that none of the firearms from Paris have been "traced." The serial number of the firearm has not been disclosed. Andre continues to pray that it did not come from his store.

Every day Andre prays that none of his guns will be used in any crime, anywhere. Every day Andre, hundreds of innocent victims and their families, and the American public must live with President Obama's legacy of "Betrayal".

Epilogue

Analyzing the past is a necessary part of understanding the present and preparing for the future. It is easy to document and comment on the events of the past. Fast and Furious is no exception. No one, other than President Obama and perhaps Eric Holder, know where the idea came from or how it started. Congress, the DOJ, and other media writers have now spent years documenting and to some extent commenting on the facts. In the process they made findings, reached conclusions, expressed opinions, and recommended actions. This book is intended to take those results to another level. It provides analysis, through the perspectives of two people who were involved in the events, that not only reports on events of the past, but critically analyzes them so we can better understand and evaluate the present and maybe anticipate and prepare for the future.

Most of what has been reported to the public is not helpful because there is too much to assimilate over an almost 8 year period. Over that time media coverage has become increasingly more one sided, and politics have changed so dramatically that the majority that said X then, now say Y. But, within this framework some things remain constant. They should be America's bedrock. They should be our litmus test to determine what is right, and what is wrong; what is true and what is false; what will keep America great or what will destroy America. The growing divide in our media, politics, and civil discourse is so extreme that the American public have not only been forgotten, but are now viewed as pawns on the chessboard of our future. They are readily sacrificed for what is better according to those holding power positions in Congress. American values and even lives have become expendable. If you needed one constituency to retain power and it didn't work, create a new constituency and cloak it with a new message, new false promises, and a vision of unattainable utopian ideas. A new plurality will adopt it because they never take the time to decipher it before they cast their ballot.

So, what are these bedrock concepts that Americans can use to make judgements that wil preserve this great nation? This is neither a trick question nor a difficult answer. Look to the Constitution of the United States. It is what either brought you here, kept you here, or makes you an American.

Most Americans understand that it defines our nation. Few understand what ethics, values, and conduct it requires of each of us to cherish and protect it.

Fast and Furious provides us important insights about how fragile values like the rule of law, equal justice under law, transparency of government, and accountability of public servants can be.

Fast and Furious was probably the most investigated and scrutinized government program since Watergate. Both Congress and the Executive branch conducted extensive investigations and issued multiple reports. Eventually the judiciary got involved in a high profile dispute between those two branches of government, which has still not been completely resolved. The lasting legacy of Fast and Furious impacts all four of these values.

The real timeline of Fast and Furious has never been concisely summarized.

Prior to Barak Obama's election in November 2008, he and his "wingman" Eric Holder ran on a platform that included their personal long held commitment to gun control. After Obama's inauguration in January 2009, it was clear that Congress, including many in his own party, would not pass any legislation that infringed on Second Amendment rights. President Obama immediately embarked on a plan to change Congress' position. He directed his top political appointees, and their high level career government subordinates, to device and execute a plan to leverage the gun trafficking issue into a gun control strategy.

Between March 2009 and September 2009 those high level Obama administration officials spent a huge amount of time on this priority directive of the Obama administration. The plan was to use a so-called gun "intelligence gathering strategy" that would take down the cartel gun trafficking networks. There was never any realistic idea, or plan, how that could possibly work. The truth is that "intelligence" meant collecting crime scene statistics involving border state gun store sales and use those in a way that could persuade Congress to pass gun control legislation.

After a little over a year, they decided they had enough statistics that they could combine with an orchestrated high visibility arrest and prosecution of dozens of straw purchasers. These plans were being finalized on December 13. They planned for a major press release in Phoenix in early January 2011. Attorney General Holder was going to be the headliner. Everything was set going in to the holiday break. Then plans changed. Border Agent Brian Terry was murdered the evening of December 14. The murderers, illegal aliens from Mexico, were armed with Fast and Furious weapons. At first there was no panic. The FFLs were already set up to be blamed because the crime scene statistics had been leaked to the *Washington Post* and were published a day or two earlier. The *Washington Post's* main target – Andre Howard and Lone Wolf Trading Company, was named the number one firearms business with crime scene traces in Mexico from 2009-2010.

Unfortunately for the Obama administration and fortunately for America, brave ATF whistleblowers came forward to Congress and blew up the planned Obama administration narrative. When Congress took it public with Senator Grassley's January 27 letter to ATF Director

Melson, the Obama administration shifted into full damage control mode.

The next five years defined the identity of the new Democratic Party, and the deep state the Obama administration left behind. Although Obamacare became the public signature legacy of his eight years as President, it was Fast and Furious that was the true signature of his administration. It was the first building block of what would become a culture of corruption, and the assembly of a deep state that Obama and the Democratic ordained successor, Hillary Clinton, thought would be in control for at least one and a half decades of power dominance.

The deep state Obama assembled bought into this anticipated future course of America. The highest levels of career bureaucrats and key administration officials that came into power under Obama believed they were secure in completing their government careers, so long as they got on board with the corrupt liberal Democrat machine. Every career employee in a key government position was well aware of the Clinton history of abusing anyone deemed an adversary and their ability to escape all consequences for criminal conduct. Obama had used executive orders with impunity. Obama's law enforcement agencies showed nothing but arrogant disdain for Congressional oversight subpoenas and other attempts to exercise oversight responsibilities. Their arrogance and corruption would later surface in their attempt to prevent the election of Donald Trump and to then target President Donald Trump for possible impeachment.

So what were the key components of the new Democratic Party? They were, and still are, the seven D's

Disregard;
Delay;
Deny;
Deceive;

Deflect;

Discredit; and

Destroy.

They were all part of the Obama administration's five year plan to get through the Fast and Furious scandal. They were so successful that not a single Obama administration official, or even low level employee, has ever been held accountable for their role in the murder of hundreds of innocent people, or their dozens of lies to the DOJ IG or Congress. They were so successful that former President Obama brazenly declared his eight years in office was "scandal free".

If anything defined the future impact of Fast and Furious it was "Disregard". President Obama, Eric Holder, Hillary Clinton and dozens of Obama administration officials simply disregarded the rule of law. They flaunted their disdain for international law, the law regarding perjury and false official statements, the laws of privacy, the laws regarding firearm trafficking, the laws regarding congressional oversight, the laws regarding obstruction of justice, and many others. Along the way they also disregarded their campaign promises, their oath of office, the best interests of America, and their own values and conscious.

Delay was an important tactic in Fast and Furious. When in doubt, delay. In politics time is a weapon. Politics change and a new crisis can replace an old scandal. Obama and Holder's illegal exercise of a fake executive privilege still denies Congress and Americans access to Fast and Furious documents. Delay has been the primary tactic of the Democrats in Congress during the Trump administration. They simply won't vote for anything. Delay and Disregard go hand-in-hand.

In Fast and Furious "Deny" was a key part of the "Delay" strategy. They both go hand-in-hand with "deceive" and of course it only worked in Fast and Furious because Obama and the members of his administration "disregarded" the rule of law and their oaths of office.

"Deflect", "Discredit", and "Destroy" are the Plan B of the Democratic strategy. Their Plan B is usually reserved for use when "Deny and Deceive" stop working. Thanks to the determination of the ATF whistleblowers and the Republican Congress they stopped working in Fast and Furious.

The Obama administration then tried to blame the Bush administration and the "bad apple" FFLs like Andre. When Andre refused to obstruct justice and join the Obama administration cover-up they used more media attacks, illegal surveillance, FBI disruptions of his business, and financial attacks under Choke Point to try to discredit and destroy him. Their multiple attacks against the ATF whistleblowers are well documented. Their disdain, and attempts to discredit and silence the Terry family, were despicable.

The Democratic Party used these same tactics against the Trump campaign, the Trump administration, the Trump supporters and President Trump. The Fake News media has been relentless in accusing Trump and his administration of things the Democrats actually have done. The liberal media and politicians disparage and attack Trump supporters as racists, deplorables, morons, and worse. There are countless incidents involving orchestrated assaults on prominent Republican politicians at their homes, their offices, and at family meals. They encourage future mob attacks on Trump supporters wherever they go. They brutally attacked Supreme Court nominee Kavanagh, and the Covington, Kentucky students.

The worst examples of Obama's deep state abuses have been committed by Special Counsel Mueller in his fake Russian collusion investigation. He has used his investigation to destroy the lives of Trump associates and their families. There have been no prosecutions for illegal conduct relating to Russian election tampering. Most have been for false statements that have nothing to do with Russian criminal activity. What is Mueller's concept of equal justice under the law? Why is there no investigation into the crimes Obama officials' committed during Fast and Furious? President Obama refused to appoint a Special Counsel to prosecute those crimes despite Congress' requests for justice. Attorney General Holder refused to hold anyone in the Obama administration accountable. The Gestapo type dawn raid on Roger Stone should horrify all Americans. It was a terrible abuse of power sensationalized by CNN, who was sent to Stone's house by Mueller and his deep state colleagues led by Andrew Weissmann to set up in advance and televise the raid.

For Andre, the Mexican families of Fast and Furious victims, the family of Brian Terry, and many other Americans, the legacy of Fast and Furious was locked in during the Obama administration. It will be with them for the rest of their lives. The lessons of Fast and Furious should be studied by all Americans because America is re-living many of the same abuses executed by the Obama deep state today. Eric Holder has indicated he wants to run for President in 2020. Hillary Clinton has hinted that she may run again for President in 2020. Robert Mueller's special counsel investigation is still in the media spotlight and will likely stay in the spotlight at least through the end of President Trump's first term.

The Trump administration has picked up the torch of promised transparency left behind by the Obama administration. It remains to be seen if it will shine.

The accountability of the Obama administration is sadly fading into political history and may well be lost.

Legacies, by definition, are lasting. Presidents of the United States try to build their legacy during their tenure. They care about their legacy. They work to build their legacy while they are in office and after they leave office. Legacies can't be fabricated. They can't be bought. They can't be molded after the fact. President Obama's legacy was earned during his eight years in office. It is a legacy of "Betrayal".

About The Authors

Andre Howard

Andre was born in San Antonio, Texas. His father was a career Air Force officer who served as a bomber pilot in World War II and then spent the remainder of his 27 year career as a fighter pilot. Growing up in a military family Andre moved frequently spending most of his time in Texas, New Mexico, Florida and Arizona. Andre served in a U.S. Army aviation unit and was honorably discharged in 1981. He has been the owner of Lone Wolf Trading Company in Glendale, Arizona, since 1991. He is also a licensed Helicopter Flight Instructor and Commercial rated pilot.

Larry Gaydos

Larry was born in Heidelberg, West Germany. His father was a career Army officer who served in the infantry in the Philippines in World War II where he got a battlefield commission making him an officer. He spend the remainder of his 24 year career as an officer in the Corps of Engineers serving in both Korea and Vietnam. Growing up Larry lived in Germany, Japan, France, Ohio, Washington, Virginia and Pennsylvania. Larry graduated from West Point where he was a Cadet Captain and graduated 18th in his class in 1973. He finished first in his class in Law and won the Eisenhower Award for graduating first in Military Psychology and Leadership. During his 13 years in the U.S. Army he graduated from Airborne School, served as a platoon leader in the 1st Infantry Division (Fwd) in Augsburg, Germany and the 84th Engineer Battalion (Construction), 25th Infantry Division in Hawaii. While in the Army he got his law degree from the University of Virginia School of Law. His first Judge Advocate General Corps assignment was as the Chief Prosecutor, and then the Senior Defense Counsel, in Hanau,

Germany, 3rd Armored Division. He attended the graduate law course at the U.S. Army Judge Advocate General's School where he graduated 1st in his class and received awards for being 1st in Criminal Law and Legal Writing.

After the graduate course he taught criminal law at the Army JAGC School. He also authored a number of articles that were published in the Military Law Review and The Army Lawyer. He resigned from the Army in 1986 as a major.

In 1986 he joined Haynes and Boone, LLP in Dallas, Texas. At Haynes and Boone he was co-founder of their White Collar Criminal Defense and Antitrust practice group. During his thirty years at Haynes and Boone he served on their Board of Directors, their Professional Responsibility (Ethics) Committee, the Sarbanes-Oxley Committee, and as the head of various legal practice groups. He also served as a Regional Chair of the American Bar Association White Collar Crime Committee, Chair of the State Bar of Texas Antitrust and Business Litigation Section, and President and Director of the Arlington Texas Bar Association. He has been recognized as a Texas Super Lawyer in the areas of Antitrust, White Collar Criminal Defense, and Corporate Government and Compliance.

For more than 30 years, Larry Gaydos represented public and private companies, their executives, and Audit Committees in federal and state government investigations involving numerous government agencies including the Department of Justice, the Securities Exchange Commission, the Department of Agriculture, Homeland Security, the Internal Revenue Service, the Texas Attorney General's office, as well as the United States Senate and the United States House of Representatives.

Larry conducts internal corporate investigations, represents clients before government agencies and litigates in both civil and criminal courts. While his clients come from many diverse business areas, his representations include many prominent national corporations in the energy field and defense industry. He has extensive experience in federal civil and criminal litigation, antitrust, federal securities, defense procurement, foreign trade, environmental and general criminal matters. His clients have included many Fortune 500 companies.

He writes and speaks frequently on Antitrust, White Collar Criminal and Legal Ethics and Compliance issues. He currently is partners with his daughter, Lauren Duffer at their law firm Gaydos Duffer, P.C. in Arlington, Texas. Additional firm and biographical information is available on the firm website www.gaydosduffer.com.

Sources **and Acknowledgements**

"Betrayal" was the culmination of a nine year collaboration between Andre Howard and Larry Gaydos. It is based in large part on our personal and professional experiences over that time frame. Because our book is being published in 2019 we have had the benefit of seeing multiple government investigations involving the Obama administration run their full course. Those investigations have been thoroughly documented in lengthy reports supported by the testimony of dozens of witnesses and thousands of documents available to the public on the applicable government websites. In addition there were many official written communications between Congress and numerous agencies within the Executive Branch ranging from the Office of the President to the Phoenix offices of ATF and DOJ. These official government documents are also publicly available. The government documents quoted in "Betrayal" come primarily from the following resources:

1. "The Department of Justice's Operation Fast and Furious: Accounts of ATF Agents," Joint Staff Report prepared for Representative Darrell E. Issa, Chairman, United States House of Representatives Committee on Oversight and Government Reform and Senator Charles E. Grassley, Ranking Member, United States Senate Committee on the Judiciary, 112th Congress, June 14, 2011.

2. "The Department of Justice's Operation Fast and Furious: Untitled Draft." Joint Staff Report prepared for Representative Darrell E. Issa, Chairman, United States House of Representatives Committee on Oversight and Government Reform and Senator Charles E. Grassley, Ranking Member, United States

Senate Committee on the Judiciary, 112th Congress, July 2011.

3. "Fast and Furious: Anatomy of a Failed Operation, Part I of III," Joint Staff Report prepared for Representative Darrell E. Issa, Chairman, United States House of Representatives Committee on Oversight and Government Reform and Senator Charles E. Grassley, Ranking Member, United States Senate Committee on the Judiciary, 112th Congress, July 31, 2012.

4. "Fast and Furious: Anatomy of a Failed Operation, Part II of III," Joint Staff Report prepared for Representative Darrell E. Issa, Chairman, United States House of Representatives Committee on Oversight and Government Reform and Senator Charles E. Grassley, Ranking Member, United States Senate Committee on the Judiciary, 112th Congress, October 29, 2012.

5. "Fast and Furious: Obstruction of Congress by the Department of Justice, Part III," Joint Staff Report prepared for the Honorable Jason Chaffetz, Chairman, United States House of Representatives Committee on Oversight and Government Reform and the Honorable Charles E. Grassley, Chairman, United States Senate Committee on the Judiciary, 115th Congress, June 7, 2017.

6. "A Review of ATF's Operation Fast and Furious and Related Matters," Department of Justice Office of the Inspector General Oversight and Review Division (Redacted), September 2012, Re-issued November 2012.

7. "Southwest Border Initiative: Project Gunrunner," United States Department of Justice, Bureau of Alcohol, Tobacco, Firearms, and Explosives, June 2007.

8. "Firearms Trafficking, Project Gunrunner: The Southwest Boarder Initiative," ATF Publication 3317.6, Revised March 2009.

9. "Project Gunrunner- A Cartel Focused Strategy," United States Department of Justice, Bureau of Alcohol, Tobacco, Firearms, and Explosives, Office of Field Operations, September 2010.

10. "Review of ATF's Project Gunrunner," United States Department of Justice Office of the Inspector General, Evaluation and Inspections Division, November 2010.

11. "DHS Involvement in OCDETF Operation Fast and Furious," Department of Homeland Security, Office of Inspector General, OIG-13-49, March 2013.

12. "Report of Investigation Concerning the Improper Disclosure of United States Department of Justice Information to a Member of the Media", Department of Justice Office of the Inspector General, Oversight and Review Division, May 2013.

13. "The Department Of Justice's 'Operation Choke Point': Illegally Choking Off Legitimate Business?", Staff Report to Representative Darrell Issa, Chairman, United States House of Representatives Committee on Oversight and Government Reform, 113th Congress, May 29, 2014.

14. "Federal Deposit Insurance Corporation's Involvement in Operation Choke Point," Staff Report to Darrell Issa, Chairman, United States House of Representatives Committee on Oversight and Government Reform and Representative Jim Jordan, Chairman, Subcommittee on Economic Growth, Job Creations and Regulatory Affairs, 113th Congress, December 8, 2014.

15. "Firearms Trafficking – United States Efforts to Combat Firearms Trafficking to Mexico Have

Improved but Some Collaboration Challenges Remain", United Stated Government Accounting Office, GAO-16-223, January 2016.

16. "A Review of the Department of Justice's and ATF's Implementation of Recommendations Contained in the OIG's Report on Operations Fast and Furious and Wide Receiver," United States Department of Justice Office of the Inspector General, Oversight and Review Division, February 2016.

Media Sources

The main media sources that covered matters related to Fast and Furious, and were cited in this book, were the Washington Post (James Grimaldi and Sari Horwitz); the Arizona Republic (Dennis Wagner); CBS News (Sharyl Attkisson); Fox News (William LaJeunesse); the Los Angeles Times (Richard Serrano); La Opinion (Claudia Nunez); Judicial Watch (Tom Fitton); the Des Moines Register (John Carlson); Univision (Jorge Ramos); Freedom Outpost (Tim Brown); the Brownsville Herald (Diana Eva Maldonado, staff reporters); the Daily Caller (Matthew Boyle); and Newsmax (Ken Mandel).

Some deserve special recognition for their long term tireless reporting and in depth analysis. Sharyl Attkisson was the first major media investigative reporter to interview John Dodson and air a television series covering the initial stages of Fast and Furious. She continued to write extensively on the matter and posted those articles on her website. Her book is discussed below.

William LaJeunesse of Fox News was also an early investigative reporter who exposed the truth about Fast and Furious and still follows that story today. He interviewed me about Andre's story in September 2011. Fox News continues to provide coverage of the Fast and Furious Scandal. Special recognition to the Fox Nation team lead by producer Rob Monaco and investigative reporter Katie Pavlich who did a detailed documentary titled "Outgunned :The Fast and Furious Scandal," which was launched on Fox Nation on February 14, 2019, and remains available there for viewing. Katie Pavlich, whose book is discussed below, interviewed William LaJeunesse and others, including Andre and myself, in an excellent expose about the corrupt legacy of the Obama administration and their absolutely disgraceful treatment of the Terry family.

Judicial Sources

The legal cases mentioned and discussed in this book are documented in the extensive pleadings in each case which are publicly available. Most of the federal pleadings cited are located through Pacer searches of the District of Arizona and Southern District of California (straw purchaser criminal cases and Brian Terry murder prosecutions); and the District of Columbia (Attorney General Holder Case).

General Background Sources

General Background information regarding the ATF history; details about the AK-47, the Barrett .50 caliber, Glock, and Herstal pistol and Operation Choke Point were taken from sources referenced in Wikipedia.

Books

The four previous books about Project Wide Receiver and Fast and Furious that both Andre and I read in the years prior to our decision to write this book are:

Sharyl Attkisson's book titled "Stonewalled – My Fight for Truth Against the Forces of Obstruction, Intimidation and Harassment in Obama's Washington" was published by Harper Collins in 2014. It included a chapter titled "Fast and Furious Redux" covering her investigative reporting on the matter from 2010-2012 including her groundbreaking television interviews of the ATF whistleblowers on CBS Evening News.

John Dodson's book titled "The Unarmed Truth – My Fight to Blow the Whistle and Expose Fast and Furious" was published by Threshold Editions in 2013.

Mike Detty's book titled "Guns Across the Boarder, the Inside Story – How and Why the U.S. Government Smuggled Guns Into Mexico" was published by Skyhorse Publishing in 2013.

Katie Pavlich's book titled "Fast and Furious – Barack Obama's Bloodiest Scandal And It's Shameless Cover-Up" was published by Regnery Publishing, Inc. in 2012. Katie, News Editor for Townhall and a Fox News contributor deserves special recognition for her steadfast determination to search for truth and fight for accountability. Her February 14, 2019, Fox Nation documentary "Outgunned: The Fast and Furious Scandal" keeps our hopes for justice alive.

Acknowledgements

First, we acknowledge and pray for the Terry family and express gratitude for their admirable charitable work through the Brian Terry Foundation.

Second, we express our sincere appreciation to Senator Grassley, Representative Issa, Representative Chaffetz and their staffs (Steve Castor, Brian Downey, and Jason Foster) for their professionalism, assistance, and dedication to fight for truth, equal justice, and fidelity to the rule of law.

Third, we acknowledge the hard work and dedication of behind the scenes patriots like Ron Coburn and Sipsey Street Irregular writers David Codrea and Mike Vanderboegh, who exposed corruption and brought actual transparency to the public during a time when our government only brought lies and obstruction.

Fourth, Andre wants to express his personal appreciation to me and the attorneys at the Polsinelli Law Firm (Cary Hall III and Troy Froderman) who provided him legal advice and assistance.

Fifth, my daughter, Lauren Duffer, and I want to express our personal appreciation to the hardworking attorneys and staff at Gaydos Duffer P.C. (Brooke M. Wilson, Courtney Harbaugh Walker, Lindsey Reynolds, and Amanda Crowder) who provided invaluable advice, support, and assistance. I want to personally express special thanks to the newest member of our firm, Courtney R. Davis, who spent countless selfless hours typing and re-typing this book which I wrote completely in near microscopic handwriting on eight column accounting graph paper (not kidding)!

Last, but not least, Andre wants to sincerely thank his family for all their support as well as his customers. He is continually grateful and thanks them for all their support because they are also victims of this criminal behavior. I also want to thank my wife, Joanne, who never wavered in her support, even while I worked on the book when we were on vacation in Aruba, my daughter, Lauren, who had to run the law firm by herself while I worked on this project, and my son, Andrew, who patiently listened to me talk about Fast and Furious so much he could probably have written the book himself.

Most importantly Andre and I thank God for all our blessings and the opportunity to share this book with America.

Made in the USA
Middletown, DE
14 April 2019